To Ruth Fornelli, my mother
To the memory of Luitpold Günsberg, my father

CW01506979

Patriarchal Representations

Patriarchal Representations

Gender and Discourse in Pirandello's Theatre

Maggie Günsberg

BERG
Oxford/Providence

First published in 1994 by
Berg Publishers Limited
Editorial offices:
221 Waterman Street, Providence, RI 02906, USA
150 Cowley Road, Oxford, OX4 1JJ. UK

© Maggie Günsberg 1994

All rights reserved.
No part of this publication may be reproduced in any form or by any means
without the written permission of Berg Publishers Limited.

Library of Congress Cataloging-in-Publication Data
Günsberg Margaret
    Patriarchal representations: gender and discourse in Pirandello's
theatre/by Margaret Günsberg.
        p. cm.
    Includes bibliographical references and index.
    ISBN 0-85496-340-5
    1. Pirandello, Luigi. 1867–1936--Criticism and interpretation.
2. Sex role in literature. 3. Patriarchy--Italy--History--20th century.
4. Italian drama--20th century--History and criticism. 5. Power
(Social sciences) in literature. I. Title.
PQ4835. I77612 1994   92-21180
852'. 912--dc20   CIP

British Library Cataloguing in Publication Data
A CIP catalogue record for this book is available from the British Library

ISBN 0 85496 340 5

Printed in Great Britain by SRP Ltd., Exeter

Contents

Acknowledgments

I would like to express my gratitude to Jennifer Lorch, not only for supporting this study at an early stage, but also for reading the entire first draft. Her suggestions have been invaluable and have contributed to a much improved final product. My thanks to Laura Lepschy, particularly for spotting some howlers; any which may still be lurking are of course my responsibility. Comments by David Forgacs on this project when it was still in its initial conceptual stages also helped it on its way. I owe a historical debt to members of the Italian Department at the University of Reading. I am thinking especially of Giulio Lepschy and Zygmunt Barański, who were there to help over a period which was crucial in terms not only of intellectual formation. Finally, I would like to thank the staff both at the University of Sussex Library and at Istat, Rome, for their assistance.

You Say That I Am, devised and directed by Mary Casey, with Austin Kenny (Pirandello) and Stephen MacCleary (Actor/Paolino); first performed Dublin, 4 May 1991; photograph by Patrick Casey.

Introduction

The purpose of this book is to examine the representation of gender in Pirandello's plays. The fundamental premise on which it is based is that of the dramatic text as one form of cultural reproduction, and indeed production, of gender relations. The specific relation of Pirandello's work to this process is one of alignment with the mainstream cultural encoding of traditional gender identities. In other words, his work can be said to typify, in the ways in which it textualizes gender issues, the dominant attitudes and assumptions of his period, class and gender. This in itself, of course, is not surprising, given his position as a middle-class male born into the archetypally traditional society and culture of Sicily in the 1860s, and taking into account the male-dominated genre for which he was writing. What is of interest, however, are the actual ways in which his narrative works to reproduce and reinforce the status quo of gender relations. An exploration of the textual strategies involved, both overt and covert, forms the primary objective of this book.

In this context, the term 'gender' is used not merely in the biological sense of male and female, but to denote the socially determined concepts of masculine and feminine. 'Gender' is, moreover, interpreted as a term which encapsulates two mutually defining positions. As a consequence of this, it would be inadequate to examine one gender without taking into account the other. The focus in this study, then, is on both genders, and specifically on the ways in which they interrelate. In the same vein, the fact that gender is a social category means that it cannot be considered in isolation from other such categories, like those of class and age. Nor can it be examined independently of the historical context, which works to define and redefine all these categories.

Interwoven with historical context, which by definition denotes flux and change, is the relatively constant ideology of patriarchy. The fundamental drive for hegemony, which is a feature of this gender-specific ideology, necessarily makes it a form of baseline to which this study constantly returns. It should be borne in mind that gender relations in these plays are situated firmly within the dominant heterosexual mode, with rare exceptions such as the fleeting foray into lesbianism in *As You Desire Me* (examined in chapter 2). Heterosexuality itself is a crucial constituent of the patriarchal base which has long informed Western mainstream cultural production. However, as Irigaray has argued, and as the plays of Pirandello show, there is a sense in which patriarchy is distinctly 'hom(m)osexual' rather than even heterosexual (with the extra 'm' shifting the meaning, though not entirely, from 'same' to 'man') (Irigaray, 1977a, p. 168). In other words, relations between men take precedence over those between men and women.

The processes whereby patriarchy seeks to maintain its hegemony are structured according to the dynamics of power relations. Given the fact that patriarchy is male-dominated, the culture which it informs is therefore set to subordinate the female gender. While it is true to say that both men and women are subject to these conditioning restraints, this clearly presents more problems for women. One key area to attend to is the range of covert ways in which their subordination in the gender hierarchy is reinforced. The specific aim of this study is to attempt to make visible the processes of this reinforcement. However, this attempt should not be interpreted as an exercise in pessimistic determinism. On the contrary, the very existence of an entire gamut of narrative strategies of reinforcement, containment and suppression is to be taken as an indication of the threat posed to patriarchy by subordinate positions. Deconstructing these strategies is one possible way of defusing them, and of laying bare the ideological processes generally underpinning cultural production.

The particular form of cultural production to be examined is the dramatic text. Of special interest, therefore, are the ways in which dramatic form works in conjunction with the more obvious and accessible ingredient of plot, to produce gender positions both on stage and in the audience. In my analyses of Pirandello's plays, I have tried as much as possible to integrate theory with practical textual analysis, in the belief that one not only complements the other, but that one without the other is unsatisfactory. In practice, this has inevitably taken the form of a theoretically-oriented introduction at the beginning of each chapter, while the main body tends towards analysis, together with some degree of theoretical explication whenever necessary.

There now follows a brief description of the contents of the six chapters, divided into two parts, which make up this work.

Chapter 1 Weeping Madonnas: The Narrative Problem

Read in conjunction with this introduction, the beginning of the first chapter acts as prelude to the rest of the book in that it addresses the issue that femininity, and in particular female sexuality, poses a problem for patriarchal culture. After noting that Western drama mirrors this problematization, it proceeds to outline both overt and covert manifestations of this in Pirandello's plays. An outline of the workings of patriarchy is then given, and the position of motherhood within it is described. Motherhood provides the main focus of this chapter, which goes on to give historical detail relevant both to this aspect of female sexuality and to its treatment in the plays, which span the period 1898 to 1935. The workings of realist drama are also related to the ideological order which underpins it. The depiction of motherhood in the plays is then examined in its links with female desire, ideal womanhood and asexuality.

Chapter 2 The Father of the Text: The Narrative Solution

This chapter opens with an account of the dominant role of the subject position in culture generally and in dramatic narrative in particular, and aligns subjectivity with masculinity, author/ity and audience identification. The processes of looking/writing/sculpting the female object position are traced in Pirandello's dramatic texts. The representation of female antagonists, rather than female protagonists, is posited. A section on monologos examines the role of logos in the construction of the male subject and includes a discussion of the soliloquy and the monologue in this context.

Chapter 3 Camaraderie in Competition: Male Bonding and Male Rivalry

The focus remains on masculinity, as this chapter develops ideas introduced previously on the prioritizing of relations between men in the particular form of exchange system which characterizes patriarchy. The first section deals with the closely intertwined relationships of male bonding and male rivalry which underlie male relations as depicted in the plays, and examines them in the context of prostitution, as well as in the light of differences in class, age and wealth. The crucial importance of female reproductive power to these relations is also examined. The second section highlights the physical and psychological forms of coercion which feature in male policing of female sexuality. While both genders suffer violence and commit suicide as a result, it is only female characters, however, who undergo virtual imprisonment, or enclosure, indoors.

Chapter 4 Danger, Women at Work

The last chapter in this part considers work as a solution to women's dependency on men and tries to establish the status of working female characters in the plays. Continuing with the notion of enclosure, the inside/outside, private/public dichotomy is examined in relation to work, and in relation to the stage presence of female as opposed to male characters. The first section analyses working female characters in the context of differences in class, age and wealth, and in relation to working male characters. Attention is paid to the related area of education, when female characters are again compared to their male counterparts. The education of child characters is dealt with and issues of class difference linked to educational opportunities. The second section looks at female characters who do not work and considers once again the relevance of class, marital status and family belonging. Factors of stasis and mobility are also taken into account. The chapter concludes with an appraisal of the price of dependency which is paid by leisured female characters in Pirandello's plays.

Chapter 5 Reconstructing the Family: The Power of Speech in *Six Characters in Search of an Author* and Chapter 6 Behind the Veil: Body Politics in *Six Characters in Search of an Author*

Part II offers two detailed analyses of what is perhaps Pirandello's most well-known play. The analyses, of speech turns and gestures respectively, are carried out in the context of the nuclear family as a social unit with a central role in structuring gender relations. The introduction to chapter 5 gives an account of the family, both from a theoretical and a historical point of view. Each chapter provides a detailed methodological background before proceeding with its analysis. Finally, the Appendix provides an analysis of a short story/article by Pirandello which features a discussion between two male characters on feminism and working women. This piece, entitled 'Feminism', appears in translation after the analysis. It is of particular interest in that it is Pirandello's most sustained, as well as being his most overt, treatment of feminism. Written in 1909, it represents the writer's position regarding this issue, a position which was not to change significantly during the remaining twenty-seven years of his life.

By now it should be apparent that what this work offers is a re-reading of Pirandello's plays drawing together recent developments in various theoretical fields. I should perhaps also clarify at this point what this study is not offering. I am in no sense attempting any sort of comprehensive study of Pirandello. My initial intention had been to include his seven novels and fifteen collections of over 200 short stories. Novels such as *The Excluded Woman, Her Husband*, and *The Notebooks of Serafino Gubbio* are of great interest in terms of the portrayal of a female teacher, a female writer and a *femme fatale*, respectively. Particularly fascinating are the ways in which information about these characters is revealed, raising issues concerning, for instance, point of view. Unfortunately, however, this project quickly became too vast and it seemed, in the end, more reasonable to concentrate on the dramatic texts for this work. There was the further complication that many of Pirandello's plays began life as short stories which he later adapted. An account of this transition from one genre to another, and its implications for gender portrayal, would in itself fill a book. There is another sense in which this study does not aim at comprehensiveness even as regards the plays themselves. I have chosen to concentrate on one aspect, that of gender portrayal. Although other aspects have clearly come into play as a result, those with no bearing on the task in hand have remained in the wings.

In effect, the orientation of this study is in diametric opposition to the *auteur*-based approach, which surveys an oeuvre in its entirety in seeking to describe and define the artist in his or her entirety, and despite, rather than in relation to, social context. This book, on the other hand, concentrates on one aspect of some of Pirandello's works in the light of various theories in an attempt to clarify the workings of one particular type of cultural re/production of identities in the social arena of gender relations. One implication of this approach is that the plays are examined according to specific, theoretically defined categories, rather than necessarily in the chronological order in which they were produced. The emphasis is therefore less on a description of the development of certain narrative structures throughout Pirandello's oeuvre than on an analysis of the narrative structures, and phenomena relating to them, at a given socio-historical moment.

It would, of course, be absurd to deny that any sort of development took place from the writing of the first play in 1898 to the last in 1935. Pirandello's life was marked by certain major events which in one way or another doubtless fed into his writing. To cite but a few, his son Stefano was a prisoner of war for part of the Great War, his wife Antonietta was confined to a neurological clinic from 1918, and in 1924 he met the actress Marta Abba, for whom he was to write several plays. His relationship with Marta is a recurrent theme in accounts of his development as a dramatic writer, as Susan Bassnett-McGuire points out in her overview of his life and work. She goes on to say:

> Plays written for Marta Abba tend to include a powerful, idealized central female figure, a part created especially for her talents, such as that of Tuda in *Diana and Tuda* (*Diana e la Tuda*) (1927) or of Marta in *The Wives' Friend (L'amica delle mogli)* of the same year. (1983, p. 19)

However, Tuda in effect becomes anorexic (see chapter 2), while Marta is portrayed with all the ambivalence attendant on the threatening figure of the *femme fatale*. The negative side of this ambivalence finds expression in the misogynist remarks of Venzi, one of her would-be lovers (see chapter 1), a misogyny which reiterates that of the earlier play *At the Exit* (1916) (see chapter 1). Similarly, while new female roles like L'Ignota in *As You Desire Me* (1930) and Donata in *Finding Oneself* (1932) actually have bigger speaking parts than, for example, Agata in *The Pleasure of Honesty* (1918) or Signora Perella in *Man, Beast and Virtue* (1919), the fundamental position of all these female characters within the patriarchal system remains unchanged. Thus while L'Ignota is a central figure, she performs the same function as her equivalent, Signora Ponza, in *That's How It Is (If You Think So)* (1918), albeit with more lines: both characters constitute the central problem to be solved, namely the problem/mystery of female identity, an identity whose threatening excess places it beyond narrative resolution.

Perhaps the closest approximation to Marta Abba in terms of dramatic character is the actress Donata in *Finding Oneself* (1932). Here again, it is true to say that much stage time is devoted to her attempt to find herself, a quest that entails solving the problem of her wish to combine her career with marriage. However, the play ultimately works its way to rediscover and reinforce the traditional notion of this combination (fought for by feminists of the time) as an impossibility. It would seem, then, that if a different type of central female character emerges at all in the post-Abba plays, it is certainly not one which is radically different from the pre-Abba equivalent in terms of achieving true power, namely autonomy, self-fulfilment and self-empowerment. In short, developments in Pirandello's dramatic writing over time in general, and after meeting Marta Abba in 1924 in particular, do not significantly affect the fundamentally patriarchal orientation which continues to inscribe his dramatic production throughout his writing life.

Finally, Pirandello's writing is often interpreted as a satire of bourgeois convention, a satire which is complemented by his philosophy of multiple identity and of flux, or life, as opposed to the constrictions of form. However, I wish to argue in this book that his satire remains predominantly at the philosophical level, without ever really touching the social. Social structures are dealt with, but they are reinforced, not challenged. Written over a period of more than forty years, a period of flux which saw feminist attempts to loosen the stranglehold of social form, the dramatic texts of Pirandello continue the work of mainstream culture in their production and reproduction, not of new multiple identities, but of the traditional gender hierarchy.

PART I

PART I

–1–

Weeping Madonnas:
The Narrative Problem

FATHER: She is not a woman, she is a mother.
Six Characters in Search of an Author, Act I

Introduction: Problematization of Female Sexuality

On the front page of the first issue of *Preparation*, the politico-military journal to which Pirandello himself contributed several articles, the following observation in a piece entitled 'Woman, the Chauffeur and the Tenor' appeared:

> I do not believe I am imparting an excessively unfamiliar piece of information to you, when I tell you in confidence that woman is an eternal character of human drama [*'commedia umana'*]. But the *chauffeur* too, to be fair, is not an oddity to be discarded . . . (Giustino Ferri,Year 1, No. 1, Tuesday, 2 February 1909)[1]

While 'human drama' or 'comedy' (echoing Balzac's *La Comédie humaine*) refers to the drama of everyday life, the so-called 'eternal' role of 'woman as oddity' therein is to be found reproduced in drama itself throughout the ages. This is noted by Ferris in her book on women in theatre: 'Argument and discussion over the nature of women appears as one of the great recurrent themes of Western Drama' (Ferris, 1990, p. 19). She goes on to describe how the mechanics of dramatic construction are particularly appropriate for the representation of femininity, in itself an archetypal cultural construction. Theatrical construction, or artifice, is pointedly exposed in its artificiality by the tradition in Western theatre, described as 'male-generated', of using male actors to portray female characters – a practice which the influential sixteenth-

---

1. Published as 'La donna, lo chauffeur e il tenore' in *La Preparazione*. The translation is my own.

century *commedia dell'arte* did much to change (Ferris, 1990, p. xiii, pp. 38ff). She summarizes the process of dramatic representation of woman-as-problem in the following way:

> The controversy over women is an issue fundamental to the very nature of theatre, for the mimetic art of acting has produced the greatest of imaginative leaps required by the spectator: the theatrical illusion involved in witnessing men playing women. 'Femininity', as feminist theory has soundly argued, exists as a cultural and social construction; central to that construction, as far as the illusionistic art of theatre is concerned, remains the fact that women had absolutely no part in their own dramatic image-making. Theatrical production provided . . . a visual and verbal performance of man's imagined women. (ibid., p. 19)

The 'eternal character' of 'woman-as-oddity', perceived by Giustino Ferri to exist in the real-life drama of 'human comedy', is, then, likewise perceived and constructed by the process of dramatic representation, the narrative of which works its way through arguments and positions on the stereotypically controversial topic of woman/femininity. It is this crucial and defining characteristic of controversiality, or problematization, which provides the essential focus for this chapter. This problematization in effect reveals the incessant cultural processes whereby patriarchal ideology is constantly obliged to reproduce and reaffirm its dominance. The important implication here is that woman/femininity as a cultural and social construction is at the centre of a site of struggle where the ideologically pertinent meanings of such constructs are contested.

One prevalent, highly successful and especially insidious form of contestation, which has the effect of concealing the fact that conflict is actually taking place, is that of simply stating a particular meaning as given. Or, as in Giustino Ferri's case, by emphasizing a familiarity and normality about the selected meaning, a tactic which has the further effect of drawing attention away from other possible meanings (for example, that the category 'woman' is not in fact problematic). This method assures a bloodless victory: by masking the ideological processes which necessarily inform the chosen meaning, combat is not even joined, and the existence of any counter-force pre-empted. This is the strategy of the Ferri quotation, which works in a covert manner to disempower any opposition. The processes whereby he actually problematizes 'woman' are rendered invisible by his statement of fact and by his claim that this fact is, moreover, not unusual. This, together with his tone of irony and confidentiality, distracts and dissuades the reader from questioning the actual bases of his statement.

In the course of this study we shall investigate a range of textual strategies which similarly work to problematize the female gender, at times in very subtle and covert ways, but always to the same effect:

meaning is not seen to be contested, ideological underpinning is not made apparent and the problematization is reinforced as a received notion. At other times, but still to the same effect, male characters talking among themselves in Pirandello's plays overtly state that women are a problem.

Let us look at two examples of comic, thinly veiled but none the less obvious problematization. The first occurs in *Belonging to One Person or to No-One* (1929). Elaborating on 'one of the three fundamental problems which need to be resolved in everyone's life' (with 'everyone' clearly referring only to men), Tito and Carlino swear by a book they have read on the subject. This particular authority, as they inform Merletti (another male character), specifies these problems as follows: somewhere to live, something to eat and woman (Act I).[2] And in the opening scene of *But It's Not Serious* (1919), two male characters discuss whether woman is more or less harmful than nicotine. The conclusion is that, without any doubt, woman is considerably more damaging, 'especially at a certain age'.

It is, then, within this context of both overt and covert problematization of woman, and specifically, as will become apparent, of female sexuality, that the examination of the representation of motherhood will take place. Internalization by female characters of the dominant patriarchal values which problematize and control female sexuality, can lead insidiously to self-policing, self-denigration and self-punishment (notably in *The Epilogue* (1898), and *A Doctor's Duty* (1912), as we shall see shortly). This type of internalization is responsible for the victim role so often assumed by female characters, who frequently refer to themselves as 'poor women'.[3] It will become apparent during the course of this chapter that an attendant humility is particularly peculiar to the portrayal of motherhood.

The male-dominated ideology of patriarchy has in effect created for itself a dependency on an Other sexuality which it is consequently forced to control. Patriarchy can survive only through the continuing process of this endeavour, with female sexuality forever needing to be controlled and possessed and forever remaining just out of reach. While operating from a position of strength, then, patriarchy is always vulnerable, to a greater or lesser degree, depending on the specific period of history

---

2. All references to Pirandello's plays are taken from the *Mondadori Oscar Teatro e Cinema* edition. Act and scene references are given for three-act, but not for one-act, plays. Translations are my own.

3. Examples of female characters who refer to themselves as 'poor women' or 'poor mothers' are: Maddalena (*The Pleasure of Honesty*, Act 1, sc. 5); Beatrice (*Cap and Bells*, Act 1, sc. 5); Mrs Perella (*Man, Beast and Virtue*, Act 2, sc. 5); Gasparina (*But It's Not Serious*, Act 1, sc. 4); The Mother (*Six Characters in Search of an Author*, Act 1); Ersilia (*Clothing the Naked*, Act 1).

involved. It is this vulnerability which lies at the root of its problematization of female sexuality and which motivates the endless process of reinforcement of appropriate sexual values, together with the recuperation and containment of those values which are not appropriate, and which pose a threat to the dominant order. These key strategies of reinforcement, recuperation and containment inform narrative structures whenever the problem-solving process is re-enacted in this particular cultural medium. Rather like the Six Characters, whose very existence depends on forever reliving certain episodes, the continuing dominance of patriarchy rests on the never-ending process of trying to appropriate female sexuality.

The two cardinal areas of female sexuality which patriarchy aims to control are those of reproduction and desire, the latter with its particularly threatening implications of autonomy and self-determination. In order to understand the reasons why efficient control over female sexuality is a major prerequisite for the continuing survival of the patriarchal system, it is necessary to consider how the ideology of patriarchy structures social relationships, especially those which are gender-specific. Before moving on to the specific historical circumstances in which the plays to be examined were written, an introductory overview of the more generalized workings of patriarchy is necessary. The following brief outline of this particular ideological basis which informs Pirandello's writing will address two main issues. The first concerns the defining characteristic of patriarchy, namely the law of patrilineality. Necessarily predicated on this is the second issue, which concerns the structure of the socio-economic system.

According to the law of patrilineality, property is inherited through the male, rather than the female, line, thereby prioritizing and empowering the male gender. Although clearly pre-dating capitalism, this law, according to the Marxist view, came into being in Western civilization with the emergence of private property, in itself one of the necessary preconditions for the development of capitalism. Hamilton provides a useful summary of this position:

> The Marxist analysis . . . has located the origins of female subordination in 'the development of surplus wealth due to the development of production' (Magas, 1971, p. 84); that is, in the phenomenon of private property. The different forms of male domination and female subjection would, therefore, reflect the different modes of production. This analysis sees the oppression of women arising not from biological differences *in themselves*, but from the acquisition of private property which made possible and necessary the exploitation of those differences. The more central the role of private property became, the more ground women lost. (Hamilton, 1980, p. 12)

She continues by differentiating between classes of women, a distinction which will prove essential in our evaluation of the position of

Pirandello's female characters throughout this study, and of his representation of motherhood in this opening chapter:

> Bourgeois women are the culmination of this process: socially useless, their role is to produce legitimate heirs for their husbands' wealth. Working-class women have made greater strides since they were forced into the factory system. While their entry into production was a crucial step, real liberation can only come, as for men, with the overthrow of capitalism and the abolition of private property. (ibid.)

Secondly, and as a direct consequence of the law of patrilineal descent, the structural organization of the socio-economic system must be taken into account. This basically functions on the principle of the exchange of commodities, which are deemed to be either of use or exchange value. Social relationships are structured according to the principles of this system. Given the privileging of the male over the female gender, it is males who are the acting subjects of the exchange system, while females are in the position of objects, and are in fact classified under 'valuables'. Lévi-Strauss describes the position of women as follows: 'valuables – viz. women – valuables *par excellence* from both the biological and social points of view, without which life is impossible, or, at best, is reduced to the worst forms of abjection' (Lévi-Strauss, 1969, p. 481). In the words of Irigaray, men are the 'subjects producing and exchanging', while women are 'productive terrain, merchandise' (Irigaray, 1977b, p. 189).[4]

Within this system, females are valued according to the particular stage of their sexuality. Virgins, for instance, are highly valued; as potential wives and especially mothers, their unused reproductive capacity will be appropriated by the husband, confident (or so the theory goes) that any child she bears will be his. Once married, she loses her exchange value and, as a mother, acquires use value. At this point she leaves the exchange system, according to Lévi-Strauss, in order to prevent the disordering occurrence of incest. This prohibition, together with other laws of the system, is still relevant in modern society, albeit in the context of complex, rather than elementary, structures of kinship (Lévi-Strauss, 1969, p. xxix).

The following summary by Irigaray of the mother's position in this system should be borne in mind for our examination of Pirandello's representation of motherhood:

> That is to say the mother, reproductive instrument marked by the name of the father and enclosed in her house, will be private property, forbidden to be exchanged. The *prohibition of incest* represents this prohibition of the entry

4. All translations of Irigaray are my own.

of productive nature into exchanges between men. As natural value and use value, the mother may not circulate under the form of merchandise without the risk of abolishing the social order. Necessary to its (re)production (notably as (re)producer of children and the labour force: through maternity, feeding, and more generally, domestic maintenance), her function is to maintain it without modifying it by her intervention. Her products will not be legal tender other than being marked by the name of the father, other than being taken up by his law: that is to say, in as much as they are appropriated by him. (Irigaray, 1977a, p. 180)

From this system, there ensues a cultural demarcation of female sexuality into specific, differently valued stages relating to different sexual phases in a woman's life. These phases are, significantly, evaluated not according to her sexual activity in terms of desire or recreation, but solely in terms of fertility or the capacity for procreation. Hastrup defines these stages in the context of cultural assumptions of an 'asymmetric relation' between male and female sexuality, in that 'the male world is generalised', and therefore not liable to this type of sexual demarcation, 'while the female is specified':

It seems, then, that the course of life of a woman is basically divided into three stages. The first stage is that of the unspecified, yet creative virgin; the next stage is that of the sexually specified, child-bearing woman, and the course is completed by a final return to unspecificity, this time of widowhood and of old women's impotence. It is a course going from an ambiguous sexual potentiality, through the unambiguous sexual fertility, on to a condition completely lacking in sexuality and devoid of creativity. . . . This course of life is peculiar to women. Only women's bodies can be used to define social states in this way. They can be used as social markers because they are marked by nature in a way that invites the use of these bodies in other than just sexual ways. Men are just men, all the time. Being the generalised sex, their identification is not tied up with their sexual states to the same extent as is the case with women. The basic asymmetrical relationship is once more conspicuous. (Hastrup, 1978, pp. 59–60)

Of particular relevance to our argument is the cultural devaluation of the 'sterile' stage of female sexuality which follows the previous two, highly valued fertile stages of virginity and motherhood. This is the post-menopausal phase, when females are no longer of any value in the patriarchal exchange system, a system which prioritizes their reproductive function above all else. It is notable that only female characters who are still fertile (in terms of age) are central to plots of sexual/romantic interest in Pirandello's plays. There are, furthermore, many negative portrayals of older women. Particularly derogatory are those that represent women desperately trying to look younger than their years, in other words 'the category of old women and widows, who are ideologically devoid of sexuality', and who conform to this ideology by default in their attempts to appear 'sexual' (ibid.).[5]

In conjunction with an understanding of the basic workings of patriarchal ideology as outlined above, it is important to consider the particular historical period and national variant of patriarchy with which we are concerned. Pirandello's dramatic writing, or adaptation for the stage of earlier prose narrative, took place in the Italy of the 1880s to the 1930s. This period saw significant demographic changes and corresponding attempts at correction by government policy. These clearly have a distinct bearing on our writer's representation of motherhood in particular. The 1880s in fact saw the beginning of a fall in the national birth-rate, which was to remain unbroken during the period 1921–36 (Glass, 1967, p. 264). Although the decline was not serious, with Italy showing a high fertility rate in comparison with other Western countries, Fascist concern nevertheless manifested itself (from about 1926 onwards) in a variety of attempts, by means of legislation and propaganda, to halt the decline and encourage an increase in population (attempts which did not in the event have much impact on the figures) (see Caldwell, 1986, pp. 110–41; Glass, 1967, pp. 219–68).

This historical situation, together with the deep-rooted influence of the Catholic Church, which has always prioritized woman's reproductive role, helps to explain the emphasis which motherhood receives, and even the specific ways in which this emphasis is portrayed, in Pirandello's plays. For example, fertility rates were class-specific, being highest among the poorer classes (Glass, 1967, p. 239). There are there-

---

5. This figure of the older woman trying desperately to look younger, with results that are described as absurd, appears to be somewhat of a *bête noire* for Pirandello. She recurs variously as Mrs Nenni in *That's How It Is (If You Think So)*, the widow Nàccheri in *As Before, Better Than Before*, the landlady Onoria in *Clothing the Naked* and Donna Fiorina Segni in *The Life I Gave You*, etc. In his essay 'Humourism', Pirandello uses the example of an old lady attempting to appear younger than her years to illustrate his theory of humourism: 'I see an old lady, her dyed hair oily with who knows what horrible pomade, ridiculously made-up and decked out in youthful clothes. I begin to laugh. I notice that this old lady is *contrary* to what a respectable old lady should be like. I can, in the first instance and in a superficial way, stop at this comic impression' (Pirandello, 1965, p. 127).

Pirandello goes on to describe the deepening of this perception of the contrary into a feeling, with a consequent progression from the comic to the humouristic. This progression entails his reflection upon, and supposed understanding of, the old lady's motives, namely to retain the love of her much younger husband. This focus on what the post-menopausal female body should be like/is like (i.e. unattractive), not only problematizes that body, but also makes it abhorrent. The 'wrinkles' and 'grey hair' which are presumed to horrify the younger husband are shown primarily as a legitimate source of anxiety for the old lady. This is done in such a way as to appear not only inevitable, but, furthermore, almost incidental (the old lady is used as an example in quite a different argument). This entire passage works in a covert manner to reinforce the cultural stereotype of the distasteful asexuality, or even anti-sexuality, of the post-menopausal woman. (The above translation is my own.)

– 9 –

fore obvious implications of low fertility on the part of the bourgeois middle class, to which the majority of Pirandello's female characters belong. Interestingly, cases of infertility, or quite simply absence of motherhood in married female characters, are restricted to these classes (for instance, the infertile, middle-class Livia in *As Others See It*, 1916). In the peasant play *Liolà* (1917), on the other hand, children abound, with two more conceived during the course of the play. Interlinked with this class element is the urban-rural polarization, with decreased fertility being associated with the towns (Caldwell, 1986, pp. 126, 128).

The overriding importance thus attributed by patriarchal ideology in general, and by the specific historical period covered by Pirandello's years as a dramatist in particular, to the reproductive phase and function of female sexuality, permeates the culture which disseminates its values and assumptions. These particular values can be seen to inform various cultural spheres concerned with narrative. In concentrating our attention on the work of Pirandello it is important to bear in mind that the mainstream cultural context within which his plays were produced featured problematization of the female gender as a narrative concern. The birth of the cinema during this era, for instance, saw this same issue transposed into a technologically advancing medium. A film such as Camerini's *I'll Always Love You* (1933), for example, examines the problematic nature of woman's place in the family and society (Hay, 1987, p. 122).

Narrative concern reveals itself not merely as far as subject-matter is concerned (and many of Pirandello's plays deal with the subject of female sexuality and matters related to it), but also in terms of the structural functioning of the text. In other words, female sexuality is portrayed not only as problematic, in that it causes no end of complications for both female and male characters alike, often resulting in violence, enclosure and even death; it is also posed as a *narrative* problem which requires resolution. (Kuhn, writing about film, describes female sexuality as the 'trouble in the text': Kuhn, 1982, pp. 84–108). This chapter explores the narrativization of this problem, concentrating particularly on the textual strategies which contribute to its reproduction in dramatic form. Female sexuality, notably in the threatening form of female desire, can often be seen to form an integral part of the plot. (Bearing in mind the definition of plot as action, an integral part of the plot is any element in the narrative which moves the action forward.) Frequently posited as a narrative problem requiring resolution, female sexuality can be found as the initial plot motivator, in other words, as the cardinal element which precipitates the subsequent action of the play. Plot motivation, or the emergence of a problem, can itself be seen in terms of the disruption of a pre-existing, ideologically inscribed order. Belsey gives a useful definition of this narrative process in the particular form of realist prose narrative, a definition which is also applicable to realist drama:

> Classic realist narrative . . . turns on the creation of enigma through the precipitation of disorder which throws into disarray the conventional cultural and signifying systems . . . [T]he story moves inevitably towards closure which is also disclosure, the dissolution of enigma through the re-establishment of order, recognizable as a reinstatement or a development of the order which is understood to have preceded the events of the story itself. (Belsey, 1985, p. 53)

One example of the disruption of (patriarchal) order by female sexuality, in the form of female desire, can be found in *A Doctor's Duty* (1912). In this play it is Angelica's desire for the reluctant Tommaso which leads to adultery and ultimately to three deaths. As in many other plays, this disruption actually takes place in a part of the story that is not included in the plot of the play; in other words, it has already taken place before the play begins. The significance of this will emerge during the course of the analyses of individual plays.[6] It is particularly interesting to note, in this context, that the term 'adultery' itself originally referred only to wives and not husbands, in so far as it consisted in 'a wife's granting of marital advantages "to another (*ad ulterium*)" rather than to their owner, her husband' (Ferris, 1990, pp. 33–4, quoting Williman, 1986, p. 69; see also Armstrong, 1976, for a study of adultery in relation to social order). In the same vein, we shall see how female sexuality in terms of female identity provides the problem to be resolved in chapter 2. Two classic examples of this occur in *That's How It Is (If You Think So)* (1918) and *As You Desire Me* (1930), where the fundamental enigma is provided by the mysterious identity of Mrs Ponza and the Unknown Woman, respectively, and where the problem in fact remains unsolved.

Motherhood itself is a common plot motivator. In the form of an illegitimate pregnancy, it gives rise to the plot of *Think it Over, Giacomino* (1917) and *The Pleasure of Honesty* (1918) (with the pregnancies of Lillina and Agata). Conversely, the absence of motherhood is seen as an unfortunate lack which sets events in motion in *Cap and Bells* (1918). At the opposite end of the plot, the closure of the narrative can also sometimes be seen to depend on issues of motherhood, especially in cases when motherhood is portrayed in a final dramatic interaction with female desire. This particular dynamic structures the plot resolution of *At the Exit* (1916) and *The Epilogue* (1898), as we shall see shortly.

In the following examination of Pirandello's representations of motherhood, a variety of traditional tenets will emerge as fundamental.

---

6. For an examination of 'antefact' in Pirandello's plays, see Lepschy (1988–9, 1991).

Embedded as they are in the overall problematization of female sexuality, these representations feature varying degrees of misogyny based on fear of female sexuality, and, in particular, female desire (pp.12–19). This misogyny reveals a rather unfamiliar dimension in the work of Pirandello, who is perhaps known more for his overall geniality and wit, even if this is at times punctuated by a certain pungency. The representations also work to promote both the asexuality and humility of motherhood (pp.26–33), while even forging causal links between female desire and bad, or undeserving, motherhood (pp.12–19). Above all, motherhood is portrayed as the embodiment and apotheosis of womanhood, and indeed as ideal womanhood (pp.19–26), to the extent that not being a mother is shown to have dire consequences if the female character is of the appropriate age and marital status. Despite this, however, motherhood is by no means portrayed as a joyful state, the predominating image being that of the *Mater dolorosa*, in other words, of motherhood as a state of self-sacrifice and suffering.

Female Desire and (or) Motherhood

Pirandello's dramatic output begins with the representation of the problems posed when female sexuality in the form of desire goes against the dominant order in *The Epilogue* (1898). There is an examination of the complications which this transgressivity gives rise to, taking place, as it does, outside the confines dictated by marriage and motherhood. The plot culminates with the containment of the threat to patriarchal order by means of the removal of the offending female character from the narrative. This takes on the insidious guise of self-punishment by means of suicide, with its origins in the internalization by the female character of alien (patriarchal) values. The mechanics of the narrative, both in its precipitation and its closure, will now be analysed in detail.

The Epilogue tells the story of Giulia, whose failing marriage has led her to take a lover (an action which precedes the beginning of the play). When her husband discovers her adultery, he orders her to leave him and their children on the grounds that she is now unworthy of motherhood. She thereupon shoots herself.[7] The initial plot motivator which provides the narrative problem is female sexuality, and in particular female desire which has transgressed the bounds imposed not only by marriage, but also by motherhood. The narrative is set in motion with the discovery by the husband, the guardian of his wife's sexuality, of her transgression. The rest of the narrative enacts an investigation of the

7. For plot summaries of the plays, see Bassnett-McGuire (1989).

question of responsibility for the transgression, which is ultimately apportioned to the female character, as both husband and lover are progressively exculpated by none other than the female character herself. This investigation works to outline, and so reinforce, the underlying premise of a problematic and culpable female sexuality which needs to be both resolved and punished. The closure of the narrative satisfies this need with Giulia's weeping, her violent treatment at the hands of her husband, and finally her suicide.

The narrative investigation and allocation of responsibility deserve close attention. The process begins during a discussion between Giulia and her lover concerning his fears that her husband has discovered their liaison. When Antonio, her lover, suggests that indiscreet behaviour, particularly on her part, has alerted her husband's suspicions, Giulia readily agrees with him. Despite the fact that he then goes on to lament what he in fact sees as their joint indiscretion, Giulia is now quick to turn his remarks into a full-scale reproof of her own participation in the affair, with the words: 'Are you reproaching me now? It's only natural. I have tricked a man who trusted me more than himself. . . . Yes, the fault is mine, in fact, principally mine.' To which he replies, 'I didn't mean that.' With these remarks, then, Giulia initiates her own trial, and appoints her lover as prosecutor.

She embarks on a lengthy monologue which begins with three self-accusations: first, that she ran away from home with her husband-to-be; second, that she practically forced him to run away with her; and third, that she then betrayed him with another man. Although the rest of the monologue explains why she became alienated from her husband (who is now a workaholic) and even accuses Antonio of having taken advantage of her needs in order to become her lover, she finds herself guilty at the end of the speech and condemns herself to the total loss of all she holds dear. She makes it clear, in particular, that her transgression deprives her of her right to motherhood, as well as to life itself: 'I no longer have the right to love anybody! Not even my children! If I bend over to kiss them, it seems as if the shadow of my guilt stains their immaculate foreheads! No... no... Will he do away with me? I will do it, if he does not.' The play is not yet at the halfway mark, the husband has not yet even appeared, but the narrative closure has already been established. The female character has single-handedly tried, judged and condemned herself. The narrative examination and allocation of responsibility has thus been enacted through a female character whose internalization of dominant patriarchal values has led inexorably to self-condemnation and self-punishment.

As if that were not enough, the narrative then goes on to repeat the same process of solving the problem of a transgressive female sexuality.

With the arrival of the husband, and his elaborate toying with Giulia's fears of discovery (a game needed, presumably, to re-activate the narrative after the anti-climax following Giulia's self-condemnation) the process of condemnation and judgment begins all over again. This time it is the husband who prosecutes and condemns, telling Giulia that she is never to see her children again. Although in her own monologue and subsequent speeches she had passed the same sentence on herself, this time she pleads with her judge for her children. When this fails, she asks him to kill her, to which he responds that she should kill herself. In other words, the same narrative process has been represented twice, once by the female character alone and again by the female character and her husband, with narrative closure taking place at the end of the second representation. This double narration of trial, judgment and condemnation serves a reiterative function which gives resonance to the reinforcement of patriarchal values informing the narrative.

The second representation, moreover, is significantly prefaced by an exchange concerning the children between Giulia and the maid, Anna, so that, just before the husband's arrival, much is made of Giulia's maternal love. Her motherhood is in fact emphasized throughout the play as being of great importance to her. This serves to underline the severity of her punishment when she condemns herself/is condemned by her husband, never to see her children again. The narrative thus works to promote a direct link between transgressive female sexuality and bad/disallowed motherhood, a process which is endorsed by the female as well as the male character. Finally, this weeping Madonna has to forfeit her life along with her motherhood as the narrative closes, in order to contain the threat of her errant sexuality.

In *A Doctor's Duty* (1912), female desire is again set in opposition to the traditional values of motherhood and ideal wifehood and, as the prime plot motivator, gives rise to a series of destructive events which culminate in the deaths of three characters. Prior to the beginning of the play, Angelica, married but apparently childless, has seduced the 'reluctant' and 'blameless' husband of Anna, who, on the contrary, is a 'saintly' wife and mother. Angelica's husband discovered the lovers in bed and fired at Tommaso, but was himself killed by his rival. Tommaso then shot himself and Angelica threw herself out of a window. The lover's life is saved by a doctor, who is then berated for his trouble when the lover realizes he will be charged with murder, because his self-inflicted injuries make it impossible for him to plead self-defence. The lover then reopens his wounds, which are left untreated by the doctor, who at this point respects his patient's wish to die.

Although it is the dilemma of the doctor which is foregrounded by the title of the play as its dramatic pivot, the narrative structure does not in fact revolve around this issue, which is full of contradictions. The lover's defence of his actions appears to conflict, in essence, with his subsequent shooting of himself once the husband is dead. Tommaso tells his wife that he was obliged to defend himself because he could not, for her sake, allow himself to die for the other woman. The reasons he gives are that he considers the other woman to be worthless, and that he was actually reluctant to be in her bed in the first place ('I didn't want to be there') and found himself there 'by chance'. These reasons clearly do not square with the fact that he did in fact try to kill himself.

Such inconsistencies do, however, reveal the basic narrative preoccupation, which lies with the disruptive potency of female sexuality, and in particular, female desire. This concern surfaces here to interfere with the supposedly central plot dilemma revolving around the lover's legal position and the duty of the doctor towards his patient. A transgressive female sexuality sets the narrative in motion, with one man's wife, Angelica, being responsible for the seduction and sexual deviance of another woman's husband. The narrative subsequently delineates the complications which arise from this seduction, culminating in the death of the husband at the hands of the lover, the suicide both of the reluctant lover and the errant wife, and the widowing of the ideal wife and mother. Apart from the lover's mother-in-law, who does blame him for the affair, both he and his wife hold Angelica entirely responsible.

The choice of the name Angelica for this dangerously seductive female character is unlikely to be fortuitous. As the archetypal seductress who drives Orlando and other knights mad with desire in Ariosto's major epic poem, *Orlando furioso*, the connotations of her name are indisputable. In this play her insatiable sexual desire is responsible for her illicit liaisons not only with one, but with several men (according to Anna). She refers to Angelica misogynistically, in rabid animal terms, calling her a 'sick monkey' and a 'mad bitch', while her husband is the innocent victim: 'Look, it wasn't even a caprice for him; it was nothing, merely the proof of a sort of weakness which no man can stop himself giving in to.' Her husband, who himself never refers to Angelica in any terms other than 'that woman', is therefore not merely accepted as having reacted, rather than acted, in the affair; his wife here actually excuses, and even justifies, *his* desire, as 'a sort of weakness'. In the case of the married male character, then, the issue is a minor one, that of loss of self-control.

No such allowances, however, are made for the married female character, who forfeits her life for her desire. This double standard reappears elsewhere in Pirandello's plays, notably at the opposite chronological end of his production, in *One Doesn't Know How*, written in 1934. Here again, gender-specific allowances are made for desire. The sea-faring

Giorgio considers it only 'natural' to indulge in sexual liaisons when he is 'far away for so long' from his wife, and even makes her aware of his affairs on the basis that she would be 'stupid' not to understand the inevitable. 'Women', on the other hand, he says, 'are another matter'. A further double standard, this time at the expense of another male character, is in evidence, when Giorgio reacts to his wife's affair during his absence by instantly shooting her lover (whose case is not helped by the fact that he is called Romeo).

As an important side-effect of female desire, the childless Angelica, as well as being responsible for three deaths, is also shown to contaminate motherhood, as the narrative depicts the unhappy separation of her lover's wife from her children (who are with her mother while she nurses her husband). A transgressive female sexuality is therefore represented as problematic on all fronts. The resolution of the problem requires containment by means of suicide, as in *The Epilogue*. The suicide, it is revealed, has taken place before the play opens, thereby effectively constituting a closure to a previous narrative (or, in Formalist terms, to the story from which the plot of the play is drawn).[8] This closure is then reinforced by the process of the play's exploration, not of the responsibilities of the doctor, but of the culpability of female desire.

The misogynist terms in which response by both male and female characters to female desire is expressed in *A Doctor's Duty*, find their apotheosis in *At the Exit* (1916), a play in which motherhood and female desire are once again set in opposition to each other. In this play, set in the afterlife, a Fat Man awaits the appearance of his wife, the Murdered Woman. He eagerly waits for her to be murdered by her lover, at which point, he says, he himself will at last find peace. During the dialogue between the Fat Man and the Philosopher, which, notably, leads (up) to her appearance, the former expresses a revulsion towards his wife in terms which go beyond her involvement with another man to delineate the fear of an insatiable and exultantly defiant female desire. The Fat Man describes how his wife was never satisfied, whether with her lover or indeed with anybody, and would undoubtedly come to grief because of this. Her dissatisfaction with her lover began immediately after her betrayal, when, the Fat Man says, 'she turned on him all the fierce hatred which she had formerly felt for me'.

Both men, the Fat Man and his wife's lover, were therefore treated identically by the wife, once her desire renewed itself for a new object; the Fat Man even refers to the lover as his own shadow, with the wife desiring a lover (the shadow) to complement the husband (the body). The shadow/lover and the body/husband, two socially defined aspects of

8. See Matejka and Pomorska (1971); Šklovsky (1976); Todorov (1968).

masculinity, work together to represent the category 'man' by means of a process of narrative doubling into two male characters. Other men would follow in their footsteps, the Fat Man says, as the wife would not be satisfied with merely one man after her husband's death: 'When she is free, why only one? Especially when that one is merely the boring shadow of a body which no longer exists? She will want another one; and then others too, maybe.' Not only are innumerable men/the category of 'man' itself, the objects of desire of an insatiable female sexuality; that insatiability is expressed as the specific desire for adulterous love.

As far as the Fat Man is concerned, the worst aspect of this insatiable female sexuality is its exultancy: it is the laughter of his wife, he believes, which will ultimately incite her lover to murder: 'The first time she laughs, he will kill her.' He then describes her laughter in the following terms: 'I can already hear her terrible laugh gurgling in her convulsed viscera/womb (*viscera*), ready to burst in his face from between the cut of her shining teeth in that ferocious red mouth of hers.' The imagery of the *vagina dentata*, in all its threatening overtones, is unmistakable, with the lover as innocent victim of these castrating, devouring female genitalia, the locus of insatiable, all-consuming female desire (Creed, 1986, p. 44; Theweleit, 1990, p. 201).

A similar uneasiness regarding the female mouth, and its analogy with the vagina, appears in the description by the frustrated male character, Venzi, of 'lips marked like a wound' in *The Wives' Friend* (1927), in a reference to the lipstick worn by a sexually provocative/desiring woman (Theweleit, 1990, pp. 192, 454 n. 8). The description ends with the unmistakably phallic cigarette positioned between these awesome lips: 'frivolous, flirtatious, shameless, provocative, simpering: almost naked, with short hair, made-up eyes, lips marked like a wound, and cigarette in mouth' (Act II). The image of the vagina as wound has a long tradition, stretching at least as far back as Rabelais, whose *Pantagruel* features an episode with a woman whose vagina is mistaken for a wound by a lion and a fox (ch. 15).

The Fat Man's description situates the origin of this fearful female threat in the 'convulsed womb', the very heart of female sexuality and traditionally the seat of hysteria (from the Latin *hystericus*, derived from the Greek for 'belonging to, suffering in, the womb', and characterized by 'convulsive fits of laughter or weeping') (OED). He then outlines the withering, earth-shaking destruction brought about by her laughter, a laughter no less powerful than Medusa's petrifying gaze:

> I told you that your philosophy could not tear the roses from my garden, but the laughter of that woman could do more than this! Every time I used to hear her laugh, it was as if the earth shook, the sky darkened, and my little garden withered to a mass of bristling thistles. It erupts from her womb, like frenzied, destructive rage. (*At the Exit*)

His repeated belief, 'Of course he will kill her', voices his/the lover's desire for the removal of the threat via the death of the woman, a desire which is already satisfied at the outset by the name 'Murdered Woman' given to the female character.

The male fear of female sexuality, and desire for its demise, works itself out further as the wish is fulfilled by the appearance of the Murdered Woman herself. What is more, the wish is not just fulfilled by, but actually evokes, her appearance: the Fat Man concludes his description of her laughter with the words: 'Of course he will kill her'; after a pause, during which he listens, staring into space with one hand raised, he continues: 'Perhaps he has already killed her. In a short while we shall see her come out of there. There she is! There she is!' His excited, sadistic description of her dancing, spinning, dishevelled figure, laughing and splattering blood in all directions from a wound in her left breast, ushers in the Murdered Woman.

The mere appearance of the Murdered Woman, in other words, the on-stage affirmation of a demise already ensured by the naming of the female character, does not, however, suffice to allay male fears and provide a narrative resolution. The repeated examination of the female problem from all angles, in other words, the reiteration which consolidates the reinforcement of patriarchal values, now requires the female character to display her own culpability. She does so precisely as outlined by the male character who preceded her on to the stage. It is not only the Fat Man, moreover, who has 'set the scene' for this: the play itself opens and closes with the words of his companion, that most familiar and ubiquitous of Pirandellian characters, the male philosopher, here quite undisguised as the Philosopher.

The female character's self-display is therefore doubly contained within a securely closed patriarchal frame. She accordingly reveals her visceral threat by laughing, the sinister implications of which have previously been described by the Fat Man, who now relives his terror; she exhibits her sexuality, inviting voyeurism by recounting how her breasts and legs were bare for all to see for an entire morning after her death; and she tells of her lover's suicide, thereby validating male fears. (Female exhibitionism and its counterpart, male voyeurism, will be discussed in chapter 2.) Most significantly, she exposes her sexual insatiability up until the very moment of death:

> No kiss has ever set me on fire. Thrown on to the bed, as the white ceiling of the room seemed to be bearing down on me, and everything was going dark, I hoped, I hoped for that final kiss, O God, to set me on fire, in the way that my frustrated womb has always yearned for hopelessly. (*At the Exit*)

Constant insatiability, then, is made synonymous with actual denial of sexual satisfaction in this uncompromising process of forbidding female desire.

The narrative investigation of the problem of her desire continues with the arrival in the afterlife of a male child trying to eat a pomegranate, a desire it needs to fulfil before finding peace, according to the laws of the afterlife established by the play. At this point the issue of motherhood enters the narrative: the Murdered Woman and the Child with Pomegranate now interact as the nurturing mother-figure helps the child to eat the fruit. (It is, notably, the female character who immediately makes contact with the Child, while the Fat Man and the Philosopher merely stand by.) Having been helped to fulfil its desire, the child vanishes. The Murdered Woman then bewails her own unfulfilled desire and begins to weep. She can satisfy *his*, the little man's, desire, but not her own. Her painful and 'salutary' transition from laughter to tears by means of a maternal experience signals the disappearance of the Fat Man.

Despite his disappearance, which betokens the fulfilment of his/male desire, and the implication that male fears have finally been assuaged, the Murdered Woman's punishment has yet another stage to go through, once again involving an experience related to motherhood. Another child, this time a Little Girl, who is not dead, comes on to the scene. Although not able to see the Murdered Woman, the child senses her 'terrible eyes staring at her from the shadows' and is afraid. When the Little Girl leaves, the Murdered Woman 'gets to her feet, violently shakes her dishevelled head, raises her arms in desperation and flees like a madwoman after the Little Girl, who has disappeared'.

This gesture, revealing as it is of thwarted maternal feelings, heralds the climax of the Murdered Woman's punishment (a similar gesture is repeated twice by the suffering Mother in *Six Characters in Search of an Author* (1921) towards her retreating Son). This punishment, all the more powerful because the rejecting child is female, warns that transgressive female sexuality, particularly in the form of female desire, is incompatible with motherhood. The anguish of the Murdered Woman at this point betokens her recuperation for the role of motherhood, a role prized by patriarchal culture as the apotheosis of womanhood. With this recuperation, the danger of female desire has been defused.

Womanhood is Motherhood

The prominent involvement of motherhood in the closure of *At the Exit* and *The Epilogue*, in that both the Murdered Woman and Giulia are punished in their maternal role for their desire, indicates the importance of motherhood in the containment of female sexuality, and, in particular, of female desire. To this end, the patriarchal ideal collapses motherhood and female sexuality together, so that womanhood *is* motherhood. This is succinctly expressed by the Father's description of the Mother in *Six Characters in Search of an Author:* 'She is not a woman, she is a mother.' In the lead-up to this definition, he puts forward the traditional, idealized viewpoint, namely that she quite simply lacks desire (an orthodox attribute of motherhood which will be explored in the next section): 'Her drama could not consist in the love of two men, for whom she, incapable, could not feel anything – apart from, perhaps, a little gratitude.' Her drama, by contrast, 'consists entirely in these four children which she had by the two men' (Act I).

This equation of womanhood with motherhood is achieved in *Liolà* (1917), a fantasy of traditional masculine wish-fulfilment, by means of a metaphor with a tradition going back to the classics. In this metaphor, woman is likened to a piece of fertile terrain which produces fruit when cultivated by man (Halperin, 1990, pp. 140–1). The effect of this is to equate womanhood with, and reduce it to, the function of reproduction: 'Here we have a piece of land. If you stand around looking at it without doing anything to it, what will the land produce for you? Nothing. Like a woman. She won't bear you any children' (Act I). Another comparison likens woman to a sow which produces piglets, and to a cow which produces calves. In *The Grafting* (1921), the same rhetorical strategy is carried out by using a botanical metaphor for the rape and subsequent pregnancy of woman-as-plant. Womanhood is thus described, and circumscribed, in terms of motherhood.

To this end, womanhood is also often represented as being incomplete without motherhood. Several plays illustrate the devaluation of the married woman who is childless, together with the predicament in which this places the husband, and work to posit the threat of the loss of the husband as a possible consequence. *The Grafting* opens with a discussion by a group of women about motherhood, during the course of which the view is put forward that there are problems between Laura and Giorgio because they are childless after seven years of marriage. This view is justified as follows: 'Do you know what happens to a woman, after so many years, if she hasn't had children? She is ruined. I tell you it's true! And the man is ruined too. Both of them are ruined. It's inevitable!' There follows the innuendo that the man will look elsewhere as a result: 'As the man gives up the idea of seeing his own wife become a mother, so . . . you know what I mean, don't you?' (Act I, sc. 1).

Laura, the daughter of the woman expressing this view, is at that very moment in the process of being raped elsewhere, and will become pregnant as a result. Furthermore, it is made clear that it is she, and not any impotence on the part of her husband, which has led to their childlessness. (We learn later that he already has an illegitimate child by a peasant girl.) Attention thereby remains firmly focused on the woman's sexuality/reproductive status. In particular, the narrative dwells on her subsequent compulsion to motherhood despite the horrific manner of conception, a compulsion to which her husband reluctantly concedes.

It is during the course of her conversation with a gardener on the subject of plant-grafting that Laura clarifies her resolve to bear the child of her rape. The gardener's explanation of the process of grafting is constructed in such a way as to set up a subtext, which Laura clearly reads. The grafting itself represents the rape, and the plant to be grafted upon is the beautiful but childless woman. The rough but skilful peasant (*villano*, with the double meaning of 'peasant' and, significantly, 'rough man') who performs the grafting, stands for the rough *but potent* rapist, and the plant's condition of being in sap/desirous of bearing fruit, is the woman's ability to bear children/maternal love:

'. . . You think you have performed the grafting; you wait . . . – what are you waiting for? You have killed the plant. – It takes skill, it really does! Ah, perhaps because it is the work of a peasant? Of a peasant who, God forbid, were he to touch you with his rough hand, would harm you? But this rough hand . . . Look here.
(He takes a huge vase with a leafy plant growing in it, and places it next to Laura.)
Here we have a plant. You look at it: it is beautiful, that is true. You enjoy the plant, but only to look at: it doesn't bear you any fruit. I, a peasant, come along, with my rough hands, and look, do you see?
(He begins to take off the leaves, in order to perform the grafting . . .)
It looks as if, in a trice, I have destroyed the plant: I have torn it up, now I am cutting, here: I cut and cut – and now I make an incision – wait a minute – and without you knowing anything about it, I make you bear fruit. What have I done? I have taken a bud from another plant and I have grafted it on here . . . .'

The plant, furthermore, must be in sap (*in succhio*), in other words, the woman must be fertile for the grafting to take: 'Yes, in sap. That's to say . . . how can I put it? . . . in love, that's it! It must want . . want the fruit which it cannot bear on its own!' (*The Grafting*, Act II, sc. 1). At this point Laura associates the love of the plant for the fruit it wants to make its own with her maternal love for the child: 'without knowing anything anymore, with no more memory of whence the bud came to it, it makes it its own, it makes it the fruit of its love.' Imagery from nature, then, is used to establish and justify the 'natural' and inevitable role of womanhood as motherhood. As a highly dangerous extension of this, the act of rape as 'skilful grafting' has not only been naturalized, but also glorified. Female sexuality characterized by deficiency, namely the absence of motherhood, thus provides the initial problem for narrative exploration, with the drive towards the fulfilment of womanhood in motherhood propelled by the botanical/biological metaphor.

The loss of the husband's attentions as one consequence of the inadequacy of the 'unfulfilled', childless wife, which is mentioned at the beginning of *The Grafting*, motivates the plot of *As Others See It* (1916). Leonardo, in a childless marriage with Livia, has had an affair and a child with Elena. Once again, the lack, or fault, is clearly seen to lie with the wife (who is described at the beginning of the play as 'cold', and so, by analogy, frigid), and not with any impotence on the part of the male character. It is interesting how, in both these plays, the husband's sexual potency is made abundantly clear by means of a child which each has fathered outside the marriage. In terms of narrative strategy, the apparent irrelevance of this fact to the actual plot is an indication that its function lies elsewhere: rather than moving the plot forwards in an overt manner, the husband's proven virility serves the precise purpose of covertly and insidiously proving, and defining, the wife's inadequate womanhood; in other words, it points up the ideological perspective which, however imperceptibly, informs the plot.

Like Laura, Livia's ultimate reaction is to internalize the values which equate childlessness with inadequate womanhood, and she accordingly accounts for her situation in such a way as to focus on the problematization of her own sexuality/childlessness. Her husband's sexuality, by contrast, remains not only unquestioned in this context, thereby rendering it unproblematic, but is actually sanctioned: 'I am neither defending him nor accusing him! I see myself, Father; and what I am lacking! Home is where the children are. And he has no children here' (Act II). Leonardo later compounds this reaction. When he reveals to Livia that Elena has suggested he leave both her and the child, Dina, and that only the child has been keeping them together, Livia asks whether Dina would prefer to live with him. To this he replies: 'You mean, if she were ours? Ah, don't even talk about it! Here, out in the open. How happy I would be! And so would she, the little girl.' Livia says 'Really? Without her mother?' (Act II). When Leonardo responds 'No, I mean if she were yours! If she were yours, Livia!', Livia's reaction is 'to darken and stiffen as if with an agonizing shudder', a sign of her acceptance that the problem, and its solution, are connected with her childlessness, with her inadequacy.

The resolution towards which the narrative moves is correspondingly centred on female sexuality being seen to solve what is made to seem *its* problem, with male sexuality standing by, unproblematic, in the wings, ready to complete the process of closure which a culpable but conveniently self-correcting female sexuality has set in motion. Livia decides she can resolve her lack through social motherhood, and asks Elena, the biological mother, to return to her not just the husband, but the father; in other words, to give Dina to the reconciled married couple, who would legitimize her as well as provide her with much wealthier surroundings. Leonardo arrives, unaware initially of Livia's plan, which he subsequently supports by playing on the wealthy upbringing Dina would have, before finally leaving with her.

As a further indication of the exclusively female nature of the central narrative preoccupation, it is not Leonardo's wealth that is being referred to here, but Livia's, as Leonardo has none of his own. Although important (as we shall see in chapter 4), wealth is not in fact the main issue. Money appears to be significant, in that Elena originally came to Leonardo for financial help and is now in difficulties with her landlord because Leonardo is having problems supporting her. Wealth therefore is used as the final lever to persuade Elena to give up her child. On the other hand, it is made clear that she would be able to support herself and Dina with her work, which is said to be more lucrative than Leonardo's. This inconsistency reveals the pivot of the narrative to lie elsewhere. What is actually at stake is the solution of a different problem, namely that of the insufficiency of the childless wife.

There is, in addition, more to the relationship between Leonardo and Elena than a simple affair which began after Leonardo's marriage to Livia. This would have been sufficient in terms of the plot. However, Elena was once betrothed to Leonardo and broke off their engagement for what are described as petty reasons. In later years she came to him for help, in the hard times that followed her husband's death, by which time Leonardo had married Livia. At this point a short-lived affair ensued and Dina was born. Elena's revelation of her initial, unwarranted rejection of marriage to Leonardo, occurring as it does during the visit of Livia which precipitates the resolution, serves the function of giving her impending loss of her illegitimate daughter the aura of a punishment. The way is clear for the childless Livia to resolve her lack and reclaim the father as her husband.

As we have just seen, the cultural foregrounding of female reproduction provokes competition between female characters. In *Liolà* (1917), Mita and Tuzza compete for the old but wealthy landowner, Uncle Simone. Lack of motherhood sets the action in motion. The play opens with the violent eruption of Uncle Simone's anger at Mita's apparent inability to produce children, followed by his abandonment of her in favour of Tuzza, whom he will support on condition that she pretends the child she is expecting is his. As Tuzza's mother says, in a manner reminiscent of Livia in *As Others See It*, 'His home will be here. Home is where the children are' (Act III). Liolà, who is in fact the father of Tuzza's child, persuades Mita to become pregnant by him too. Mita claims this child to be her husband's, successfully ousts Tuzza and regains her place as Uncle Simone's wife.

At issue once again, then, is the threat of the loss of the husband on the part of the childless wife, openly associated here with the loss of economic support. Uncle Simone is a wealthy farmer. Mita, whose mother died at birth and who was left fatherless at the age of three, is therefore said to have married well above herself. With her failure to become a mother, however, she runs the risk of losing not merely a husband, but considerable financial security. Her low position in the Sicilian peasant economy thus differs radically from that of the upper-middle-class Livia in *As Others See It*. The latter's well-connected father, friend of a newly appointed government minister, ensures her material stability, so that losing her husband carries no financial threat in her case.

While Mita loses both husband and economic security, he, as possessor not only of wealth-producing land but of his wife's reproductive capacity, can simply jettison the unproductive (Mita) in favour of the 'officially' productive (Tuzza). This play clarifies one of the underlying reasons behind the importance given by patriarchy to motherhood within marriage, namely the property interests of a culture in which inheritance is patrilineal. As Aunt Croce says of Uncle Simone's continual lament that he has no children, 'No, what he is lamenting – let's be honest about it – what he is lamenting, is his wealth: so much beautiful wealth which would end up, at his death, in other people's hands. He can't get it out of his mind' (Act I) (a concern also explored by Verga in his novel *Mastro-Don Gesualdo*, 1889). Moreover, Uncle Simone's illtreatment of the childless Mita is made possible by the fact that, as her aunt suggests, she has no male relatives to protect her: 'I should like to see what would happen if she at least had a brother. Then he wouldn't treat her like this, I assure you' (Act I). Such 'protection' is necessitated precisely by a patriarchal culture in which female reproductivity is in the possession of men, who therefore police and protect 'their' women from other men. For that reason, the fact that Mita's aunt might afford her adequate protection is not even considered as a possibility.

Even when the childless wife does not lose her husband to another woman who has borne him a child, as she does in *As Others See It*, or to one who will officially do so, as in *Liolà*, her inadequate womanhood can result in her losing him quite simply to another woman. This is what happens in *Cap and Bells* (1918) (a reference to the cap worn by mad people). Beatrice, the wife in question, is introduced by the stage directions as hysterical (*isterica*) and unbalanced (she is prone to outbursts of temper followed by sudden exhaustion). This is significant information in the light not only of the closure of the play, which ends with her madness, but also in view of the traditional association of hysteria with frigidity, and hence childlessness.[9]

9. For an account of the significance of hysteria, particularly as the impotent underside of feminism, in certain of Pirandello's female characters, see Günsberg (1992).

As Beatrice bemoans the unfaithfulness of her husband, La Saracena's comment supplies information about the original plot motivator which has set in motion the husband's adultery, and thus all the ensuing events of the play: 'A household where jealousy has taken hold? It is destroyed! Finished! A perpetual earthquake, let me tell you! If only there were children involved.' Fana agrees: 'This is the real problem here: that there aren't any!' (Act I, sc. 1). The issue of the childless marriage is hereby raised as a problem, indeed as *the* problem leading to the husband's infidelity, with the implication that it is the childless wife who is at fault.

As the plot unfolds, Beatrice moves ever nearer her punishment, as she attempts to take action against her husband's adultery. She sets a trap for her husband and the other woman, who are found together, and officially denounces them. However, she has reckoned without the other woman's husband. Ciampa is aware of his wife's infidelity, but has preferred to remain silent so long as her adultery remains a secret. With Beatrice's denunciation the matter becomes public knowledge, and he is revealed as a cuckold. He feels obliged to kill both his wife and her lover as a consequence, when another solution presents itself to him. If Beatrice can be declared mad and confined in a sanitorium for three months, everybody will save face. As the other characters, including her mother and brother, urge her to agree to this solution, she suddenly appears to go mad and is ushered away at the end of the play. Everybody saves face, then, except Beatrice. It is she who must pay for everyone else and, ultimately, for her childlessness, without which the situation might never have arisen. Her denunciation of a situation which is 'inevitable', given her childlessness, compounds her culpability and triggers the narrative resolution which will culminate in her punishment and removal from the 'normal life' of the play.

The narrative construction of her actual collusion with these values and their enforcement is anticipated by the description of her as already unbalanced at the beginning of the play. The final enclosure, which constitutes her punishment, is foreshadowed by various other references to the enclosure of women. Beatrice herself speaks of wanting to 'get out': in her letter to La Saracena asking for help, she writes 'My house is an inferno; I want to get out at all costs!' She repeats to both La Saracena and Fana 'Yes, yes, and I want to get out! At once! Once and for all!' (Act I, sc. 1). Ciampa, meanwhile, always keeps his wife locked up on the following principle: 'Wife, sardines and anchovies: the last two, under oil and brine; the wife, under lock and key' (Act I, sc. 4). Only the window is left open for her to breathe, and even then, he says, he does not want to hear reports of his wife having been seen doing herself an injury trying to get out. His solution to the 'problem' of Beatrice is consistent with this: 'She must be locked up! She must be locked up!' (Act III, sc. 5). The narrative problem of a non-reproductive and generally subversive female sexuality is thus resolved by means of its en/closure.

Asexuality and Motherhood

The patriarchal drive towards the reductive and limiting equation of womanhood with motherhood is further reinforced in its strategies of containment by the construction of motherhood as asexual. To this end motherhood, and particularly asexual motherhood, is idealized in patriarchal culture. This idealization is necessary in order to compensate for the actual deprivation and isolation experienced by mothers in devoting themselves exclusively to this activity. In the words of Bridenthal, 'It is now clear that our form of raising children is historically specific, a product of advanced capitalist society, which idealizes mother*hood* while isolating and marginalizing mother*ing*, in a classic demonstration of the mystifying function of ideology' (Bridenthal, 1982, p. 232). The historical reality behind the cultural idealization and prioritization of motherhood is, in effect, one of marginalization. The development of capitalism and the consequent separation of the workplace and home, she argues, have resulted in the isolation and marginalization of women, and especially mothers, in the low-status, private zone of the home. Men, on the other hand, dominate the high-status, public world of work, now located outside the home, which previously accommodated both home and workplace (ibid.).

The consequent cultural idealization of motherhood sanctifies not merely asexuality in particular, but also humility, self-sacrifice and suffering. Humility and obedience, as prescribed by the vows of marriage, are encouraged precisely in order to camouflage the unavoidable conflict of basic interests involved in complete and enforced abnegation of the self. Catholic religion and its iconography, especially in Italy, provide a highly influential array of illustrative material, ranging from the asexual conception of Christ by a virgin, to imagery of the Madonna and Child foregrounding motherhood as the only possible female occupation, while even her suffering is idealized and immortalized by her identity as *Mater dolorosa* (Hastrup, 1978, pp. 60–3; Warner, 1976). The Mother in *Six Characters in Search of an Author* wears a mask described in terms of sculptures and paintings of the *Mater dolorosa* found in churches, with fixed tears of wax in the dark rings under her eyes and down her cheeks. Later plays, such as *The Life I Gave You* (1924) and *The Fable of the Changeling* (1933), also focus on maternal suffering and anguish (with the characters Donna Anna and the Mother, respectively). The religious association of suffering, of the 'Passion', and of mystical experience itself, with sexual arousal (viz. Bernini's *The Ecstasy of St Teresa*), would seem to indicate that sublimation of female desire is necessary for 'true' (i.e. idealized) motherhood/womanhood. Beardsley writes: 'It seems likely that most women sublimate in love for their children a considerable part of the drives that might otherwise be expressed in sexual relationships' (Beardsley *et al*, 1959, p.333, quoted in Michaelson and Goldschmidt, 1971, p. 342).

An interesting effect of such sublimation is evident in cases of narrative doubling of identity, namely in some of the discordant mother–daughter dyads represented in Pirandello's plays, where the daughter appears in effect to be her asexual mother's sexual Other. This is partly related to a process which Chodorov describes as follows: 'Mothers, especially in isolated nuclear family settings without other major occupations, are also invested in their daughters, feel ambivalence towards them, and have difficulty in separating from them' (Chodorov, 1978, p. 135). The situation of this particular dynamic within psychoanalytical discourse takes as its starting point the entry of the female subject into patriarchal culture via the Oedipus complex. At this point the little girl 'takes her father as a love-object. Her mother becomes the object of her jealousy. The little girl has turned into a little woman' (Freud, XIX, p. 256, quoted in Silverman, 1983, p. 143). In addition to this, as Silverman notes, 'the female subject learns of her "castration" only by means of a cultural mediation in which the mother plays a key role' (Silverman, 1983, p. 146).

This may illuminate the particular dynamic which characterizes some of Pirandello's mother-daughter dyads. The Mother in *Six Characters in Search of an Author* (1921), for instance, physically prevents her daughter's sexual liaison taking place. In this play, the daughter plays the laughing, defiant Eve to the patently asexual Mother's *Mater dolorosa*. Matilde in *Henry IV* (1922) is jealous of her daughter Frida, who now looks as she herself did when she was young and beautiful, in a clear case of projected desire, or desire to desire. And while Marta in *The Wives' Friend* (1927) is sexually desirable and unattainable, her mother is described in such a way as to suggest that she is repressed (she appears impassible and rigid in her bearing, yet her voice is full of passion).

It is clear, then, that one major threat which patriarchal idealization of asexual motherhood and womanhood aims to obviate, is that of female desire. *At the Exit*, as has been shown, outlines the misogynist fear of an insatiable female desire, a desire which is to be curbed by motherhood. And in *The Epilogue*, the sexual mother is punished by the loss of her children and her life. In *The Pleasure of Honesty* (1918),

Agata is told that 'in you, inevitably, the lover had to die with the arrival of motherhood. You see, you are no longer anything other than a mother' (Act III, sc. 5). At the latter end of Pirandello's dramatic production, Mommina, in *Tonight We Improvise* (1930), is similarly informed by her husband that her children are all she should think about, in a case where not only her sexuality, but also the possibility of working as a professional singer, are suppressed.

In *The Pleasure of Honesty*, asexuality appears under the guise of 'honesty' or 'respectability'. Agata's pregnancy as the result of an affair with the unhappily married Fabio is the plot motivator of this play. Baldovino agrees to marry Agata, thereby legitimizing the child and saving the honour of the family, for the pleasure of living out an honest role in the eyes of a society which has, until now, spurned him. Honesty is also a specifically female sexual attribute connoting chastity and absence of desire as prescribed by patriarchy, and one which it is now crucial for Agata to uphold. The stage directions introducing Agata delineate her progress in attempting to maintain this honesty and to forgo her desire for Fabio. For her, being honest has the significance not, as in Baldovino's case, of pleasure, but, on the contrary, of driving necessity: 'Twenty-seven years old, proud, almost hard, as a result of the effort involved in resisting the downfall of her honesty (*onestà*). Desperate and rebellious in the first act, she then proceeds, proud and dutiful, straight to her fate (*sorte*).' The use of the notion of fate here works to essentialize a process which is, in fact, determined solely by patriarchal values.

Baldovino, on the other hand, is characterized by intellectually, rather than sexually, defined attributes, and particularly by 'a strange philosophy, full of both irony and indulgence.' While Baldovino pursues the rational pleasure of honesty, Agata's part of the bargain requires her to relinquish her desire for Fabio in favour of asexual motherhood, a transition which is marked by her rejection of Fabio as soon as she and Baldovino are married. In the words of Baldovino warning Fabio of the consequences of the pact of honesty: 'And in order to preserve my dignity, in these circumstances, it will be enough for me to see, in the woman who will be mine in name – a mother' (Act I, sc. 8).

This consequence of the reduction of sexual womanhood to asexual motherhood has been possible for Agata, Baldovino maintains, precisely because motherhood automatically brings with it the demise of female sexual desire. Speaking to Agata about the consequences of the pact, he says that, unlike Fabio and Agata's mother: 'You have accepted them, in fact, you have been able to accept them, on your part, because unfortunately the lover in you inevitably had to die with the arrival of motherhood. You see, you are no longer anything apart from being a mother' (Act III, sc.5). Agata's mother also reiterates this 'natural law' of the asexuality of motherhood: 'now that she is nothing other than a mother, only a mother' (Act III, sc. 1).

When Baldovino colludes with an attempt by Fabio and Agata's mother to bring the pact to an end by committing a theft, he thereby provides Agata with a socially acceptable opportunity to separate from him. However, sexual womanhood (represented by her liaison with Fabio before the beginning, and for the first part of the narrative) has been replaced by asexual motherhood (represented by her marriage to Baldovino). Her painful transition is ultimately sealed by the closure as she chooses not to separate from Baldovino and not to revive her liaison with Fabio. The stage directions describing Agata at this point make it perfectly clear that her choice is not dictated by desire for Baldovino. She is 'pale and decided', ready to do her duty ('It is what I must do'). Fulfilling the indications at the outset of the narrative, she 'proceeds, proud and dutiful', having completely internalized the values necessitating this transformation of her sexuality, values which are disguised as her 'fate'.

A similar case is that of Evelina, in *Mrs Morli, One and Two* (1922), whose sexual desire (in the form of her enduring passion for her first husband) is portrayed as inevitably giving way to asexual marriage/ motherhood. This occurs at the point when the young child of her subsequent common-law marriage (a relationship which does not engage her desire) sickens and prompts the mother's return home. The very fact that the narrative includes the existence of a child from her first marriage, a child who, by contrast, is now old enough not to need constant maternal attention (he is eighteen years old), is an essential narrative ingredient governing the 'choice' which the female character must make between the two husbands. Closely intertwined with this particular portrayal of the two children, is the 'choice' Evelina must make between desire and asexuality. Once again, the fact that it is her *second* husband with whom her relations are not passionate (rather than the first, which might have been the case), and the fact that they have had a child (which again need not, in narrative terms, have existed at all), combine to create a position for Evelina which actually allows her no real choice at all.

In a culture and historical period which envisaged motherhood strictly within the realm of marriage, the asexuality of motherhood is inextricably interwoven with the asexuality of wifehood. This is underlined and idealized by patriarchal culture in general, and by Catholic teaching in particular. In a papal encyclical of 1933, designed to reinforce the status quo of received views on sexual conduct (and issued just over a decade after the publication of *The Pleasure of Honesty*), Pope Pius IX emphasized the purely procreative function of sex, viewed exclusively within the confines of marital relations, and denies it any recreative function.

The mandatory asexuality of the proper mother and wife (but not of the father and husband) is a basic tenet of *Man, Beast and Virtue* (1919). The female character in question, Mrs Perella, is described in the list of characters as 'virtuous', and is in fact the 'virtue' of the title (her lover being the 'man', and her husband, the 'beast'). It is her sexuality in relation to the two male characters which provides the plot motivator. The actual narrative problem to be solved can clearly not be her virtue itself, but, rather, her departure from it. Faithful adherence to the values of the status quo would not make a good plot; as observed in the introduction to this chapter, this would fail to provide the necessary disturbance of order which the narrative works to investigate and set to rights.

The resulting paradox of the virtuous wife and mother who nevertheless becomes pregnant by her young son's Latin teacher, and thereby provides the narrative problem of disruption of the status quo, is dealt with, initially, by the use of irony in its description: 'Mrs Perella is the personification of virtue, modesty and pudency; which, unfortunately, does not prevent her being two months pregnant – however unnoticeably – by Mr Paolino, Nonò's private teacher.' However, the irony of the paradox described in the stage directions accompanying Mrs Perella's first appearance as she enters her lover's study to inform him of her pregnancy, immediately slides into ridicule of the character herself. She is described as 'much afflicted, for to be sure she does not deserve to be treated like this by fate, on account of her many virtues and her exemplary pudency.' Even her virtue itself is parodied: 'She dresses, it is to be understood, with awkwardness, as fashion, by its very nature, has the task of making virtue appear awkward, and Mrs Perella is indeed constrained to go around dressed according to the fashion, and God knows how much she suffers because of this.'

She exhibits the stigma of pregnancy in the form of a curious physical sign, by involuntarily opening and shutting her mouth like a fish, which causes Nonò great amusement. The fact that her son is portrayed with much charm ensures that the audience will laugh with him and at her. Her querulous voice has a distant quality, 'as if in reality it were not her speaking at all, but the invisible puppeteer who makes her move, imitating badly and awkwardly the voice of a melancholy woman.' A later reference to her like a puppet being shaken furiously by Paolino (an action which is, furthermore, performed with such violence that she is actually dazed as a result) reiterates the involuntariness and lack of control on the part of the female character which lie at the heart of the ridicule.

Unlike either of the male characters (the 'man' and 'beast' of the title), who are ostensibly equally caught up in the problem of her pregnancy, it is only the female character who is not merely ridiculed, but also deprived of any volition, control or status. We shall return to her reduced status in the next chapter. She is the butt of humour and violence, and is the object of manipulation, both physical and emotional, by lover and husband alike. While a few lines in the stage directions suffice to describe the lover and the husband, an entire page is devoted to what amounts to an overkill of the female character, to the extent that not even her virtue, which in fact represents the cardinal ideological tenet informing and structuring the narrative, is left unridiculed and intact.

It is the female character who *is* the narrative problem. Her 'fall from virtue' is occasioned, and openly justified by, her husband's neglect of her in favour of his Neapolitan mistress and their four children, a neglect which is seen purely in terms of motherhood (he does not allow her to have more children) and not in terms of any sexual desire she might have. Nevertheless, it is she who is exhibited and her body made a spectacle, in order for the problem to be resolved. So that her husband will believe her pregnancy to be due to him, thereby ensuring that everybody's 'honour' remains unbesmirched, he must be persuaded to depart from his custom of not sleeping with her. While the lover provides a cake laced with an aphrodisiac for the husband's consumption, the wife/mother/mother-to-be must dress seductively, baring her cleavage and wearing excessive amounts of make-up. When she appears, a ludicrous figure of coy embarrassment, in her own version of a seductive outfit described as 'extraordinary attire', the lover takes charge of her transformation, issuing instructions and applying her make-up himself. He effectively acts as pimp, placing her on display for another man. She is the incarnation of the problem-to-be-solved: 'It is your martyrdom,' he tells her by means of consolation, 'You must face it courageously.' Meanwhile she is shown as completely impotent; a hysterical fit of weeping and laughing (the latter also induced by his efforts) ends in convulsion, followed by more weeping. At this point 'he shakes her angrily and forces her to her feet, like a puppet which is falling to pieces in his hands' (Act II, sc.5).

The transformation from asexual to sexual is met with horror by the personification of virtue: 'I am a poor mother!' she exclaims, when she sees the result of her lover's work. 'That is how he wants you,' replies the lover, 'he doesn't want you as a mother' (Act II, sc. 5). The connection between asexuality and motherhood is paralleled by that between asexuality and wifehood, when the husband himself comments to the lover at dinner, having temporarily overcome his amusement at her appearance: 'Very nice, yes. I'm not saying anything to the contrary! That is, if she were someone else, I mean! If she were a . . . you know what I mean! As a wife, no . . . come on! As a wife, like this, go on, tell the truth: she's hilarious!' (Act II, sc. 6). While the husband and lover discuss the wife's appearance, her own contribution to the conversation is limited mostly to unfinished fragments of phrases and exclamations of 'My God!'

The female voice is again completely excluded, this time by its total absence, from a later discussion between the two male characters, again about women. When the lover begins to talk about wives, the husband asks: 'Excuse me, but where do wives come in? We are talking about women.' The lover replies, 'And are wives not women, then? What are they?' To which the husband grudgingly responds, 'Well, they may well be women too . . . sometimes. . . Yes' (Act III, sc. 3). The link between asexuality and wifehood is thus made once more. While the lover clearly views the husband's wife as a (sexual) woman, for the husband she is, predominantly, an (asexual) wife. Between the two male characters, then, female sexuality is defined and regulated, with the female character conspicuously absent.

Male appropriation of female sexuality is further evidenced in this play by the use of the metaphor of woman-as-fertile-terrain, which we saw in operation in *Liolà* and *The Grafting*. Here it is used by the lover, in enlisting the help of a doctor friend, to explain the pregnancy of Mrs Perella and in order to exculpate himself, laying the blame instead on the 'proprietor of the terrain', the husband:

> Look: it is as if you had a piece of land, and left it abandoned. There is a tree on this land, and you do not take care of it. It's as if it belonged to no-one! Well. Someone passes by. Picks some fruit from that tree; eats it; throws away the kernel. You throw it away . . . just like that, for the simple reason that you have picked that abandoned fruit. Well. One fine day, from that kernel there, another tree is born. Did you wish for that? No! Neither did the land which received the kernel in that way. I ask you: to whom does this new-born tree belong? To you, the proprietor of the terrain! (*Man, Beast and Virtue*, Act I, sc. 7)

As in the other two plays, the woman-as-fertile-terrain metaphor completely disempowers the woman, who has no volition or desire of her own and whose passive fecundity is worked by her owner, or indeed any passing male. And yet again, the collapse of female desire into fecundity guarantees the womanhood-is-motherhood equation. This process receives an apocalyptic celebration a decade later in La Spera, the ex-prostitute recuperated for a triumphant maternity which ensures her survival, together with that of her child, as the rest of the island sinks into the sea in *The New Colony* (written for Marta Abba in 1928).

Male management of female sexuality is thus couched in this terrain imagery whereby one male (the passer-by/lover) admonishes another (the proprietor/husband) for bad management. It is also in evidence when the lover/Pirandello quite literally constructs a male version of the sexual woman (a version which is, significantly, degradingly comical) by 'painting' sexuality onto asexual motherhood/wifehood. None of which would have been necessary, the lover maintains, if the husband had not neglected her – or if she had *brothers* who might 'legitimately take him by the scruff of the neck and remind him of his duties as a husband' (Act I, sc. 7). The policing by males of female sexuality, seen as particularly justified if they are relatives, again places female sexuality in the powerless position required for the survival of patriarchy. As males guard female sexuality for, and against, each other, they totally occupy the subject position, to the complete exclusion of female subjectivity. Male definition and management of female sexuality structure the narrative of this play, working towards a form of closure in which the female character is reinstated by the narrative/a male character, as 'Virtue personified.' This happens as a result not only of these final words, uttered by the lover, but by his actions, which have successfully resulted in the resolution of the initial problem.

As we have observed, then, the terms in which motherhood is represented throughout Pirandello's plays are male-defined and male-oriented, in conformity with the patriarchal ideology which these definitions work to construct and reinforce. This strategy is of course employed not only in the case of motherhood, but also applies to other aspects of female sexuality. In the following chapter we shall look more closely at the whole issue of subjectivity itself, and in particular at the various ways in which male characters control and dictate definitions of female identity.

–2–

The Father of the Text:
The Narrative Solution

ERSILIA: I want to be just as you have imagined me
Clothing the Naked, Act I

Introduction: Subjectivity/Masculinity

The problematization of female sexuality by the narrative, as discussed
in the previous chapter, interlinks closely with, and indeed helps to produce, narrative processes engendering subject positions and setting up
systems of identification. This chapter explores the workings of these
processes through the complex of Father-as-author/ity, in conjunction
with the traditional binary allocation of cultural creativity to the masculine, and biological procreativity to the feminine domain. This will lead
to a focus on the predominance of the role of logos in the quest for
identity on the part of the male protagonist, as opposed to the emphasis
on sexuality-as-identity in the case of what must logically be termed
the female antagonist. The latter construction, it will be argued, is produced by its positioning in an object rather than a subject position,
compounded by its association with discourses which are negatively
valued.

The fundamental notion of subject position is a key element in theories of the signifying process (linguistics, psychoanalysis, semiotics).
These equate access to language in the position of speaking subject, as
indicated by the subject pronoun 'I', with subjectivity (Silverman, 1983,
pp. 3–53). In other words, 'the subject is a position in terms of a linguistic field or an artistic device such as narrative' and as such 'is now perceived as a cultural construction and a semiotic function. The subject is
an intersection of cultural codes and practices.' More specifically, 'the
subject represents a point of view' (Case, 1988, p. 121).

Theorizing subjectivity in classic narrative of theatre and film has
raised issues concerning the position of the audience, with crucial impli-

cations for the narrative construction of the subject position itself. It has highlighted the actual lack of subject position for the audience, for viewers, 'who are spoken and not speaking, and whose gazes are controlled, not controlling' (Silverman, 1983, p. 223). This basic lack is concealed by narrative processes which work to produce a subject position for the audience to identify with. A subject position necessarily implies a corresponding object position, and it is precisely in the relation of the subject to the object position that identification procedures are set up, with the audience being made to align itself with the subject position of speaking, and looking at, the object position.

This narrative engendering of subject and object positions is gender-specific in mainstream texts which produce and reproduce the dominant cultural values of patriarchal society. 'The traditional subject has been the male subject with whom all must identify', albeit in different ways, depending on the gender, class, age, race, etc. of the particular audience concerned (Case, 1988, p. 121). This situates the female object as Other and as subordinate to and derivative of the male subject position (ibid., p. 122). The female object position comes to signify the *actual lack* of subjectivity for any of the audience, male or female, while the male subject position signifies the *illusory plenitude* of desired subjectivity and control. Identification between audience and the male subject position is set up by narrative processes constructing the relation of the male subject to the female object position. These processes include those of looking at and speaking/writing the object, thereby placing the object in a position of being looked at, spoken and written.

In the sphere of looking, feminist psychoanalytic film theory has identified masculine voyeurism and feminine exhibitionism as two gender-specific forms of scopophilic drive which are activated by subject and object positions respectively. Silverman notes, 'This opposition is entirely in keeping with the dominant cultural roles assigned to men and women, since voyeurism is the active or "masculine" form of the scopophilic drive, while exhibitionism is the passive or "feminine" form of the same drive' (Silverman, 1983, pp. 222–3). In classic film and theatre narrative, the audience looks *with* the male subject *at* the female object on display.

It will be remembered that the female object position epitomizes the lack of audience subjectivity, and thereby fuels other anxieties regarding lack or absence, in particular loss of power and control, represented in psychoanalytic theory by the lack of a phallus, or castration. Female exhibitionism, in its excessive overplaying of, and attracting attention to, its object position of lack, produces itself/the female body, as visual fetish actually denying lack, and thence moves into an illusory phallic position of power. This:

involves the transformation of the female body into a fetish, substituting either one of its parts or the whole for the missing phallus. This privileged zone (legs, ankles, breasts, face, hair, general 'shape') is subjected to an overvaluation, and in this way compensates for the deficiency which is always associated with the female genital region, although it is in fact broadly cultural. The mechanisms of fetishism function to reassure the male subject that the woman to whom his identity is keyed lacks nothing, that she has not been castrated after all. Examples of this . . . include not only the song-and-dance number, but the entire star system. (ibid., p. 224)

One striking example of female fetishism in Pirandello's work is the song-and-dance routine performed by the Stepdaughter in *Six Characters in Search of an Author*. In chapter 5 we shall see how the Stepdaughter gains access, with this routine, to the verbal turn-taking process as both she and the Father vie for the Director's attention. She then proceeds to waste her speech turn by not putting forward her point of view in the controlled, reasoned and above all prioritized discourse of cause and effect argumentation, which is the discourse already established by the Father and the Director. Instead, she switches discourse to the lesser valued one of the body, of herself as spectacle. In so doing, she temporarily interrupts the narrative, as her action here bears no relation to narrative progression. Writing about the conflict between narrative and spectacle in film, Mulvey notes how 'song-and-dance numbers interrupt the flow of the diegesis'. She goes on to say: 'The presence of woman is an indispensable element of spectacle in normal narrative film, yet her visual presence tends to work against the development of a story-line, to freeze the flow of action in moments of erotic contemplation' (Mulvey, 1989, p. 19). Commenting on Mulvey's analysis, Kuhn writes: 'The assumption here is either that the spectator is male or – a more complex position – that cinematic address works to constitute the spectator as such' (Kuhn, 1982, p. 61).

In focusing the attention of the other characters on stage on herself as spectacle in this way, the Stepdaughter is therefore not only playing out the exhibitionist and fetishist functions of the object position. She is also providing the object for the looks of both characters and audience, as the audience looks not only at her, but also at the characters on stage looking at her. In other words, the audience is made to identify with the subject position of looking, and not with the object position of being looked at. Mulvey continues: 'This alien presence then has to be integrated into cohesion with the narrative' (Mulvey, 1989, p. 61). The narrative of *Six Characters* indeed resumes with the interchange of two males in subject position, as the Director turns to the Father and asks, 'Is she mad?' This seals the object position of the Stepdaughter as regards both the subject position in this scene and that of the audience and, what is more, suggests the expulsion of the object position *to a point outside* the social norm of sanity, a norm inhabited by the subject position and an identifying audience.

The identification of the audience, in the sphere of looking, with the male subject position of plenitude, conceals the narrative processes, or apparatus, which actually produce the subject position. Silverman describes this process of cinematic subject production, or suture, as follows:

> One of the chief mechanisms by which the system of suture conceals the apparatuses of enunciation is by setting up a relay of glances between the male characters within the fiction and the male viewers in the theater audience, a relay which has the female body as its object. (Silverman, 1983, p. 222)

The same process of subject production is achieved by the Stepdaughter's song-and-dance routine. Moreover, 'the representation of the male subject in terms of vision has the effect of attributing to him qualities which in fact belong to that same apparatus – qualities of potency and authority' (ibid., p. 223). It is precisely the male subject's 'qualities of potency and authority' which I wish to address, qualities which, however illusory, appear as manifestly overpowering. I shall focus not just on the area of looking in Pirandello's plays, but also on those of speaking and writing, on the basis that audience identification with, and the construction of, male subjectivity, takes place not just in the narrative mechanics of looking (at the female object) but also in that of speaking/writing (the female object).

Furthermore, speaking and writing are not simply categories to be interpreted literally, but are also to be understood in a metaphorical sense. For instance, the 'writing' of an alternative female identity in *Diana and Tuda* (1927) takes place in marble, as Sirio attempts to 'rewrite', or translate, the living, sensual Tuda into the dead, chaste marble statue of Diana (or, in terms of conventional Tilgherian Pirandello criticism, transmute life into form). I shall be looking at instances, then, when the male subject position, as I have outlined it above, is occupied by a male 'writer', the most direct example of such seamless suture being the novelist Ludovico Nota in *Clothing the Naked* (1923). Before doing so, however, I wish to elaborate on the roots of the stereotype of masculine cultural creativity vs feminine biological procreativity. This will, I hope, add a particular resonance to what I have already said about the subject position.

The formation of the subject position takes place with entry into culture, into language, initially through the process of looking (at a reflection of oneself), according to the Lacanian exposition of the infantile mirror stage (Lacan, 1966, pp. 89–97). Thereafter it is continually re/formulated with each action of speaking, writing, looking, and other cultural procedures, such as exchanging goods of value (see chapter 1). According to Lévi-Strauss, the basic feature characterizing cultural processes is their regulating tendency. It is the regulation of nature, he says, which constitutes and defines culture. Regulation occurs most importantly in the definition of familial relationships (with the social notably taking precedence over the purely biological) and particularly in the restriction of sexual intercourse to certain of these relationships, as exemplified by the incest taboo.

The family, then, is the primary locus of regulation, and so of culture. The actual identification, or naming, of familial relations (father, mother, sister, etc.) is clearly a prerequisite of this process, so that language/culture/family are in effect mutually defining. Silverman, writing about Lacan's work on the Oedipus complex (a key phase in the development of familial relationships), says:

> Lacan indicates that the Oedipus complex and language do not merely resemble each other, but that they are 'identical.' He supports this claim by pointing out that the incest taboo can only be articulated through the differentiation of certain cultural members from others by means of linguistic categories like 'father' and 'mother'. (Silverman, 1983, p. 181)

The association between subject position, culture and masculinity becomes clear in what she goes on to say:

> Lacan further consolidates the relationship between the Oedipus complex and language by defining the patriarchal signifier – what he calls the 'Name-of-the-Father' – as the all-important one both in the history of the subject and the organization of the larger symbolic field. (ibid., p. 181)

A closer look at the cultural process of the exchange of goods of value (in object positions) between male subject positions, deepens the gender-specific link between subject position, culture and masculinity, when it is considered that in exogamous kinship systems, women are exchanged by men, as goods of value. Silverman quotes the following passage from Lévi-Strauss:

> The law of exogamy . . . is omnipresent, acting permanently and continually; moreover, it applies to valuables – viz., women . . . without which life is impossible . . . It is no exaggeration, then, to say that exogamy is the archetype of all other manifestations based upon reciprocity. (ibid., pp. 179–80)

This system of reciprocity operates, by definition, between equals, namely, between subject positions which are equally empowered to exchange and regulate necessarily subordinate object positions.

Ultimately, then, a scheme emerges whereby the subordinate object position/woman/nature/being/the Imaginary, is regulated, tamed, defined and transcended by the dominant subject position/man/culture/meaning/the Symbolic.[1] (It goes almost without saying that this type of scheme is, of course, in itself 'a construct of culture rather than a fact of nature', as Ortner concludes in her study 'Is Female to Male as Nature Is to Culture?' (Ortner, 1974, p. 87).) For the purposes of narrative analysis, the key zone in this scheme is the activity of regulating, taming, defining and transcending the object position, in the specifically narrative terms of looking/writing/speaking, on the part of the (author)itative subject position. In other words, it is the (author)ity of the Lacanian patriarchal signifier, the *nom-du-père*, which occupies the dominant looking/writing/speaking subject position, with all the attendant connotations outlined above, and which I have subsumed under the specifically narrative complex Father-as-author/ity.

Author/izing the Female Object

The power of authority subtending the subject position is at the root of a range of notions associated with 'author'. This divides into three basic areas; first, 'author' as fount of wisdom, as teacher and guide to be obeyed; second, as father, creator and ancestor of genealogies and ideas; and third, God as the ultimate Author (the *verace autore* of Dante and the Bible).[2] The exclusively patriarchal bias of this fundamental cultural complex clearly has implications for a female subject position, the most obvious implication being that of its absence. In other words, there is no genuine representation of a female subject position. The position

---

1. On the Imaginary and the Symbolic, see Lacan (1966); Laplanche and Pontalis (1980); Silverman (1983). For an analysis of a literary representation of the passage from the Imaginary to the Symbolic during the Lacanian mirror phase, see Günsberg (1983).

2. The *Enciclopedia Dantesca* tells us that 'the term "author" derives from the Latin "auctor" in close connection with the concept of "auctoritas" ["authority"]' and that 'in the Latin tradition, "auctor" refers to whoever possesses the power of initiative, promotes an act, perfects and guarantees, by integrating and reinforcing it, the insufficient will or personality of another (like the "patronus", the "pater", the "tutor")' (*Enciclopedia Dantesca*, 1970, p. 454, my translation. See also OED). Dante provides early examples of the three basic associations of 'author'/'authority'. First, the notion of 'author' as fount of wisdom, teacher and guide to be obeyed appears in his reference to Virgil: 'Tu se' lo mio maestro e 'l mio autore' (*Inferno*, I, 85). Second, 'author' as father, creator and ancestor of genealogies occurs in his reference to Dardanus: 'Dardanus Iliacae primus pater urbis et auctor' (*Monarchia*, ii, 3, 73). This line is itself a quotation from a much older work (*Aeneid*, VIII, 134), thereby illustrating the long history of the association of 'author' with 'father'. Third, Dante refers to God as the ultimate Author in the phrase 'la voce del verace autore' (*Paradiso*, XXVI, 40), taken from *Exodus*, 33, 19.

constructed for/by the male subject for the female is either that of object position or of no position at all, the latter signified by absence, a relegation outside the text and outside representation. In either case, female identity/subjectivity is absent. In an object position, the resulting female 'identity' is no more than a construct, an extension, of male identity/ subjectivity, and is no more representative of female identity than non-representation through absence. In the words of Diamond, 'What remains is a dress, a palpitation, a scream, all encoded female behaviors adding up to a trace denoting absence. The *woman* . . . is not represented; *she* lacks symbolization in culture' (Diamond, 1990, p. 97). A striking stage representation of a female character who is quite literally in an object position appeared in a recent production of *Man, Beast and Virtue* (Act II, sc. 5). In this production, Mrs Perella was represented, not by an actress, but by a mere prop, in the form of a double-faced head on a stick, held and painted by the actor playing Paolino (as shown in the frontispiece).[3]

Access to cultural subjectivity is problematic for the female, who 'never enters as fully as does her male counterpart into the symbolic order' (Silverman, 1983, p. 234). As a consequence, representations of female identity revolve around its Otherness. This Otherness, or 'out-siderness', centres on sexuality, and is invariably problematized, to be investigated and rendered harmless in various ways. On the other hand, the identity of the male subject, as we shall see, is associated with rational, non-sexual issues relating to, for instance, public or philosophical spheres. Examples of this are, respectively, the conflict between Mattia Pascal's private/individual and public/social identities in Pirandello's novel *The Late Mattia Pascal*, and 'Henry IV''s ruminations on the boundaries between his sane and his mad selves as perceived by others. Moreover, even when the identity of the male subject is apparently ruptured in this way, it in fact remains unified. The Mattia Pascal/Adriano Meis split is chosen, effected and controlled by the male subject who is, furthermore, the foregrounded first-person narrator of *discours*.[4] And 'Henry IV'/Anon remains in control of the public examination of his identities, retaining the one of his choice, so that we never even know his 'real' name prior to the accident.

This narrative device of identity doubling, a traditional topos used for the exploration of identity, works differently when female object identi-

3. This scene formed part of *You Say That I Am*, devised and directed by Mary Casey, and performed at University College, Dublin, on 4 May 1991. For interesting discussions of the semiotics of the relationship between actor and prop, see Honzl (1976) and Veltruský (1964).

4. On the opposition between *discours* and *histoire* (Benveniste's terms approximating to 'I' and third person narration respectively), together with other formulations of this distinction, see Ducrot and Todorov (1981).

ty is involved.[5] One example of this is Mrs Ponza (*That's How It Is (If You Think So)*, 1918), whose 'real' identity (either Mr Ponza's second wife or Mrs Frola's daughter) is the object of what amounts to a public enquiry managed by the philosophical Laudisi in the position of male subject. Even this so-called 'real' identity, which is the cause of so much curiosity and intrigue, is merely that defined and circumscribed by the culturally regulating language of familial relations, coterminous, as we have seen, with patriarchal law. Female identity here remains fractured and incomplete throughout, with no controlling subjectivity, as evidenced by the character's ultimate denial of any identity of her own ('And as for myself, I am no-one, no-one'). Her identity is, precisely, constructed by others: 'As for me, I am who I am believed to be' (Act III, sc.9).

Forces outside female identity are again implicated in its construction by the title itself of *As You Desire Me* (1930). In the words of the female character under scrutiny: 'I came here; I gave myself completely to you, completely; I told you: "Here I am, I am yours; there is nothing of myself in me any more, nothing: make me, make me as you want me to be!"' (Act II). Her identity, no more in her control for the fact that this character was written specifically for Marta Abba, floats between the perception of her by two males in subject positions (Salter and Pieri). The female character is called 'L'Ignota', the archetypally unknown – and unknowable – woman. Female identity is once again depicted as problematic, as ultimately indefinable, uncontrollable and fluid. Named variously as Elma by Mop ('Elma', interestingly, being the Arabic for water), and as Lucia or Cia by Pieri, L'Ignota remains unidentifiable and Other, and finally leaves Italy for the second time to return to an Other place, to an Outsider culture beyond the confines of Italy (Germany). Her identity remains unlegitimated, and she returns to her sexually foregrounded roles of mistress, dancer and object of desire in Berlin, having failed to be inserted/reinstated in the (culturally) less sexually-charged role of wife in Udine.

The question of her identity is clearly linked throughout to her sexuality; if she is indeed Lucia/Cia, then the reason for her disappearance from Udine ten years previously is due to her rape and abduction by German soldiers during the Great War. Furthermore, not only the reason for her disappearance, but also the nature of her re-appearance, centre on her sexuality. She is rediscovered in the streets of Berlin by Boffi, sur-

5. There are many instances of doubling in the case of female characters in Western culture. To cite just a few: the two Maria's in Lang's film *Metropolis* (1926), Clara and Olympia in Hoffmann's short story *Der Sandmann* (1815), Lucy and Mina in Stoker's novel *Dracula* (1897) and, of course, the fundamental example from Christianity, Mary and Eve. For an examination of an example of the female double in Italian literature, see Fanning (1991).

rounded by drunken admirers as she returns home from her performance as a dancer (an activity with clear sexual connotations in the 1930s). With this scene L'Ignota actually makes her entrance in the play. Her appearance is preceded by a tense interchange defining her as a problem, an interchange between father and daughter who both desire her passionately. As inspirer of desire in numerous admirers, and in both sexes, L'Ignota is an archetypal object of desire, the embodiment of sexuality itself. This representation of female identity is saturated, and synonymous with, an excessive and Other sexuality in a way that no male Pirandellian character ever is.

The issue of desire raises more questions regarding the implications for the construction of female identity for and by a male subject position. Misconstruction of female identity into an object position necessitates the particular omission of a desiring female subject, for the reason that, 'in revolt against the psychoanalytic model of subject construction in which desire is articulated as exclusively male, it is female desire which is most disruptive. As lack, reflecting only men's desire, women are not permitted or even conceived of as having or owning their desire' (Forte, 1990, p. 259). So, just as L'Ignota has no definable identity of her own, so she is desired but does not herself desire. There is no indication of any desire on her part for any of her admirers; her time is spent reacting to the desire of others. In the words of Jacobus in 'Is There a Woman in This Text?', 'The function of the object of desire is thus to mediate relations between men; female desire is impossible except as a mimetic reflection of male desire' (Jacobus, 1982, p. 130).

A clear illustration of this is the doubling of the female object position in relation to the male subject ('Henry') in *Henry IV*, whereby the two female characters, the young Frida and the older Matilde, reflect and embody, in terms of their desirability (and not desirousness), *his* youth and *his* old age, respectively. Along similar lines, the aged sculptor Giuncano refers to his erstwhile lover, the now aged Rosa, as a mirror in which he sees *his* age reflected (*Diana and Tuda,* Act I). In this context, the characterization of Salter's daughter Mop is of great interest, in that her desire for L'Ignota clearly suggests the possibility of female desire. However, this possibility is defused from the start by the description in the stage directions of Mop as a *manly* woman (her hair is cut in a masculine style), and whose deviation from the feminine into the ambiguous zone of androgyny is characterized as disgusting, and disturbingly tragic. Furthermore, her ambiguous, semi-male, semi-female status undercuts the subject position she appears to occupy in naming the object of her desire (Elma) (bearing in mind the Lacanian association of the act of naming with power and subjectivity).

Absence of female desire, then, is an important element contributing to the lack of female subjectivity. However, mis/representation of the female object position sometimes goes further than positing the female subject as merely absent, or lacking, in some way. Acting at the expense of female subjectivity, prohibitive male cultural creativity/subjectivity is, at times, actually destructive. Or, to describe this process more accurately, the female character is made to internalize this destructiveness and turn it on herself. This covert mechanism conceals and thereby exculpates the male subject position/characters, by making the female object position/characters appear responsible for their own destruction.

Such narrative sleight of hand is at work in *Diana and Tuda*. The title itself already signals the doubling of the female object position, in this case not represented by two live female characters, but by a marble statue (Diana) and its human model (Tuda).[6] As indicated earlier, a male 'writing' subject/sculptor (Sirio Dossi) plays with this object position by attempting to translate one version of female identity (the live, sensual Tuda) into another (the dead, chaste, marble statue of Diana). In terms of the culture vs nature dichotomy, he attempts to use his creative subjectivity to transcend, and so improve on, an objectified nature, a positioning indicated no less by his firm belief in the superiority of art (culture) over life (nature). The fact that the subject position is occupied by *male* sculptors (Sirio, Giuncano) and painters (Caravani), while women pose for them as models (Tuda, Sara, Jonella), will be taken up again in chapter 4. What is of immediate relevance here is the highly sexualized profile of the female as model, and the network of looks which contributes to the construction of this profile, thereby continuing, on a complementary level, the work of writing/sculpting the object position.

First of all, the nudity of Tuda/the actress playing her is emphasized erotically in that it cannot be fully seen, but appears in the form of an enormous silhouette cast on the wall, as her body is illuminated by a light while she stands behind a curtain. (This visual device is further foregrounded on the verbal level by Tuda, who emphasizes its invention by Sirio.) The workings of desire are thereby closely observed, in the sense that desire is located precisely in the difference between the pres-

---

6. In the stage directions for Act 1, Pirandello says that Tuda's shadow should resemble the posture of Cellini's bronze statue of Diana. The plot of the play, with its focus on the creation by a male artist of an idealized female form, appears almost to reverse the myth of Pygmalion. In this myth, the legendary king of Cyprus, having fallen in love with a statue of Venus, sculpted a replica in ivory. In answer to his prayers, Venus brought the statue to life (Ovid, *Metamorphoses*, 10: 243–97; see Hall, 1974). *Diana and Tuda* appears to reflect the opposite process, in that, for the artist, the statue (Diana) derives its beauty from, and takes precedence over, its human model (Tuda), very much to the detriment of the latter. Interestingly, other examples of the female double in Western culture also consist of one artificial and one live female character, with the former personifying the male ideal of the female form: the mechanoid Maria in *Metropolis*, and the doll Olympia in *Der Sandmann*, both constructed by a male character/author.

ence and absence of the desired object. The naked female body is rendered absent yet still present by the device of the curtain and the light, which allow only a silhouette, a partial nudity, to appear. The play opens with both Tuda and Sirio behind the curtain, she posing and he sculpting, while Giuncano is positioned on the audience side of the curtain.

A clear network of looks is thereby set up, in which the audience looks at Giuncano looking not just at Tuda's nude silhouette, but also in the direction of Sirio and Tuda behind the curtain, with Sirio himself looking at Tuda's actual naked body, as well as at its enlarged silhouette. This complex, concentric series of looks works in a vicarious and voyeuristic fashion for both Giuncano and the audience: vicarious because they merely see the silhouette, while being aware that Sirio is looking at the body itself, and voyeuristic because the object of their look cannot see or look at them. The audience is in a particularly vicarious position here, in that they are looking at someone who is himself already looking at one remove from the ultimate master of this look, Sirio.[7] The complementary zone of this scopophilic field, that of exhibitionism, is occupied by Tuda, whose naked body, in its entirety and, what is more, enormity, provides the excess of fetish. Audience identification, from the very beginning of the play, is thus positioned in alignment *with* the looking male subject position, and *against* the fetishized female object position. The scene is now set for the process of diminishing the enormity of this female sexuality, and it is during this process that the destructive activity of the 'writing' male subject position comes into play.

Diminution of the threat of female sexuality, and with it management and containment of the female object position, is inscribed on to the actual body of Tuda (another Marta Abba role). She literally wastes away, losing weight and becoming, to all intents and purposes, anorexic, as the statue of Diana, conversely, becomes more perfect and more completely written. Tuda's deteriorating body bears witness that, at a deep level, she has internalized, and turned upon herself, the destructive force of the male subject position. Her open accusation of Sirio as author of her physical deterioration only serves to underscore her actual powerlessness in resisting the mechanism of internalization and consequent self-destruction and, in the last resort, it is she who is seen to be damaging herself. This is also borne out by several references she and Giuncano make to her death, while at the same time she continues to allow herself to degenerate. In a similar way, she repeatedly complains of tiredness, yet masochistically suggests that Sirio continue sculpting.

---

7. For an analysis of a similar system of looks in Tasso's *Gerusalemme liberata*, see Günsberg (1991, p. 201).

Her sense of identity, in other words, is completely tuned in to Sirio's perception of her, even though this perception is destructive in nature. This culminates in her blaming his death, at the end of the play, on what she sees as her own failure in having being unable to satisfy his demands: 'I, who am to blame for everything. I, yes, I, for everything – because I didn't know how to be what he wanted me to be.' After his death, or rather, after the disappearance of the 'author' of her identity, she feels bereft of any identity: 'I, who am now like this – nothing, nothing any more', a refrain we have heard before in *That's How It Is (If You Think So)* and *As You Desire Me*, and which we shall hear again in *Clothing the Naked*.

Tuda's life is saved, not by her own actions, but by the violent eruption of male rivalry, which has been simmering throughout the play. When she moves threateningly towards the statue of Diana, the older Giuncano strikes the younger Sirio to prevent him attacking her. Such salvation is not the lot of Candelora/Loretta, a male painter's model and wife in Pirandello's short story *Candelora*, published in 1917 and bearing striking similarities to the later *Diana and Tuda*. The doubling of the object position is indicated here by the naming of the female character, who is called both Candelora and Loretta. Paintings of this female character, and indeed the character herself, form a medium of exchange between the painter, interestingly surnamed *Papa*, and their consumer, the Baron, who becomes the painter's patron, while Candelora becomes his mistress. Candelora, the actual object of exchange, over-self-destructs, taking poison as well as shooting herself.

In her case, as in Tuda's, sexuality is foregrounded as the major feature of her identity, this time by the use of bestial imagery in addition to narrative systems of looking. She is described, for instance, as having 'the air of a she-goat fallen asleep in the midst of voluptuousness' (p. 9). So, while Papa remains placid and in control, she screams and even roars with rage (pp. 7, 8). At one point she 'opens her mouth like a wild beast and sinks her teeth into his arm (p. 8), upon which her rational companion, pale but still smiling, coolly observes 'I know you are one of those little beasts that bite' (p. 8). In addition to these associations of bestiality and animal sexuality, Candelora is described as a creature of nature, sunburnt and covered in sand and salt as she returns from the sea.

Much of the narrative is in free indirect discourse, narrated from Papa's perspective.[8] The reader thus looks *with* Papa's artistic eye *at* Candelora. His gaze, and that of the reader, have the power to transform this 'natural' being into an artefact: 'She is a marvel of forms and

---

8. See Ginsburg (1982). References to this story are taken from the *Mondadori* edition of the collection entitled *Candelora*.

colours, Candelora, a derisory challenge to his painter's eye which reveals her as forever new and different' (p. 9). His artist's eye, together with the reader's, becomes that of the voyeur, as it proceeds to wander over her scantily clad body and examine its nudity, apparent despite, or rather because of, her flimsy, clinging dress (the equivalent of the dramatic projection of Tuda's silhouette from behind the curtain, and similarly producing an erotic effect). The words *nuda/nudità* appear five times in the twelve lines describing her. The voyeuristic gaze is cut short when Candelora looks up and leaves. The narratorial viewpoint remains with Papa, while Candelora leaves to commit suicide, elsewhere and unnarrated, neither in subject nor object position. With Papa's discovery of her 'doubly' dead body, the voyeurism of the reader and Papa continues into necrophilia, with the Baron joining in the communal gaze at her exposed, bare thigh.

(Self)-destruction of the female character, the ultimate narrative containment of the female object position by the male 'writer', both opens and closes *Clothing the Naked*. As in *Diana and Tuda*, female identity is keyed to, and constructed by, the activity of the male subject. In Ludovico Nota, the male subject position is occupied not by the 'writer'/sculptor, but by the 'writer'/novelist, who literally writes female identity, a writing with which Ersilia identifies (the verb 'notare', from which his surname derives, actually means to note down or to observe). When she learns that he has imagined the novel, or the narrative, of the events which led up to her first suicide attempt, she wants to know all the details about herself, saying 'I want to be just as you have imagined me' (Act I). In the second act she similarly declares, 'But I swear to you that I would have done anything to be who you had imagined me to be! For you, indeed, for you, indeed, I could: because it meant living in the fiction of your art!'

However, by then events have conspired to undermine not only Nota's version of her identity, but also the version of Franco Laspiga, to whom she says, in the same vein: 'But if you find out that I am not the one you believed me to be, the one you had imagined me to be' (Act II). Nota himself had originally read about Ersilia's case in the writings of Cantavalle, 'writer'/journalist. In this archetypically cultural system of exchange *between* occupants of the active, male-dominated subject position, and *of* the female object of exchange, by means of their writing, the female position is rendered passive and helpless. Ersilia herself has not read the newspaper article, and repeatedly asks for a copy (which, incidentally, she never receives). What is more, Cantavalle has not respected her wishes and has written his own version of events, rewriting and recreating the account of events which Ersilia had chosen. The female character herself, then, apart from providing the *natural*, raw material for her story/public identity, is allowed no control, no active part in the entire process of its *cultural* construction, whether at the stage of writing, or that of reading.

The actual result is that more of the story is made public than she would have wished, particularly the part concerning certain of her actions and the identities of the other participants, who are now re-written into her life. In other words, the identity which Ersilia had chosen for herself and which, almost paradoxically, would have allowed her to align herself with the identities written for her by Nota and Laspiga, is sabotaged. Her *real* identity, comprising all the events and persons in her life, and particularly all her sexual activities, is thrust into public view by one male subject, simultaneously making it impossible for the other male subjects, especially Nota, to construct their versions. In the end, as a result of what can ultimately be seen as rivalry between male versions of her identity/story, her 'real' identity, which she in fact rejects, is exposed and prevents her from assuming the 'other' identity written for her by Nota.

The process of Ersilia's rejection of her 'real' identity, as constituted and reconstituted by each of her own actions and reactions, is underscored by her emphatic denial of ever having possessed any identity of her own:

> I have never had the strength to be anything . . My God, not even a thing . . .
> I don't know, of clay, put together by hand, which if you drop it, shatters, and
> at least the pieces on the floor tell you that it was something, something that
> it now no longer is – My life . . . one day after the other . . . and not one that
> might ever have been mine. . . I, all things, just as they wanted me, haphaz-
> ardly . . . without ever being able to get my bearings . . . pulled one way and
> then the other . . . torn apart . . . and never anything that might make me say:
> I exist, too! (*Clothing the Naked*, Act II)

Speaking to Nota, she says, 'I have never been able to be anything.' He contradicts her in such a way as to locate her identity specifically in her sexuality: 'But, for one thing, you are a beautiful girl.' Her response to this, as she remonstrates that she has not even been able to capitalize on her looks ('Hardly beautiful. And anyway, if I haven't known how to turn it to my advantage', Act I), does not merely continue her pattern of self-rejection. It also implies her acceptance and internalization of Nota's viewpoint, namely that her sexuality *is* her identity, and that she should, furthermore, use her looks (the classic double-bind, in that it is precisely for her sexuality that she is to be socially punished). This characteristically abject and negative self image repeats itself each time she refers to herself as wretched ('my wretched life', 'I am a wretched invalid', Act I).

In fact, even the so-called 'real' identity which Ersilia rejects cannot be described as her own, in that this construction of her identity is already prescribed, in this case by her inferior social position. (The post of live-in governess was low in status and, as sole means of income, a highly precarious one, in that no laws protected her from instant dismissal accompanied by immediate eviction.) Ersilia rightly rejects this identity as a false construction, but has no identity *of her own* to put in its place. Instead, she tries to vest herself with an 'other' identity which is similarly produced by an outside agency (Nota). However, she lives out Nota's fantasy of her to excess, and he rejects her as a result. The problems surrounding Ersilia's identity are entirely bound up with her sexuality, and are marked by the stigma attached to her sexual activity within, or because of, the restricting context of her inferior social position. She cannot, in the last resort, live up to men's expectations of her. Of course, this is completely paradoxical as Nota's fantasy was precisely of her as prostitute, turning her sexuality to financial advantage. According to patriarchal rules she is in a no-win, double-bind situation. Her internalization of this position is apparent when, for instance, she pre-empts Laspiga's rejection of her, condemning herself for having had sexual relations with Grotti, her employer, after Laspiga abandons her. She does not even give Laspiga the opportunity to choose to stay with her after his discovery of this relationship, assuming, correctly, that he would not do so.

Ersilia is, then, unable to provide her own identity, and Nota can no longer write one for her. This apparently contradictory, but in patriarchal terms complementary, combination (in other words, the absence of female identity in the former case, and its undefinable, 'unwritable' excess in the latter) means that there can be no place for this unfathomable female identity, which is ultimately written out of the narrative with Ersilia's second, successful suicide attempt. It has, in short, proved impossible for the male subject position to write a satisfactory female object position, or, in terms of the title of the play, to give it a discernible appearance, to clothe its nakedness. Furthermore, the precise wording of the title, *Clothing the Naked*, implies a passive nakedness which is to be clothed by an agent external to it (any agency on the part of 'the naked' would have been expressed by wording such as 'The Naked Clothe Themselves' [*'Gli ignudi si vestono'*]). In addition, the generalized, masculine plural/EveryMan gender of 'the naked' (*'gli ignudi'*) serves to mask the fact that it is *female* nakedness, with all its concomitant eroticism, which is actually the issue.

In contrast to the total demise of the female position, for the male subject the exercise in 'writing' the object position, although ultimately unsuccessful, is accompanied by all the pleasures of cultural creativity and of subjectivity itself. When Nota establishes that his fantasy of Ersilia as prostitute, which was triggered by his reading of Cantavalle's account, was correct in all its details, he congratulates himself ('Ludovico, as if to himself, hurriedly, pleased with himself: "Ah, look . . . Look how accurate my intuition was!"', Act I). The fact that he has 'guessed correctly' is not at all surprising: in the last resort she is, after all, a male construct.

He continues to press Ersilia for further verification of the details he has imagined; she, meanwhile, becomes progressively more emotional and finally breaks down in tears. He nevertheless continues to recount, and so lay bare, her innermost responses with a perseverance bordering on sadism. His primary concern is with his own pleasure-in-writing: 'Didn't you see? I've guessed perfectly . . . It's so right!', to which she replies, 'But I'm so ashamed' (Act I). It is significant that, immediately after these words, the noise of a death in the street outside invades the room, thereby foreshadowing her own imminent death, which is thereby inescapably linked to the sense of shame she has just expressed.

Cantavalle is similarly delighted with his creative efforts: 'I shouldn't boast about it, but the effect of my 'piece' has been colossal, truly colossal' (Act I). The ultimate result of his writing will be, in effect, Ersilia's suicide. Indeed, the pleasure of the male writing subject is sharply contrasted throughout with Ersilia's reactions. She is in an almost constant state of anxiety, anguish, shock or confusion, indicated not only by what she says, but by the manner of her expression. The stage directions describe her a 'afflicted', 'frightened', 'smiling painfully', 'confused', 'shocked', 'terrified', 'anxious', 'downhearted', 'mortified', etc., and she also has a hysterical attack accompanied by a fainting fit (Act I). Male pleasure-in-writing becomes narcissistically self-referential when Ersilia, made to commit an embarrassing social gaffe, refers to Nota's novel *L'Esclusa* (The Excluded Woman), likening herself to its main character. Nota's humourous rejection of this novel, which he dislikes, as having been written not by him but by Pirandello, serves to reinforce the 'writing' male subject position even further, and completes the narrative circuit which establishes and enthrones the Father of the Text.

The pleasure of writing in the male subject position can thus be seen to produce a variety of self-destructive resolutions for female objects literally embodying the internalization of the values of a system gendered stereotypically along patriarchal lines (suicide for Ersilia and Candelora in *Candelora*, anorexia for Tuda in *Diana and Tuda*). This pleasure, which is actually pleasure in destructiveness, has distinctly sadistic overtones (as we noted above in the case of Nota's pressing interrogation of Ersilia). The sadism accompanying the 'writing' male subject position is matched by a corresponding masochism on the part of the female object position which is being written. We have already pointed out Tuda's masochistic behaviour in urging Sirio to continue sculpting when she has just complained of tiredness, thereby colluding with and encouraging his ill-treatment of her. More drastic instances of masochism are, of course, the utter denial of self in female characters who express their lack of identity and, in particular, cases when such denial, inscribed by the character on to her own body, finds its ultimate expression in suicide.

Sadism and masochism as tendencies inherent in the actual form of traditional narrative have been explored by feminist film theorists influenced by Freud and led by Laura Mulvey. As Case comments in her book *Feminism and Theatre*, 'An even deeper analysis which has recently emerged in the realm of psychosemiotics suggests that the form of narrative itself is complicit with the psychocultural repression of women' (Case, 1988, p. 124). In her seminal article 'Visual Pleasure and Narrative Cinema', Mulvey makes the link between sadism and the activity of 'looking' on the part of the male subject. Earlier in this chapter, I mentioned the activity of 'looking' the female object position, alongside that of 'speaking' and 'writing' it, as one of the narrative means of constructing not only male subjectivity but, concomitantly, the non-subjectivity of the female object position. Mulvey's association of sadism with a certain type of looking (voyeurism) can therefore be extended to the 'speaking' and 'writing', as well as 'looking', male subject positions which I have been examining. She says, citing voyeurism as one avenue of escape for the male subject from castration anxiety:

> voyeurism . . . has associations with sadism: pleasure lies in ascertaining guilt (immediately associated with castration), asserting control and subjugating the guilty person through punishment or forgiveness. This sadistic side fits in well with narrative. Sadism demands a story, depends on making something happen, forcing a change in another person, a battle of will and strength, victory/defeat, all occurring in a linear time with a beginning and an end. (Mulvey, 1989, pp. 21–2)

The exhibitionism of the female character/object position, on the other hand, shows complementary masochist tendencies: 'Her exhibitionism, her masochism, make her an ideal counterpart to . . . active sadistic voyeurism' (ibid., p. 24). Summarizing the ideas of De Lauretis on the implications for a culture which popularizes the sado-masochistic orientation of the structure of traditional narrative, Case writes:

> within the typical narrative, the male is the one who makes something happen (the typical hero), who forces a change in another through a battle of wills. He is given the role of the sadist. In love stories, the defeated one is typically the female. Within the narrative structure, the female plays the masochist to the male sadist. Freud has also drawn the character of female

sexuality as a masochistic one, locating female masochism in the natural development of the child. The popularity of such stories indicates the sado-masochistic nature of desire in the community at large. The reader or audience member who gains pleasure from this narrative structure joins in the reification of male and female sexuality as a battle in which the female is defeated. Desire, which propels the story forward, is sadistic and encoded in terms of male and female genders. The structure of narrative as well as its broad appeal enacts this process in the culture. (Case, 1988, p. 124)

The narrative structure which situates the male subject as 'writer' of the female object position, and aligns the subject and object positions with those of sadism and masochism respectively, similarly encodes logos in the position of the male subject, while the female object is identified with the negatively valued discourse of the body. Sadism and logos come together in the Father's relation to the emotional, instinctual position occupied by the Mother in *Six Characters in Search of an Author*. It is in his violent establishment of the power of the discourse of logos over the Mother's discourse of the instincts, that the Father occupies a sadistic subject position. This finds its culminating expression in his demeaning verbal and non-verbal attack on what *he names* as her 'terrifying mental deafness' (her lack of logos). With his next comment ('attachment to her children, yes') he does not go on to counterbalance this 'defect' with her instinctual position of doting mother, but implicates this position as being distinctly inferior to that of logos. His is the discourse of reason/culture which regulates instinct/nature, a regulation which, it will be remembered, distinguishes culture from nature, and which has all the characteristics of sadism as described above by Mulvey: assertion of control, subjugation, forcing a change, a battle of will. Let us now take a closer look at the role of logos in the narrative configuration we have identified as Father-as-author/ity.

Monologos

The role of logos in constructing the subject position in general is an important one, as I indicated at the beginning of this chapter. I now want to focus on the predominance of logos in the quest for identity on the part of the male protagonist, as opposed to the emphasis on sexuality-as-identity in the case of the female antagonist. In the context of what I have already said about the narrative construction of subject and object positions, I want to argue that in Pirandello, as in traditional narrative in general, there is a problem with female *protagonists*. As a rule, genuine female subjectivity is not represented; the version of it which appears in the text is constructed entirely by, and in relation to, the male-dominated subject position and is characteristically identified with sexuality/ instinct. In other words, it is identified with what is represented as the inferior discourse of the body in a way that male subjectivity never is. Male subjectivity, on the other hand, is identified with reason, philosophy and the (heroic) quest for 'truth'.

In this narrative quest, the 'truth' or objective of 'reasoned' enquiry is frequently inscribed on to the female body, with invariably sexual implications for that body. The sexual element may be submerged, for instance, by the use of symbolization of an idealized kind. Such is the fate of Mrs Ponza whose identity is, as we have seen, the subject of a public enquiry managed by Laudisi in *That's How It Is (If You Think So)*. With her veiled appearance at the end of the play, and at the end of an unsuccessful search for 'truth', Mrs Ponza symbolizes the unattainable, unfathomable 'truth' on a general epistemological level (the exclusively male subject's realm of enquiry) which is, however, inscribed on to the female body in an *idealized* symbolic state. This idealized state denies and suppresses the *real* state of female identity, which is fragmented according to culturally determined procedures inherent in the patriarchal naming of family relationships (Mrs Ponza is both Mr Ponza's second wife and Mrs Frola's daughter). At the same time, the threat of female sexuality is contained by imprisonment (Mr Ponza does not allow his wife to leave their apartment). Like Shakespeare's Cressida, 'her value as an object of masculine fantasy requires that she keep herself veiled in mystery, unattainable and unreadable' (Cook, 1990, p. 192).

In this play the discourse of logos is in the power, or rather, works to constitute the power, of the male protagonist, Laudisi. He is the central authority to whom all information is communicated, and whose point of view regarding the meaning and value of this information is prioritized, not just for the other characters, but also for the audience. The audience is privy to his reasoned, philosophical soliloquy as he ponders on the meaning of meaning in the mirror scene (Act II, sc. 3). The basis of Laudisi's philosophical ruminations is that there is more than one 'truth', a stock Pirandellian theme, and this 'realization' makes him the embodiment of the authorial point of view. Laudisi's recognition of the multiple nature of truth ends each act, and the play itself, on a triumphant note.

The play's conclusion translates on to a philosophical plane the fact that female identity, which has objectified the sought-after truth, remains unknowable, fractured and multiple. While Laudisi the philosopher has no problem with this, the female character remains trapped in a state of non-subjectivity, dependent, as she says, on what others believe her to be: for herself, she is no one. Unlike Laudisi, who, in the mirror scene, develops similar ideas regarding his own identity, Mrs Ponza is not portrayed philosophizing about the nature of truth. She is the object of the philosophizing of others, only appearing at the end of the play to speak about nine lines. She is certainly never accorded the privilege of a soliloquy, the classic theatrical vehicle for the prioritization of a character's innermost thinking processes. In short, she is not the subject of the discourse of logos, but its object; not a protagonist in the play, but an antagonist.

An examination of the realist structure of this play offers further evidence of the discourse of 'truth'-seeking logos as a discourse of power. Belsey defines realist narrative as follows:

> Classic realism is characterized by . . . narrative which leads to 'closure', and a 'hierarchy of discourses' which establishes the 'truth' of the story. . . [A] high degree of intelligibility is sustained throughout the narrative as a result of the hierarchy of discourses in the text. The hierarchy works above all by means of a privileged discourse which places as subordinate all the discourses that are literally or figuratively between inverted commas. (Belsey, 1985, p. 53)

The high status of this discourse invites audience or reader identification with the reasoning subject (Laudisi) and acquiescence with his findings. Belsey continues:

> By these means classic realism offers the reader a position of knowingness which is also a position of identification with the narrative voice. To the extent that the story first constructs, and then depends for its intelligibility, on a set of assumptions shared between narrator and reader, it confirms both the transcendent knowingness of the reader-as-subject and the 'obviousness' of the shared truths in question. (ibid.)

With this typically seamless and imperceptible realist device, the audience is aligned with the subject position and against the object position: we join Laudisi, who is almost always on stage, in the quest for Mrs Ponza's 'true' identity, rather than positioning ourselves with Mrs Ponza, the enigmatic object, who comes on stage only at the end of the play. Mrs Ponza provides the enigma necessary for the realist structure to be activated, for the plot to be set in motion; the problem of female identity, identified in the previous chapter as *the* narrative problem, must be solved, and the search for the narrative solution is very much under the management of the reasoning male subject.

Realism's quest for truth via the powerful discourse of logos is not in fact successful in this play; access to truth, alias definition and hence circumscription of female identity, is not achieved. The sought-after closure via disclosure of truth does not take place. The unknowableness of female identity, presented as fragmentation, is imprisoned, veiled and 'raised' to the status of idealized symbol, (mis)appropriated by and for logos on to a seemingly genderless epistemological plane. The mechanism of this attempt at recuperation lies in transforming the actual failure of the discourse of logos into a triumph, by a distinctly tautologous sleight of hand, as the 'discovery' of the multiplicity of truth (the unfathomableness of female identity) is itself made into a truth. At this point the text can be seen to deconstruct itself by exposing the precise juncture at which subject and object positions collide; in other words, by revealing its suturing processes and their basis in patriarchal ideology. It is also at this point that we see the extent to which Pirandello's satire is restricted to the philosophical plane. In a play which has been heralded as a masterpiece of social satire with bourgeois convention as its target, traditional patriarchal values regarding female identity are in fact reinforced.

A denial of the subversive potentialities inherent in the very unknowableness of female identity, potentialities made possible by readings of realist narrative which expose its workings, in other words, by reading against the text, is expressed by Case:

> [T]he violence released in the continual zooming in on the family unit, and the heterosexist ideology linked with its stage partner, realism, is directed against women and their hint of seduction . . . [T]he closure of [the] realist narrative chokes women to death and strangles the play of symbols, the possibility of seduction . . . Cast realism aside – its consequences for women are deadly. (Case, 1989, p. 297, quoted in Dolan, 1990, p. 42 n. 9)

The fact that deconstructive readings of texts are not, by their very definition, the norm, of course substantiates Case's viewpoint. However, pushing up against the philosophical 'coup' which closes *That's How It Is (If You Think So)*, there is, undeniably, the excess, the insoluble mystery, and therefore threat, of female identity. Patriarchal ideology maintains its hold only by a continuous process of countering the threat to its hegemony. This threat cannot be allayed once and for all, and necessitates constant surveillance and punishment. One positive strategy might be to attempt to make this threat visible, thereby increasing its power even more.

A crucial stage in the continuing process of suppression is the tendentious construction of subject and object positions in narrative of all kinds. Narrative undoubtedly plays a key role in informing the construction of these positions in other, non-narrative contexts which combine to give shape to the ideological topography of a culture. In the narrative context of the function of the discourse of logos in empowering the male subject position, I should now like to return to a specifically dramatic device which has already been mentioned in relation to *That's How It Is (If You Think So)*, and which contributes, on a structural level, to the dominance of the reasoning subject. This is the soliloquy, and the closely related monologue.

In her chapter 'Playing The Woman's Part', Helms signals the high profile of this particular theatrical device:

> Soliloquy, by convention, allows an actor to establish a privileged relation to the audience, either to tell the character's side of the story by creating the illusion of interiority or to restructure the theatrical event by breaking through the dramatic fiction. (Helms, 1990, p. 199)

In discussing the implications for female characters of the way in which the soliloquy functions in Shakespearean theatre, she comments that:

> female characters are rarely alone on stage and even more rarely do they address the audience directly. When they do, the conventions of the soliloquy are regularly adapted to the female character, revealing the extent to which the Shakespearean soliloquy is ordinarily gendered as male. (ibid.)

While comic soliloquies 'seem to offer greater possibilities for feminist intervention', in *Hamlet* and *Macbeth* the

> subjectivity of the female characters, even in soliloquy, is, for the audience, mediated through their shared concentration on the male protagonist. The text insistently interposes a male presence between the female speaker and the auditor. (ibid.)

Helms concentrates on the Elizabethan period, the heyday of the soliloquy, which fell out of favour in late nineteenth-century theatre, and in fact is little used by Pirandello. In the words of Roessler, citing Matthews (and using the word 'monolog' for soliloquy), 'This revulsion of feeling occurred in the final decades of the nineteenth century, when "the leading playwrights of every modern language began to display a distaste for the monolog, with Ibsen setting the example of renunciation"' (Roessler, 1966, p. 1). The other reason for the decline first recognized by Ibsen, is Edison, 'as the introduction of electric lighting together with the picture-frame stage created a setting so realistic that the stepping out of the picture to talk intimately with the audience was felt to be entirely out of place' (ibid., pp. 2–3). However, most of the salient features of soliloquy are shared by its close relative, the monologue, which is rather prominent in Pirandello's plays. Here, in the form of passages of rational argumentation made up of complete, sustained sentences (rather than unstructured collections of frequently only half-finished syntactic constructions), the monologue is 'ordinarily gendered as male' (Helms, 1990, p. 199). (For an example of the latter, unstructured type of monologue, see Ersilia's speech quoted on p. 47). As we shall see in our analysis of turn duration in chapter 5, the Father in *Six Characters in Search of an Author*, for example, has the longest speech turns compared to the other Characters, and the lowest proportion of short turns. In the category of turn continuity, he has the highest number of unbroken turns (of ten lines or more).

At this point, some definitions of 'soliloquy' and 'monologue' are in order, before moving on to an examination of the role of these devices in structuring the discourse of logos in the speaking subject in some of Pirandello's plays. To begin with, no definitions specify the minimum number of lines which either a soliloquy or a monologue must contain. Cuddon, for example, defines soliloquy as 'a speech, often of some length', while Roessler gives a brief history of critical responses to 'long' soliloquies (Cuddon, 1982, p. 637; Roessler, 1966, p. 6). Strictly speaking, then, the information given above on turn duration and turn continuity is of relevance in that it deals with relative lengths of speeches, rather than monologues as such. As far as any distinction between soliloquy and monologue is concerned, most definitions imply that there is much overlap between them without attempting to account for any differences. Etymologically, both terms mean 'speaking alone', with 'soliloquy' deriving from Augustine's late Latin 'soliquum' ('solus', 'soli', adj. = 'alone', + 'loqui', verb = 'speak'), while 'monologue' derives from the Greek equivalent (OED). 'Soliloquy' thus contrasts with 'colloquy', and 'monologue' with 'dialogue' and 'chorus'.

Roessler does attempt to establish a distinction between the two terms, noting that definitions of 'monologue', unlike those of 'soliloquy', invariably specify a dramatic context, and concludes: '[t]he difficulty can be peacefully settled, however, and both of the contestants put upon an equal footing by prefixing "dramatic" to soliloquy' (Roessler, 1966, p. 3). However, he also mentions that English and American critics for the most part employ the term 'soliloquy', while French and German usage prefers 'monologue', a fact for which he can find no explanation (ibid., pp. 2–3). What is more, the 'monologue' may be a 'general literary composition', as well as specifically a dramatic one (OED). In fact, it is probably more correct to say that in English usage, it is the term 'soliloquy' which has distinctly dramatic associations, whereas 'monologue' also suggests a wider, non-dramatic range of connotations.

The problem of establishing a precise distinction therefore appears unresolved. For the purposes of this discussion, both terms will be used. I shall adapt Cuddon's definition and use 'soliloquy' for instances when the speaker is alone on the stage, and 'monologue' for cases when the speaker is not alone on the stage.[9] In these terms, the speaker of the soliloquy, compared to the other characters in the play, is in the most privileged relationship possible with the audience. The speaker of the monologue, on the other hand, shares audience attention with the other character(s) on stage, but is nevertheless in a more privileged relationship with the audience than these other characters. In this sense, the monologue often appears within a dialogue. One definition of the term 'monologist' as 'one who monopolizes the conversation', or, in our case, the dramatic dialogue, is particularly relevant here (as well as serving to illustrate the wider semantic range of 'monologue' and associated terms, as compared to 'soliloquy').

The purpose of this clarification of the use of soliloquy and monologue, it will be remembered, is to help ascertain the dramatic workings of the discourse of logos. Looked at now from the perspective, not of the theatre, but of the discourse of logos itself, the monologue appears as a natural component of that discourse, in that philosophical argumentation gives rise to, and indeed entails, relatively prolonged periods of speaking. By contrast, the 'lower status' discourse of the body does not necessitate prolonged, sustained verbalization, but can find expression in actual verbal incoherence, as well as in non-verbal behaviour. (This is the case of the Mother and the Stepdaughter in *Six Characters in Search of an Author*; see chapters 5 and 6.)

In this way the monologizing characteristic of the discourse of logos appears to dovetail neatly with the dramatic monologue. The use of the dramatic monologue to place this discourse with the male subject can now be examined in some of Pirandello's plays. We have already discussed the implications of Laudisi's soliloquy above. While the incidence of soliloquy in Pirandello's drama is rare (its popularity having generally waned towards the end of the nineteenth century, as we saw earlier), the same cannot be said of the monologue, which makes a frequent appearance. The soliloquy is 'a kind of talking to oneself, not intended to affect others', although the 'others' are clearly implicated by their actual absence; the monologue, on the other hand, has the effect of monopolizing and controlling the dialogue, or, if more than one other character is on stage, the colloquy, of which it forms a part (Shipley, 1970, p. 203, quoted in Clemen, 1987, p. 193).

The first area of interest, then, is the use of the philosophical monologue as a means of ensuring dominance of the stage, in other words, of

9. Cuddon's definition of 'soliloquy' does in fact specify that a character is 'alone on the stage'; for 'monologue' he gives 'a single person speaking alone – with or without an audience', and I am therefore opting for the former possibility only (i.e. with an audience), in addition to taking 'audience' to refer to the other character(s) on stage as well as to the audience in the auditorium (Cuddon, 1982).

the 'speaking space', and thereby of audience attention, together with the implications of this process for other characters/positions. An interesting variant of this dramatic strategy occurs when a dialogue between two male characters, during which one of them may predominate, becomes what amounts to a monologue to which they both contribute. This is particularly striking when a female character who could take part in the philosophical discussion does not do so, especially when philosophy turns into a problematization of the female character herself. This can happen in a variety of ways: the object of the discussion may appear on stage and speak, but nevertheless not take part in the philosophizing, which takes place before her entry and resumes after her exit (as in *At the Exit*); or when the object of the discussion is effectively absent, in that she is an evanescent, shadow-like presence with no voice, occasionally materializing on the boundaries of the male arena, conjured up by the discussion (as in *The Man With the Flower in His Mouth*).

In *At the Exit*, the (male) Philosopher and the Fat Man philosophize on life and death until almost halfway through the play, when the problem of female identity/sexuality, in the form of the Fat Man's wife, is introduced into the discussion. She appears on stage (as the Murdered Woman), effectively conjured up by his words, for approximately the final third of the play. This shows her laughing and crying, in direct contrast to the sustained, unemotional reasoning which preceded her entry on to the stage. Her laughing account of her own murder, in the allocutionary mode and punctuated by direct addresses to the Fat Man, although not short, is very different from the lengthier, sustained monologues spoken by the two male characters. These monologues are characterized by mostly non-personal subject matter, a predominant 'emphasis on the speaker; little reference to the allocutionary situation [and] absence of metalinguistic elements' (Ducrot and Todorov, 1981, pp. 303–4). The Philosopher, alone on stage, ends the play with words which imply, however coyly, the primacy of logos: 'I fear I alone shall remain here forever, continuing to reason.' A similar, but non-dramatic, example of male-dominated dialogue-as-monologue is to be found in Pirandello's article 'Feminism' (discussed in the Appendix). In this case the discussion moves from abstract matters to the problem of female identity (this time in the politicized form of feminism). The dialogue takes place with a woman present in the room. However, she does not join in their dialogue/monologue, even though the subject matter clearly concerns her, speaking only to say that she in fact cannot hear, or is not listening. She is in effect excluded from their philosophical-political discourse and relegated to a position *behind* her father's books and papers.

The female voice is excluded to an even greater extent by male monologizing in *The Man With the Flower in His Mouth*. The dominant male philosophizer of the title discourses on his perceptions of life, and both male characters lament the problems caused them by the women in their respective families. For the Peaceloving Customer, sent on a shopping expedition by his wife, his daughters and their female friends, it is their consumerism which aggravates him (a common topos in the literature of discord between the sexes, see p. 105). The references by the Man to his wife are more deprecating, violent and sadistic. He says she is more like a rag or a duster than a woman, and compares her to a stray bitch which refuses to go away, however much it is kicked. Furthermore, he expresses a wish to strangle her. He also paints a revolting picture of female desire: she wounds herself on the lip with a hatpin and tries to kiss him on the mouth, where he has an epithilioma (a cancerous, flowerlike growth) so that she may die with him.

This female character never speaks, and only her shadow puts in an occasional, fleeting appearance with its head, conjured up by his references to her. She is not listed as one of the characters (the only characters being the Man and the Peaceloving Customer), appearing only as a reference in the initial stage directions ('Towards the end, at the places indicated, the shadow of a woman dressed in black with a small old hat of weeping feathers will stick its head out from the corner'). Like the Murdered Woman in *At the Exit*, this shadow of a woman is not allowed access to the discourse of logos. As objects, and not subjects, of this discourse, both are excluded, and upstaged, by its monologizing male proponents. Another form of exclusion is to pre-empt any use of this discourse on the part of a female character by actually explaining it to her, thereby constructing her position as one of instant ignorance. In *But It's Not Serious*, Loletta calls Memmo's behaviour illogical, at which point Magnasco launches into a patronizing explanation of logic: 'Because you see, Loletta, the triumph of logic was that marriage of his. Eh, you don't understand, my Loletta! Do you know what logic is? Look: imagine a sort of pump . . .' (Act II, sc. 1). A similarly patronizing use of simile occurs in 'Feminism', when Dr Post explains feminism in terms of a balloon filled with air.

Shifting focus now to the ways in which logos in the male subject can lead to plot resolution, we see that the monologue as a dramatic device contributes to the movement of the narrative towards its closure. In these instances, it is the male character who has all the answers, more often than not expounded in monologue form, and whose ideas and solutions solve the problem which has set the plot in motion (a problem more often than not associated with a female character).

In *Cecé* for example, the plot is resolved by the outwitting of the female character (who is described as 'ingenuous' in the stage directions) by the male character of the title, together with the help of his male friend, Squatriglia. As a result of a bet with male friends, Cecé has managed to acquire Nada's sexual services, and the plot of the play hinges on the return of three cheques which he felt obliged to give her. Returning a favour Cecé has done him, Squatriglia persuades Nada to return the cheques, worth 6,000 lire, and gives her 1,650 lire instead. In so doing, Squatriglia speaks the longest monologue of the play (31 lines). During their dialogue, Nada speaks only one monologue (of 10 lines). Cecé, who is responsible for managing the resolution of the plot, has the most monologues (four in total, of 29, 20, 10 and 13 lines). In the male-dominated context of the original bet concerning her sexual favours, and the ingenuity of intellect employed by the male protagonist in establishing an appropriate payment for them, the female character is excluded from the discourse which articulates her function as object of exchange, and which names her price.

Leone Gala exercises his intellectual faculties with similar success in *The Rules of the Game*. In a later play, *Six Characters in Search of an Author*, he is referred to as representing reason itself: 'You are reason, and your wife is instinct' (Act I). He uses his reason to outwit both his wife and her lover, and the play ends with the latter's unexpected participation in a duel to defend the wife's reputation, a duel which the wife had meant the husband to fight and in which her lover is fatally wounded. Gala is allocated the highest number of monologues (five, of 19, 10, 27, 10 and 13 lines) in his steering of the plot to its conclusion, a plot which the wife (who has only two monologues, of 10 and 12 lines) sets in motion with a scheme arising from her adultery.

In *A Doctor's Duty*, on the other hand, the male protagonist uses the discourse of logos to validate his own death. By an absurd process of logic, Tommaso Corsi decides that the injuries he has received at the hands of his mistress's husband, as a result of having been 'coerced' into an affair by her, are justified, and re-opens his wounds. The narrative dilemma is posited as being that of the doctor, who must decide whether to save a patient who does not wish to live. However, it is a dilemma brought about by the discourse of logos being taken to extremes by the male protagonist (who has four monologues of 20, 15, 11 and 21 lines, while his wife has only one, of 25, and two other male characters each have one of 11 and 14 lines respectively).

Another male character who 'lives out', or embodies, this discourse is Baldovino in *The Pleasure of Honesty*. As a result, he 'wins' the female character whose illicit pregnancy sets the plot in motion. Baldovino is given financial remuneration to marry Agata and thereby legitimate both her and the child. He reasons that, in order to fulfil this function properly, his position as husband and father must not be jeopardized by the presence of the lover. He 'becomes' his new social role so completely that Agata becomes his wife in more than name. Once again it is a male character whose reasoning powers dominate the outcome of the plot, reasoning which is conveyed with the help of eighteen monologues, while two other characters, one male and one female, each have only three. Agata herself has none. The process whereby she moves towards acceptance of her marriage to Baldovino is not governed by the workings of her intellect, as far as we can see. We are certainly not acquainted with any lengthy, intricate thoughts of hers, as we are in Baldovino's case.

Rather than her reasoning faculties, it is 'fate' which propels her forward, so that she is portrayed as reacting passively (to the thinking activities of Baldovino). While the notes for the performance describe her in the following way: 'haughty, almost hard because of the effort involved in resisting the downfall of her honesty. Desperate and rebellious in the first act; she then moves proudly and submissively straight to her fate', the more extensive description of Baldovino, on the other hand, refers to his 'strange philosophy, full of both irony and indulgence'. As we saw in the last chapter, the use of the notion of fate to explain Agata's reactions serves to essentialize behaviour which is in fact ideologically determined. The title of the play similarly obscures the existence of two very different types of honesty which are at issue: first, there is Agata's socio-sexual honesty, in the context of mores forbidding extra-marital sex for women, particularly for reasons of recreation (she at least has the goodness to procreate); and second, there is Baldovino's logical honesty, or integrity. In this play, then, it is the discourse of logical integrity which establishes control over, and recuperates, a transgressive and rebellious female sexuality.

The problem of pregnancy outside wedlock is again solved by the application of reason on the part of the male protagonist, namely the man of *Man, Beast and Virtue*. While the masterly schoolmaster, Paolino, with the help of another male character, his brother the pharmacist, manoeuvres the plot towards its resolution, the virtuous Mrs Perella, wife of the beast, Captain Perella, weeps and sighs her way through the play. In a now celibate marriage, and pregnant with Paolino's child, she literally becomes a puppet in Paolino's hands, as he applies make-up to her face and generally rewrites her virtuous purity. His transformation of her appearance into that of a prostitute, in order to tempt her husband who is also fed a cake containing an aphrodisiac, ultimately ensures that the pregnancy will be attributed to Captain Perella, and not himself. Once again, it is a male character who has all the answers, who uses his reason to engineer the narrative solution, and who does so with the help of the monologue (Paolino has six monologues, two other characters have one, but Mrs Perella herself has none).

In *Cap and Bells* it is similarly a male character, Ciampa, who 'all of a sudden, absorbed in an idea which comes to him in a flash there and then, beamingly', arrives at a solution to the narrative problem. This entails publicizing the fictitious insanity of the female character, an insanity which, once invented, appears to come true. The play closes with the enclosure of Beatrice, whose scheming, or rather transgressive appropriation of the discourse of logos, is rewritten as madness, and contained with her confinement. The monologue is, throughout the play, mainly in the possession of Ciampa, who, as well as directing the plot towards its resolution, spends much time ruminating on multiple identity. (He has ten monologues, Spanò, the legal deputy, has five, and La Saracena, the second-hand dealer, has one.)

In this play, the appropriation of the discourse of logos by a female character is punished. This discourse has, of course, already been appropriated by the male subject in the wider ideological context of a patriarchal culture, which assigns reason and order to the masculine domain, and emotion and disorder to the feminine. This male order is constantly threatened with disruption by an oppressed, and suppressed, female identity, against whose potential and actual subversiveness as a lower-status gender, patriarchy, in order to survive, is committed to legislate and, through its cultural media, to manipulate and persuade. In the continuing dialectic between the activities of oppression, on the part of the dominating force, and those of transgression, on the part of the subordinated, control over the discourses of power is also constantly contested. In this context, the discourse of logos, as a discourse of power, is highly valorized, while stereotypically feminine discourses of the body (of emotion, of instinct and particularly of sexuality) are attributed a lesser status.

As we have seen, certain of Pirandello's plays play out this dialectic in a variety of ways, with the discourse of logos repeatedly placed in the possession, or rather, forming an integral part of the construction, of the male subject position. Enmeshed with this dynamic of discourse/power appropriation is dramatic form itself, in the use made of the monologue and, in some cases, of the dialogue-as-monologue, when two male characters dominate this discourse between them to the obvious exclusion of a female character. Such exclusion is of course by no means always only gender-specific. Male characters among themselves constitute a hierarchy based on class and age. Indeed, it is not always only female characters who are marginalized from the discourse of logos. Other male characters, particularly domestics, are similarly barred, often becoming the object of comedy as a direct result.

One example is Councillor Agazzi's manservant, who comes upon Laudisi soliloquizing before the mirror, and who is clearly made to appear out of his depth intellectually. He is described as 'bewildered', 'dumbfounded' and, open-mouthed, is unable to sustain a dialogue on multiple identity with Laudisi (*That's How It Is (If You Think So)*, Act II, sc. 3). In another example, Henry, the epitome of the idle rich at play, toys with his four manservants, making them appear dimwitted when they, too, prove themselves inept at philosophizing, this time about madness. They are described three times in the stage directions as 'bewildered' and twice as 'stupefied', while Henry addresses one of them, who stands open-mouthed, as 'imbecile' (*Henry IV*, Act 2). In both examples there is a reinforcement of class difference, as the upper-class male character outwits the male servant class, the latter functioning as an ignorant and laughter-provoking foil to the mighty discourse of philosophy.

In the case of the dialogue-as-monologue, on the other hand, when two male characters share the discourse of logos to the overt exclusion of a female character, the process of male bonding can be seen at work. These male characters, in the texts mentioned above, are ostensibly from the same social class (for example, the Philosopher and the Fat Man in *At the Exit*, the Man and the Peaceloving Customer in *The Man With the Flower in His Mouth*, and also the 'I' narrator and Doctor Post in 'Feminism'). It is notable that the opposite process, namely that of male rivalry, is also in evidence. This, too, normally entails the two characters concerned belonging to the same class. In this particular dynamic, however, it is age which frequently provides the socially differentiating factor. Unlike the reinforcement of class difference between male characters, which involves a cross-class and not a cross-gender opposition, male rivalry inevitably takes place in the context of gender. Indeed issues of both male rivalry and male bonding can be seen played out characteristically in the arena of female sexuality itself. These issues form the basis of the next chapter.

–3–

Camaraderie in Competition:
Male Bonding and Male Rivalry

MERLETTI: And now they are left with the child,
which has turned them, from the close
friends they used to be, into enemies.
Belonging to One Person or to No-One, Act III

Introduction: Conditions of Bonding/Rivalry

In the last chapter we saw male bonding at work in examples of collaboration between male characters occupying the subject position and, by extension, alignment of the audience with this position. We shall now turn our attention to the conditions in which both bonding and its opposite, rivalry, take place. As far as the cultural representation of bonding in narrative, and particularly in the sphere of drama, is concerned, one formal device which we have already encountered is the dialogue-as-monologue, examined in the last chapter. Another such device is the construction of a system of looks; for instance, the look shared by the Father, Director and the other characters on stage (and the audience) at the fetishized, exhibitionist display of the female character (the Stepdaughter) occupying the object position in *Six Characters in Search of an Author*. Moreover, the interchange between the Director and the Father which follows this display (while the actors and actresses merely laugh and applaud) places them, for the first time, on the 'same side'. It is they who, between them, will set up a reasoned dialogue which the Stepdaughter will counter with her emotional, fragmented discourse of the body. Another example of male bonding as an effect of a collaboration of looks, this time involving a system of voyeuristic, vicarious looks shared by Sirio, Giuncano (and the audience), takes place as part of the process of 'writing' the highly sexualized object position occupied by Tuda in *Diana and Tuda*, described in the last chapter.

The underlying dynamic which brings about male bonding is again the fundamental process of the exchange of women, a dynamic contributing to the gender-specific link between subject position, culture and masculinity. We have already noted the particular relationship of reciprocity which maintains between male subjects. Reciprocity leads, in turn, to bonding. One aspect of male bonding, namely homoeroticism in latent or overt form, may be seen to derive in part from this relationship of reciprocity.[1] Irigaray has pointed out that a system in which reciprocity/subjectivity is under male domination, is occupied not by two interrelating genders, but by one gender relating only to itself. She has coined the term 'hom(m)osexualité' for this self-referential gender, on the grounds that heterosexuality 'is only an alibi for the smooth workings of the relations of man with himself, of relations between men' (Irigaray, 1977a, p. 168). In this system, women function fetishistically as 'manifestation and circulation of Phallic power, establishing relations between men' (ibid., p. 178). While men are 'subjects producing and exchanging', women are 'productive terrain, merchandise' (Irigaray, 1977b, p. 189). We have encountered the metaphor of woman-as-fertile-terrain in relation to *The Grafting* and *Liolà*, where it is used to reinforce precisely this function for women, and we shall be returning to it later in this chapter. The role of women in this exchange system between men is that of mediation, of providing an arena in which relations between men can take place. These relations may be divided into bonding, or collaboration, and rivalry, or hostile confrontation, taking place between men and about women.

Before examining instances of male bonding and male rivalry in Pirandello's plays, some clarification is needed concerning the relationship between these two opposing forms of interaction. As will become apparent in the analysis of the plays, bonding can change abruptly into rivalry, and vice versa; and at times there appears to be remarkably little to separate them. This in itself is not surprising; although bonding and rivalry are clearly opposites, they are nevertheless both variants of the same relationship, namely that between male subjects. In other words, although relations may fluctuate between camaraderie and hostility, the basic parameters of a relationship of exchange 'between at least two men' remain constant (Irigaray, 1977a, p. 177). If anything, hostility, rather than camaraderie, is the dominant marker of this relationship, ever-present as an undercurrent when not in action as overt rivalry. These relations of exchange (which are basically subject to social and market forces, and founded on competition for a never-sufficing quantity of 'rarefied commodities'), are characterized by Irigaray as 'more or less rival'

1. Halperin writes interestingly about active and passive in relation to erotic reciprocity, which the ancient Greeks saw as the particular province of women. In ancient philosophy, erotic reciprocity was also believed to be present in the dialogue form (Halperin, 1986, 1990).

(ibid., p. 167; 1977c, p. 31). Ultimately, then, even when male subjects are involved in hostile rivalry via women, they are operating within the rules of their own system, a system which oscillates between collaboration and confrontation, depending on the immediate circumstances.

Male Bonding and Male Rivalry

A classic example of the transformation of rivalry into bonding occurs in *Cap and Bells*. When Beatrice publicly exposes her husband's adultery with Ciampa's wife Nina, Ciampa, who had been aware of the affair, suggests that Beatrice be declared insane, a solution which invalidates her denunciation and exculpates not only his wife, but her husband (Ciampa's rival). This solution does not merely remove the need for Ciampa to kill him, which he first thought necessary; it establishes a bond between the two men, a bond which is all the more significant in that its author is employed by Beatrice's husband and is therefore his social inferior.

Because Beatrice's husband never appears on stage, the actual rivalry/relation between the two men is translated and relocated, appearing as conflict between her and Ciampa. This is an illustration of men's relations in the exchange of, or competition for, women, taking place in a mediated fashion. In other words, they do not relate *with* each other directly as subjects, but *by means of* a woman-as-object-of-exchange. It is to be noted that, in this play, the mediation takes the form, not of *the* woman-as-object-of-exchange (Nina) but of *a* woman-as-object-of-exchange (Beatrice). This is because Beatrice has interfered with a system which is not her own; in other words, she has contravened the male code of honour (a code informed by relations of exchange). Cuckoldry is only a crime, and in fact can only even be said to take place, if it is by definition 'public' (issues of male honour, such as paternity and potency, being defined not by biological, but by socio-cultural criteria). Beatrice's action of taking her husband's adultery into the social domain, an adultery kept private by Nina, brings to the surface the rivalry between the two men, a rivalry which is translated into bonding at the expense of Beatrice's sanity.

In another play, *Man, Beast and Virtue*, the transition from potentially overt rivalry to bonding is once again masterminded by one of the relationship's male characters, namely Paolino. He does so by means of a solution which similarly involves the manipulation of a woman-as-object-of-exchange, Captain Perella's wife. The rule of secrecy being difficult to obey once pregnancy occurs (the marriage itself being a celibate one, it will be remembered), issues of paternity and legitimacy inevitably arise to disturb relations between the husband and his wife's male lover. In order to resolve these issues, the pregnancy must be attributed to the husband, who must somehow be made to sleep with his wife, an act he is usually reluctant to peform.

It is at this point that Paolino becomes a pander, a sexual entrepreneur who acts as a middleman between another man and his wife's sexual availability. Two other male characters, a doctor and chemist, also join in the pandering process. Paolino himself grooms a weak and powerless Mrs Perella for her role, liberally applying cosmetics to her face and arranging her clothing so as to make her appear like a prostitute. These exclusively male machinations prove successful; the Captain and Paolino even have a comradely discussion about the nature of women after the deed is done. The latent rivalry between them has been transformed into bonding, and eventually one will even rear the other's child as his own (albeit unwittingly), as the patriarchal rules of social (rather than biological) paternity are reinforced.

The woman-as-object-of-exchange is similarly passed from one male character (Fabio) to another (Baldovino) in *The Pleasure of Honesty*, in this case from the lover to his male cousin's former schoolfriend. Again, paternity and legitimacy are the guiding factors; here it is the unmarried Agata whose pregnancy by Fabio must be made legitimate by marriage. The necessary social paternity is provided by Baldovino, a solution devised by Fabio's cousin, Maurizio, who acts as entrepreneur between Fabio and Baldovino. Money changes hands as Maurizio employs a male financial speculator to negotiate terms with the prospective husband and social father.

In this business transaction, the woman-as-object-of-exchange is 'sold' to an insolvent Baldovino for 300,000 lire and the position of managing director in Fabio's newly established joint stock company. As far as Baldovino is concerned, he considers himself to be picking up the bill for Fabio's actions, a payment which buys him long sought-after vindication in a society which has hitherto denied his signature credit. He explains the mutual benefits of this deal to Fabio in terms which echo the economic basis of their new bond:

> You must now pay for your consolation, Marquess. You have before you the menacing shadow of a protest which will not brook postponement. – I come along to sign as guarantor, and to assume responsibility for paying your bill. – You cannot imagine, Marquess, how much pleasure it gives me to be able to carry out this vendetta against a society which denies my signature any credit. (*The Pleasure of Honesty*, Act I, sc. 8)

The forging of this bond between two male characters, and its organization by various other male characters, takes place via the exchange, in the form of the actual purchase, of the female character. It is according to the rules of this system of exchange that Agata must behave, and by which 'her' 'honesty' will be 'saved'. She is manipulated from a position of initial reluctance to one of acceptance with such a degree of success that for her, too, social paternity (legitimated by marriage to Baldovino) eventually comes to outweigh biological paternity (an illicit affair with Fabio). With this development male bonding turns to male rivalry, as Baldovino now clearly outranks Fabio in the hierarchy of the exchange system, an outranking for which, in the last resort, another mediating object-of-exchange is responsible. This is Fabio's wife, who never appears on stage, but who is blamed for their unsuccessful marriage, in other words, for unsuccessful mediation.

Prostitution

The financial transaction which takes place between Fabio and Baldovino in this system of exchange, of woman-as-object-of-value for money highlights the economic structure of the system governing relations of bonding and rivalry between men as exchanging subjects. Several of Pirandello's plays deal with the related, if different, business deal which takes place when a female character is paid for her sexual services. While a woman's use value lies in her *potential* reproductive power which, in turn, gives rise to her exchange value in the case of the prostitute, her use value lies in the sexual services (not leading to reproduction) which she has *already* provided. Her use value and exchange value are therefore less clearly differentiated from each other. (Irigaray gives a definition of prostitution as 'use which is exchanged'; Irigaray, 1977a, pp. 170, 181.)

It is not a prostitute's potential use value, but the already-effected nature of her use value, which determines her exchange value: 'It is by virtue of having already served that the woman's body acquires its price. Indeed, the more it has served, the more it is worth.' The valued commodity is not, then, the actual body itself or the use of it, but the fact that the body has already been used by other men. Once again, the woman-as-object-of-value, the female body, can be seen to mediate in relations between men. Irigaray continues: 'It is not that deployment of its natural riches has thereby taken place, but, on the contrary, because its nature . . . has again become the simple vehicle for relations between men' (ibid., p. 181).

Even when women are not prostitutes, as in the case of Agata, they are nevertheless still evaluated in economic terms on account of 'their submission by/to a culture which oppresses them, uses them, "moneys" them, without them deriving great profit from the process' (Irigaray,

1977c, p. 31). In other words, 'her valued form goes back again to what man inscribes in and on her matter: her body' (Irigaray, 1977a, p. 182). So, although the prostitute is paid for her services, it is not she, but the male customer, in the context of market forces, who fixes her price. *Cecé* is a play which, as we have seen, deals precisely with this issue. In a situation of male rivalry, Cecé is goaded by other men who challenge his ability to obtain Nada's services, in other words, who question his potency. It is then Cecé who, having succeeded in his quest, decides what she is worth. The entire plot revolves around his decision to reduce this price, and the collusion of a male friend who helps him to outwit Nada into accepting the reduced rate.

Pirandello's plays make a variety of references to prostitution. In *Man, Beast and Virtue*, the 'virtuous' Mrs Perella is made up to look like a prostitute by her lover-turned-pimp. Back in the realm of direct financial reimbursement, which we encountered in *Cecé*, in *But It's Not Serious* a female character (Loletta, one of two 'dubious little women') is paid for her sexual services by the hero, Memmo Speranza (Act II, sc. 2). In *Six Characters in Search of an Author*, money almost changes hands, as the Father nearly becomes one of the Stepdaughter's clients in Madama Pace's boudoir; and Ersilia makes a similarly unsuccessful attempt at earning money, this time in the streets, in *Clothing the Naked*. Goods, rather than money, are paid to the nameless young wife with expensive tastes by her lovers in *I Dream (But Perhaps Not)*, as they vie for her sexual favours with a pearl necklace.

Progressing from the payment of money and goods to the subsidy of living expenses in exchange for sexual services, we find the figure of the kept woman: Flora, kept by Mauri in *As Before, Better Than Before*, L'Ignota, kept by Salter in *As You Desire Me*, and Melina, who services two men, Tito and Carlino, in *Belonging to One Person or to No-One*. In the transaction of prostitution, the actual exchange value of the woman-as-object-of-exchange is based on her sexual services. In the different, but nevertheless contiguous context of marriage, on the other hand, the exchange value of the woman-as-object-of-exchange derives, as we have seen, from her reproductive power, with sexual services as an optional extra. When the reproductive function crosses over from the domain of marriage to the purely sexual sphere of prostitution, problems arise which underline the strict demarcation between these two areas of patriarchal exchange. This is precisely what happens when Melina becomes pregnant in *Belonging to One Person or to No-One*.

In this play, bonding between two male characters turns to rivalry at the point when their mistress becomes pregnant and is unable to identify which of them is the father. Until then, Melina had performed a positive mediating function, bringing the two friends closer together. Tito and

Carlino are inseparable, sharing the same rented room, while financing *her* accommodation *elsewhere*. As Merletti, their older male friend, and also the play's 'voice of reason', comments, 'You didn't know how to separate from each other' (Act I). With Melina's unexpected pregnancy, her formerly positive mediating function is transformed into a negative one and the entire category 'woman' is problematized, as the two men speak as one: 'One of the three fundamental problems to be resolved in everybody's existence . . . a roof over one's head – food – woman' (Act I).

As procreation trespasses into the recreational sphere, Melina's new negative mediating function transforms bonding into rivalry, and the two men, who 'now hate each other ferociously', move into separate lodgings (Act III). This negative mediation is rectified by the removal of the object-of-exchange from the exchange system: Melina dies a few days after giving birth, and the two male characters finally fall weeping into each other's arms. This focus on the relationship between the two males concludes the play, as, with this emotional reunion, the bond between the two males is re-established. The female character, far from being involved in a relationship with the two male characters herself, performs the mediating function of putting men in touch with each other, of 'bringing about relations between men' (Irigaray, 1977a, p. 178).

This mediating function of the female object-of-exchange is far from unimportant to the exchange system, as is illustrated by the actual necessity for her elimination after she has, in patriarchal terms, 'mal'-functioned. In a system based on a traffic in women, the strict adherence by women to the performance of specific functions in the appropriate context is a crucial factor. This accounts for the 'suppressed centrality' of women, an indicator of the actual power of women to subvert a system to which they, or rather, their conformity, are essential (Rackin, 1990, p. 219). In order for women not to become aware of their centrality, and so for their potential power to be contained and suppressed, stereotypes of ideally-conforming patterns of behaviour are attributed to female characters, who are thereby seen to accept and acknowledge subordination.

This patriarchal double-bind, namely the actual vulnerability of a system involved in a perpetual process of maintaining and reinforcing its dominance, goes a long way towards explaining the apparent paradox inherent in the enigma of the narrative necessity for the death of Melina, a seemingly unthreatening female character imbued with many submissive traits. It explains, on the one hand, her death (this is necessary because she poses a threat to the patriarchal order by performing the wrong function – reproduction – in the wrong context – sexual servicing), and, on the other, her idealized qualities (introduced as part of the strategy of suppression).

These idealized qualities all suggest acquiescence and docility, and are recognized by Tito and Carlino, who describe her as 'sweet', 'humble', 'modest', 'doleful', 'resigned', 'good' and 'submissive' (Act I). Even though Melina does put forward her point of view regarding the fate of the child, she does so in a deferential and pleading manner, in accordance with her ideality as a woman (this does not, however, prevent Carlino from describing her intervention as 'making a scene', Act II). Nevertheless, despite her submissive character, the underlying patriarchal structure makes Melina necessarily responsible for the rivalry between Tito and Carlino, and she is disposed of by the narrative. The demands of this structure are transformed into plot detail when she develops problems of the heart, in both the emotional and the medical sense, and dies. 'I am dying for them,' she says (Act III). Like Tuda in *Diana and Tuda*, she is made to appear aware of, and even openly declare, her status of victim, with the effect that she is rendered doubly impotent (once for being a victim, and again for realizing her situation without managing to effect a change):

> For everything that they have made me suffer! for how I have worn myself down on their account during this whole period! . . . They have separated; they have become enemies because of me! I had even submitted to what they wanted to do . . . just to get them back together again – No! no! – They themselves, as you are my witness, wanted me to keep the child – they paid every month – as if that were enough for me! And my heart has fallen apart . . . it has fallen apart. (*Belonging to One Person or to No-One*, Act III)

As well as victim, she is the cause of their problem; or rather, she is made a victim because she is the reason for their rivalry. Merletti says, 'she has died of the torment of having made you enemies' (Act III). More accurately, however, and on a more covert level, the female character is quite literally punished; it is, after all, still *her* pregnancy and *her* inability to identify the father, which are ultimately to blame. It is, more specifically, her misplaced reproductive power, in the form of a child whose paternity cannot be established, which activates basic patriarchal fears and leads to fatal retribution. In short, the woman can be shared by more than one man, but not the child, the child being the embodiment of her reproductive power, which can have only one owner.

Without clarifying the issue of paternity, then, the two men are inevitably on opposite sides, 'enemies as a matter of course, with this child between you', 'the child which has turned them, from the close friends they used to be, into enemies' (Act III). The situation is resolved with the entrance of a 'third', adoptive father, at which point the paternity issue disappears, and Tito and Carlino can again be friends. In other words, the child, symbol and embodiment of highly valued reproductive power, can belong only to one (male) person or to no-one, and certainly not to the mother, in a system of exchange where female reproductive power is owned by male subjects, and females function as objects – of exchange. What appears on the surface as the tragedy of a physically and emotionally fragile female character, then, is in effect a morality play informed by a patriarchal system of exchange.

Age, Class and Wealth

In this play, rivalry between male subjects takes place between two characters of the same age, with an older Merletti acting as paternal adviser. Often, however, the representation of male rivalry in Pirandello's plays is characterized by a difference in the ages of the opponents, thereby continuing the familiar, age-old topos of the old husband with a younger wife who takes a lover of her own age (examples from earlier Italian literature include some of the stories in Boccaccio's *Decameron*, and Machiavelli's play *La mandragola*). Several variations of this topos appear as a constituent of male competition in the interlinking areas of paternity, legitimacy and potency. Age is one category in which differentiation plays a crucial role; class and wealth are two other important factors which contribute to the position of the male subject within the dominant male hierarchy, in other words, to the status of one male subject measured in relation to other male subjects.

These categories of age, class and wealth do not figure in the particular case of Tito and Carlino, as we have seen. These two rivals are both young, belong to the same social class and, since they pursue identical careers (as state-employed clerks), they both have the same earning power. It is perhaps precisely because they are so evenly matched in all these areas, that one is not, in effect, more 'potent' than the other. In other words, neither of them can actually be identified as the father, because neither qualifies to be more potent than the other. Potency itself is measured in relative terms. Like paternity, its extent, and even existence, is defined only in relation to other males. These considerations are socially, and not biologically, determined; hence the privileging of social paternity over biological paternity.

This in fact shapes the plot resolution of *Belonging to One Person or to No-One*. In the end, neither of the two possible biological fathers, Tito and Carlino, is allowed to possess the child, despite contemporary pressures on men to marry (Carlino refers to the injustice of the bachelor tax then in force).[2] Instead, a deus ex machina in the form of a third

2. See p.148

male character appears, fortuitously, to adopt the child. He is, significantly, the wealthy owner of a nearby villa (whose wife has at that moment only survived childbirth at the cost of the baby's life). His superior class status and greater wealth combine to earn him the right to social paternity. The two young clerks are thereby manoeuvred out of the arena of potency and paternity by, in effect, a third rival.

One of the plays in which age, class and wealth do figure as categories of difference in male rivalry, is *Cap and Bells*. It was noted earlier in this chapter that Ciampa's solution to the exposure of his wife's adultery, as well as having the desired effect of reinstating his own potency rating, also does the adulterer himself, Fiorìca, a good turn. It is significant that Ciampa is employed by Fiorìca (as a clerk), and is therefore of a lower status in class terms. He is also older than Fiorìca.

This age difference is portrayed in interesting ways. The stage directions in fact indicate Ciampa to be forty-five years old, but no mention is ever made of Fiorìca's exact age. It is, first, by means of the ages of their respective wives that the age difference between the male characters is communicated. Both wives are described in the stage directions with the same phrase, as being 'around thirty'. Ciampa's wife, however, is differentiated from the wife of Fiorìca in the list of characters, where she appears as his *young* wife, whereas there is no age-related epithet in the case of Fiorìca's wife. This is a clear signal that Ciampa, unlike Fiorìca, is considerably older than his wife (and consequently, in terms of the topos of old husband–young wife–young lover, a likely candidate for cuckolding). The class difference between the two male characters is also indicated in the way their two wives are named in the list of characters: Ciampa's wife appears, untitled, as 'Nina Ciampa, young wife of Ciampa', while the wife of Fiorìca bears the formal title of respect, 'La signora Beatrice Fiorìca' (the nearest translation of 'signora' is 'Mrs', but this does not convey the status of upper-middle-class respectability associated with this title in Italian).

The second way in which both age and class differences between Ciampa and Fiorìca are constructed is through the former's precise and definitive exposition of their relative positions in these categories, as well as in the associated category of wealth. He refers to Fiorìca as 'rich, young and handsome', and to himself as 'ugly, old and poor' (Act III, sc. 5). Of the two rivals, it is the one who is higher in the male hierarchy in terms of age, class/wealth (and looks) who is the more potent: it is he who 'possesses' two women. And it is the potent Fiorìca who is too busy with his affairs, both sexual and professional, ever to appear on stage, leaving his older, poorer and more unattractive employee to devise a way of saving the honour of both.

It is the younger, wealthier male character who similarly triumphs over an older, poorer rival in the arena of male potency in *But It's Not Serious*. In this variation on the age topos, it is the husband who is young, while the would-be suitor is old. Speranza is young, handsome and wealthy enough to give Gasparina a property in the countryside, as well as pay her an annuity, on her agreement to a marriage in name only. This is a 'logical' device he has invented in order to avoid any future full marriage, with its high emotional and financial costs (Gasparina, in his eyes, being both unattractive and thrifty, and so unlikely to present any threat). However, she is not perceived in this light by Barranco, who is the only one to treat her with respect. Barranco is described as a 'gentleman from the provinces', but he is also 'mature', 'old' and suffers from a stammer. As far as wealth is concerned, Barranco lives in a boarding-house, while Speranza lives in a 'charming bachelor flat' and only visits the boarding-house in order to dine.

Given these preconditions, it is not surprising that Barranco fails in his attempt to take over the position of husband, which he does by trying to have the marriage annulled on grounds of non-consummation. It is, in fact, his very attempt to do so which triggers a hostile reaction from Speranza, despite the latter's desire, until that moment, to extract himself from an arrangement which has become intolerable. The reason for the sudden reversal in Speranza's attitude lies in that most highly valued commodity in patriarchal ideology, female virginity. What Barranco perceives as a solution to everybody's problems, namely proof of non-consummation leading to annulment, in fact alerts Speranza to the fact that, to his great surprise, Gasparina is a virgin; that she 'has managed, despite all the hardships of poverty, to keep herself intact' (Act III, sc. 6). This knowledge has the effect of filling Speranza with desire for Gasparina, and from this point onwards he is determined that the marriage should become 'serious'. Barranco concedes defeat, particularly in the category of age, with a remark which implicitly acknowledges the youth, and therefore greater suitability, of his rival as husband to a woman who is also young.

Gasparina's virginity, which suddenly raises the stakes in the rivalry between Speranza and Barranco, is now eagerly coveted by Speranza. She is not desired for herself. As 'woman-virgin . . .[i]n herself, she does not exist: a simple envelope enclosing the stakes of social circulation . . . . She is merely the possibility, the place, the sign, of relations between men' (Irigaray, 1977a, p. 181). In a system where 'goods, women, are the mirror of value of/for man', the virgin represents exchange value in its purest, most highly prized form (ibid., pp. 173, 181). To have, or to appear to have, exclusive possession, or rather, private ownership, of a woman's potential reproductive power, ensures verification of paternity and is the measure of male potency.

One major implication of exclusivity is that of relativity, in other words, reference to other, rival owner-subjects who must be excluded at all costs. Virginity is therefore an ideological construct necessarily predicated on relations between male subjects. In its attendant transformation of actual female subjects into ideological female objects-of-exchange, this construct epitomizes patriarchal strategies of setting up ideologies characterized by male occupation of subject positions. While an impotent Gasparina, then, is portrayed as 'confused, convulsed and on the verge of tears', the dominant Speranza is seen to assert his ownership before the rival Barranco, shaking her and repeatedly claiming 'You are mine!' (Act III, sc. 6).

Owners of Reproduction

The stereotypical passage from virginity to motherhood, which is the next step along the patriarchally-defined path of womanhood, signals departure from the exchange system by means of marriage, as use value replaces exchange value. The woman's proven reproductive power passes into the sole ownership of her husband and, more importantly, the child acquires a father. In a system which privileges paternity over maternity, the product of the mother's reproductive power belongs to men. As we have seen, Melina in *Belonging to One Person or to No-One* is ultimately not allowed sole guardianship of her child; although Tito and Carlino, the two possible biological fathers, grudgingly agree to this after much argument, Melina herself does not allow it. She is portrayed as dying of heartbreak because the two men abandon her, not financially, but emotionally. Constructed so as to internalize an alien code of values, this female character is made to deny any matriarchal legitimacy, along with her own life, in the last resort. The child, which can belong either to one person or to no-one, could have been a female 'someone's', but this possibility is excluded from the very beginning by the title of the narrative, which is entirely male-oriented, as well as by the plot resolution, which sees the removal of the mother and her replacement by a male character who appears on the scene at the end to provide social fatherhood.

The Pleasure of Honesty also sees social paternity overshadowing any notion of the child being brought up by the mother alone, which never even enters the narrative as a possibility, as it did in *Belonging to One Person or to No-One*. This is perhaps due to the difference in class status of the two female characters involved. Melina is an impoverished (ex)-prostitute who is initially illiterate, appears to have no family at all, and probably belongs to the working class. Agata, on the other hand, comes from a respectable middle-class family, a class which at that time

– 75 –

would not countenance single motherhood (see chapter 5). The difference in their class status may also help to account for the fact that marriage (to the social father) is sought as a solution in Agata's case, while for Melina a respectable solution of this nature is pre-empted in a variety of ways from the very beginning.

Both these plays share a prioritization of issues of paternity. In *Think It Over, Giacomino*, considerations of maternity are similarly cast into the shadows, as the interplay of social and biological paternity determines the resolution of the basic, underlying rivalry between two male characters. Toti, an elderly schoolmaster, offers the young, impoverished and pregnant Lillina, a cleaner at his school, marriage. His declared motives are to raise her from her state of poverty, and at the same time take revenge on his parsimonious employer, the state, which would be obliged to pay his wife a pension after his death. During the course of the play he also inherits his brother's fortune. At the other end of the hierarchy is Giacomino, a young ex-student of Toti's, and the biological father of Lillina's child (the youth of Giacomino being particularly evidenced by his name, which is the diminutive version of 'Giacomo', obtained by the addition of the suffix -ino). His low status as a penniless, unemployed 'poor orphan' means that, unlike Toti, he cannot support a wife and child. The 'well-meaning' older, wealthier and higher status social father (and husband) then uses his influence to find the younger, poorer, lower status biological father employment in an arrangement of apparent male bonding which also allows Giacomino daily visits to Lillina and their child.

However, the paternalistic benevolence of the older male character masks his actual dominance over the younger Giacomino. The underlying dynamic of rivalry surfaces when the latter decides to withdraw from a situation which effectively emasculates him as the arrangement becomes public knowledge. The final scene features a prolonged dialogue between the two, with Toti asserting his dominance through a monopoly of lengthy monologues. 'Am I not the boss?' he says, as he tries to prevent Giacomino from nullifying the arrangement by marrying another 'poor orphan' and ceasing to frequent the Toti household. The central importance of this dialogue, which culminates in the closure of the plot as Toti outmanoeuvres the younger man, is signalled by the fact that it contains the words of the title, namely an imperative addressed by the dominant male character to another, subordinate male character. The dialogue plays out the concerns of male rivalry in an exclusively male context, in which maternity functions merely as a zone of mediation between the two men.

Lillina is absent from the decision-making process which concludes the play, making her final appearance, briefly and tearfully, in Act II. In

Bellavita, the mediating wife/mistress/mother character does not figure at all; she is written out of the narrative by virtue of being dead. Not only is she not given a name; her death before the beginning of the play is never explained (a curious lack of detail, given that she appears to have been quite young). These indicators of marginalization serve to highlight, once again, the primary importance of the relationship between two male characters (Bellavita and Denora). This relationship focuses, not on the unnamed female character, but on the named product of her reproductive powers, Michelino. As in *Belonging to One Person or to No-One*, the issue of paternity exposes the competitiveness underlying relations between male subjects. Male bonding has changed into, and indeed given rise to, male rivalry, as Denora's attempts to improve marital relations between Bellavita and his wife, by taking up Bellavita's defence against her criticisms, have led to an affair and the birth of Michelino.

The property factor at the heart of paternity considerations now surfaces with the 'old bachelor', Denora, anxious to make Michelino his heir, whether he is the boy's biological father or not. The two rivals are evenly matched. Bellavita's age is never made clear; however, the overriding impression is one of similarity. As far as class and wealth are concerned, Denora as notary is not significantly superior to Bellavita, a confectioner with his own shop. The outcome is one of stalemate. Bellavita does not allow Denora to make Michelino his heir and, moreover, determines to devote himself to the transformation of the traditionally low status accorded to the cuckold. He does this by focusing public attention on Denora; in other words, by exposing the situation, rather than trying to keep it hidden, thereby moving himself from the position of victim and into a position of control. In so doing, he does not internalize the values of the system, but attempts to subvert its values from within.

Interestingly, then, not only is such subversive strategy allowed, it is even foregrounded as a resourceful solution to a situation whereby one male character has been manoeuvred by another into a subordinate position within the male hierarchy. Significantly, however, this successfully transgressive type of strategy is in the hands of a *male* character. It seems that subject positions in a competitive system based on exchange may be dominant or subordinate in relation to each other, while object positions by definition must always be subordinate. Submission to, and internalization of, these values is the stereotypical response built into representations of idealized femininity. In fact strategies of subversion potentially provide subordinate (female) object positions, as well as subordinate (male) subject positions, with opportunities for resistance and change. That such strategies operate from within the system (rather than from outside it) means, of course, that the ideologically determined structures of the system may ultimately remain intact. So, while Bellavita exits the play (which bears his name) a hero, the two rivals nevertheless remain locked in conflict, trapped in a system which, for once, does neither male subject any favours, although it does, of course, endow them with the rights of speaking, acting, thinking subjects. The mediating female object-of-exchange and means of reproduction, on the other hand, is silenced before the narrative even begins (a fate which also befalls Silvia in *All For the Best*).

The property concerns foregrounded in *Bellavita* are translated from the context of a provincial township to the rural surroundings of peasant life in *Liolà*. Once again, male competitiveness and rivalry take place in the arena of female sexuality, as female reproductive powers provide the channel for the patrilineal flow of land and wealth. In an exposition of the traditional topos of old, rich husband, young wife and her young lover, the play shows the young male protagonist of the title glorying in his three children (all male), and producing two more by Act III. The characterization of this gloating male stud represents him as living out the ultimate male fantasy of ubiquitous impregnation (his name means 'here or there', and three of his known offspring are fathered on women from indefinite locations, somewhere 'out of town'). This fantasy takes on an added dimension when one takes into account the fact that Liolà is the equivalent of the 'I' narrator in Pirandello's earlier novel, *The Late Mattia Pascal* (1904), an episode of which provides the basis for the play (chs. iv–v).

This young personification of male potency is in stark contrast to old Uncle Simone, owner of a farm and desperate for a male heir to inherit 'so much beautiful wealth which would end up, at his death, in other people's hands'. An heir does not, however, appear forthcoming. Due to a dexterous sleight of hand on Liolà's part, as a result of which Simone's wife becomes 'miraculously' pregnant, it will ultimately be his child (destined, of course, to be male), and not Simone's (he is impotent) who will inherit the old man's property. At the other end of the spectrum, old Simone plays out the archetypal patriarchal nightmare implicated in impotence, namely of his name disappearing as his property is taken over by another male line, and of bringing up 'the sons of other men', a preoccupation voiced by propertied males in the Alessandretta episode in Ariosto's *Orlando furioso* four centuries earlier.[3]

His young and successful rival competes not just in deed, but also in word. His is the lengthy 'woman-as-fertile-terrain' discourse with which he browbeats Simone, gloating over his abilities as farmer/man-

3. See the section 'Chastity and Virginity' in Günsberg (1991, pp. 203–4).

ager of fertile female bodies. I now want to isolate one aspect of this metaphor, namely that of female passivity. The metaphor is yet another male fantasy; the male subject, in order to 'farm' and 'manage' female fertility, must invent an obligingly submissive, if not completely inert, female object position. Passivity and submissiveness, in other words basic disempowering, are essential features in this construction of what passes for female 'identity'. The metaphor unfolds in 'natural', static images of land which 'receives the kernel', in contrast to active images of the roaming, far-ranging farmer/manager figure who 'passes by', inseminating or grafting as he goes.

In the case of *Belonging to One Person or to No-One*, male control of female fertility can be seen to operate through the particular discourse of morality subtended by pseudo-science. Supposedly sterile on account of her previous life of 'vice' as a prostitute, Merlina herself, as well as Carlino and Tito, are taken aback when she becomes pregnant. The two male characters 'diagnose' that Merlina has actually been made not merely pregnant, but actually fertile by their action of 'having raised her from that ugly life of hers ', from 'the burning of vice ... which had previously made her sterile' (Act I). The child is then described as 'the fruit of all the good which has been done *to her*', and paternity itself seen to be determined by the degree to which the female body was possessed by each of the two contenders. Pseudo-scientific 'fact' continues to make a passive female sexuality the arena for male competition and concerns. The female body is declared to be separate from, and therefore no longer in the control of, the woman herself, as she gives herself up to the 'unconsciousness of abandon'. This is the crucial moment of total passivity when possession takes place. 'It is undeniable that . . . her body, not her – must have been taken – more by one than by the other' (Act I). The pregnancy advertises the 'fact' that one male has surpassed the other in the competition for potency, a pregnancy made possible in the first place by the 'fact' that both of them had restored her fertility in the process of bonding with each other. For female sexuality, the phenomenon of alienation from the body itself, and the concomitant loss of coherence due to this fragmentation, is a prerequisite for passivity and impotence.

This fragmentation, with its implication of lack of self-determination, results in the unhappy schizophrenia of a female sexual identity which is defined exclusively in relation to male concerns. The title of the play *Mrs Morli, One and Two* epitomizes this process of splitting: while the name of the female character defines her relation to her husband, the remainder signals her split identity. Within the play, her Christian name (which can be said to describe her, rather than her position in patriarchy) appears only in the list of characters at the beginning, and rarely anywhere else. Even this name (Evelina) is split into two by the two male characters in relation to whom she is defined: her husband names her Eva, and her lover/common-law husband names her Lina. We have come across the fragmentation of female identity before and noted the sexual context in which this takes place, in contrast to the purely philosophical connotations accompanying the (self-managed) splitting of male identity (see chapter 2). Of particular interest here is the relationship between the two male characters concerned, which has Evelina as its common denominator, and its precise location in the property/wealth sphere of patriarchal interests. This problematic relationship resolves itself, yet again, around the issue of ownership of the means of reproduction. Ultimately it is the father of Evelina's younger child with whom the mother 'chooses' to remain.

The original reason for the actual existence of two males in relation to whom Mrs Morli's identity is thus fragmented is her husband's bankruptcy and his subsequent disappearance fourteen years before the beginning of the play. Her lawyer later set up home with her, having paid off her husband's debts. The play opens with the husband's return; he is now wealthy and only recently aware that his old debts have been settled. On his return he visits, not Evelina, as one might not too unreasonably have expected, but Lello, who has long been regarded as her husband in the eyes of society. The two male characters then discuss Evelina at length in a financial and legal context. The cardinal relationship which is at issue here is not that between husband and wife, but that between a husband presumed missing or dead and his common-law successor. Moreover, the relationship between the two males clearly reveals its underpinning by economic and essentially contractual structures which constitute the framework of the patriarchal exchange system, a system whereby male subjects exchange objects of use and exchange value.

The particular object of exchange under negotiation at this point is the wife whom the two males now appear to share, owing to the unorthodox circumstances occasioned at the outset by financial concerns (the losses of one male, his disappearance, their restitution by another, and the latter's appropriation of the former's wife). Basically, the rights of the returning husband, Ferrante Morli, take precedence over those of his common-law successor, Lello Carpani, a situation reminiscent of the reappearance of the not, after all, late Mattia Pascal towards the end of Pirandello's novel, *The Late Mattia Pascal*. Pascal's successor, however, had actually married the wife, or rather, 'widow', of the apparently deceased protagonist after a body had been wrongly identified as Mattia's. That Carpani has not married Evelina Morli now raises issues which lay bare the patrilineal orientation of the exchange system.

It is, specifically, the use value generated by her reproductive capacity, in other words, the channel facilitating the patrilineal flow of inherited property, which is the focus of attention as the two 'husbands' confer about the absent Eva-Lina. For the wife has borne each of them a child: a son to Ferrante (the now eighteen-year-old Aldo) and a daughter to Lello (the now seven-year-old Titti). It is precisely because Lello's child is female, and not male, that he has not taken steps to legalize his 'marriage' to Lina and thereby legitimise his offspring. Their discussion around this point clearly emphasizes that males, not females, inherit, and that patrilineality, not matrilineality, governs the system:

LELLO: I tell you that, for the mere fact of your return, my marriage, now, would be annulled.

FERRANTE: That's right, but I'm talking, you see, about your daughter, Mr Lawyer. I'm not an expert in law, but I maintain that, after the annulment of the second marriage, contracted in good faith on account of the disappearance, as you say, of the first spouse, the children of this second marriage don't lose their right to legitimacy, do they?

LELLO: No, No!

FERRANTE: That would be iniquitous! Now, as you haven't done it, your daughter . . .

LELLO: That's right! Of course . . Now I can no longer do it. But that is only relevant up to a certain point. My daughter is recognized, and that's enough. She is a woman; she will find a husband. If the child had been male, then perhaps I might not have had scruples about drawing the mother's attention to a condition of fact.

                                  (*Mrs Morli, One and Two*, Act I)

The situation of Ferrante's son in Lello's household, moreover, is not a happy one. There is obvious friction between Lello and Aldo, as well as between Aldo and Titti. (And Ferrante is also described in the stage directions at a certain point as 'understanding many things about the conditions of his son in that household'.) The root cause is undoubtedly the underlying resentment felt by Lello in having to bring up 'the sons of other men'.

    The dilemma of which of the two husbands Eva-Lina should be wife to is ultimately resolved through her reproductive function. The narrative appears, on the surface, to give the female character the choice, as she leaves Lello to visit Ferrante, with both eager to have her as 'wife'. However, the key factor, which is never overtly stated, is that Titti, at seven years, is still very much dependent on her mother, while Aldo, at eighteen, and with an affair with Mrs Armelli already under his belt, has clearly already passed into manhood. This does not prevent him, in collusion with his father, from attempting to persuade Eva to reformulate the prior family unit. He does this precisely by playing on her maternity, sending her a telegram saying that he is ill, a cry to which she instantly responds. While she is away, Lello's child develops a genuine fever. Her subsequent return to the sick young child thus signals her return to the second family unit, which is privileged by her exclusively maternal role within it. 'You are men, you two – and that's all there is to it!' she says to Lello, 'I am a mother!' (Act III).

The narrative device of the child falling sick, or even dying, at the moment when the mother is absent for what are implied to be the wrong reasons, particularly when these are sexual or work-related, is not unfamiliar in cultural representations of patriarchy. (It appears, for instance, in *Mildred Pierce* (1945), as a *film noir* device to contain the threateningly sexual and ambitious female character, and recuperate her for patriarchy via marriage. Mildred's young daughter falls fatally ill at the precise time when Mildred is starting both an affair and her own business, only to be reunited with her husband at the close of the narrative.) In *Mrs Morli, One and Two*, Evelina denies any actual sexual liaison with Ferrante during her visit. However, much is made earlier in the play of the passionate love which existed between them before his disappearance and which still exists, at a more or less repressed level. Her split identity, as 'one' and 'two', clearly falls into a sexual and an asexual type, respectively. As Eva, according to the archetypically sexual connotations which this name evokes, she is passionate and emotional. As 'stuffy old Lina' (in the words of her son), she is 'placid' and 'ordered'.

The play ends with the abnegation of Eva, of female sexuality, in favour of the asexuality of motherhood. Lina replaces both Eva and Evelina, as female sexuality, and indeed female identity itself, are fragmented, split into serviceable components and (mis)appropriated into the service of patriarchy. So, while the two 'husbands' appear on the surface to be dependent on her decision, the patriarchal system to which all three belong has already structured the outcome, pre-empting any real choice she might have had. Male rivalry, together with its partner, male bonding, has once again resolved the concerns of patriarchy, with an appropriately constructed, or rather, deconstructed, female 'identity' serving as the zone of mediation.

The next section will explore one particular effect of male bonding and male rivalry, namely male policing of female sexuality.

Male Policing

Male policing of female sexuality has its roots in the dependency of patriarchal culture on the acquiescence of both male subjects and female objects in a system based on use and exchange values centred on female sexuality. (Male) subject status is reinforced, both within the dominant male hierarchy of subjects and in relation to the subordinate female hierarchy of objects, by the greater appropriation of objects of value. The appropriation of female sexuality is particularly important as the means of reproduction, vital in its role of providing male heirs for the preservation of the patrilineal base. Within the male hierarchy, which is consolidated by relationships of bonding, the structure of competitiveness which subtends it leads to situations of rivalry as male subjects compete with each other for (greater) status. This necessitates the policing of female sexuality *by* male subjects *against* other male subjects.

Furthermore, as female sexuality is itself (mis)appropriated to serve the ends of patriarchy, a system based on the denial of female subject identity, it must also be prevented from falling under the control of females themselves. To this end, patriarchy tries to pre-empt a unified female subject identity incorporating its own sexuality, by representing female identity as fragmented. Female sexuality is thus split off and separated from other constituents of identity, such as motherhood and work which, when brought together in real life, make up a coherent and self-determining whole. A classic example of this type of representation is the traditional madonna–whore/Ave (Maria)–Eve dichotomy. This basic formulation of a split female identity is rooted in the religious bedrock of Western patriarchy, namely Christianity, which idealizes the asexual figure of Mary as the archetypal Virgin-Mother who gave birth to a son without having sexual intercourse, in other words, without any sexual desire.

The fragmentation of female identity within patriarchy is an example of policing at its most insidious, and as such is dealt with in various ways during the course of this book. In this section I wish to draw attention in particular to the ways in which Pirandello's plays represent more overt forms of policing. This will involve an examination of violence towards women in its more obvious forms which are, in effect, socially and culturally 'acceptable' precisely on account of their underpinning by parallel but invisible structures of coercion. One particular, and essentially violent, form taken by the policing of female sexuality will be explored under the heading 'enclosure'.

References to male policing of female sexuality, often perceived as a necessity, are made quite openly by male and female characters alike in Pirandello's plays. Brothers, husbands and fathers are all responsible for policing and protecting female sexuality from the incursions of rival males. For example, Paolino, in *Man, Beast and Virtue*, describes the legitimate duty of a wife's brothers in bringing an errant husband to task:

> If she were your sister, if Perella were your brother-in-law and you knew that he was treating his wife in that way . . . And if this poor lady has no brother? and has no-one? No-one, I mean, who can legitimately take him by the scruff of the neck, this Captain Perella, and remind him of his duties as a/husband. (*Man, Beast and Virtue*, Act I, sc. 7)

A similar view is expressed in *Liolà*, namely that Mita's ill-treatment at the hands of her husband would not be tolerated if she had brothers to defend her:

> Abandoned at birth by her mother and at three years a fatherless orphan too! I brought her up, God knows how! I'd like to see what would happen if she had at least one brother! He wouldn't treat her like this, I assure you! It's a miracle that he hasn't trampled her underfoot: you've seen how it is! (*Liolà*, Act I)

The character who speaks these lines is Mita's aunt, Gesa: a clear indication, then, that female policing and protection are deemed valueless and that, once again, it is only males who are empowered to police female sexuality against each other in a dialogue of activity from which women are excluded as agents.

The extent of this exclusion is exemplified by the reaction of the husband whose wife has been raped in *The Grafting*, and whose initial reaction is to want to kill *her*. As far as he is concerned it is he, as much if not more than she, who actually suffers as a result of the attack. He considers the incident a threat to his name and to his role as husband: 'I am the husband . . . not even she can feel this horror more atrociously and more keenly . . . Do you know that my name is at stake here?' (Act I, sc. 9; Act III, sc. 4). His raped and consequently pregnant wife has become the symbol of his inadequate and abused policing powers, and his initial desire is for the removal of that symbol (rather than solely for retribution against the actual rapist).

The husband's function of guarding the wife recurs in *Liolà*. Reference is made by a female character to Simone's inadequate surveillance of Mita when it is learnt that she, like Tuzza, has become pregnant by Liolà. 'Is this how you have guarded your wife, you old imbecile?' she remonstrates (Act III). It is not Mita herself, but Liolà who is ultimately held to be the responsible party for the pregnancy. Mita is not an active, desiring subject; it is, rather, that she has been poorly guarded by one male against another. In a different case in which the female character has managed to contravene the wishes of her brothers by marrying the man of her choice, animosity between the brothers and their brother-in-law is highlighted as still being rife many years later. In *The Epilogue*, Andrea tells Giulia that he has encountered her two brothers, who repeatedly ignore him. His explanation points to the primacy of the role played by male family members in the choice of marriage partners for female members, a primacy which, even when thwarted by the female herself, asserts itself in unremitting hostility towards the rival male. It is then the rival male who is considered the agent of her successful misappropriation.

That female sexuality is not allowed an active, let alone autonomous, role is signalled by Agata's mother in *The Pleasure of Honesty*. 'We are two poor women on our own and we are the ones who would have to bear the shame' (Act I, sc. 5), she says, as she argues in favour of a marriage of convenience for her pregnant daughter. She indicates here that they have no male relatives, in whose domain the regulation of her daughter's sexuality would have fallen, and thereby relinquishes any powers of agency and choice for her daughter. Such regulation is indeed bemoaned by the urban equivalent of the ultra-potent Liolà, the ever-hopeful Memmo Speranza in *But It's Not Serious*. He would have access to the large numbers of women required by his outstanding potency, 'if it were not for the fathers, uncles, brothers, brothers-in-law, male cousins, appointed to guard the oath' (Act I, sc. 7).

Women who are not well guarded, on the other hand, fall prey to the rampant male urge for possession. Such are the three young girls from 'out of the way' who have each borne Liolà a child. When he is taken to task for having ruined their lives by making them pregnant, he justifies himself in these words:

> You know very well how those boys of mine were born, and who their mothers were! Everyone knows! – Young girls from out of the way. – It's bad to force open a well-guarded door; but he who goes along an open, well-trodden road . . . (*Liolà*, Act I)

Here the stereotype of female passivity in a male-dominated context of competition and possession is once again intimated and reinforced. As Ciampa warns Beatrice, she cannot expect to take action and avenge her husband's infidelity if there are other men involved:

> You could have allowed yourself this luxury, had you believed that your husband had been with some girl without, take note, father or brothers. You would have been giving your husband a lesson, there being no other men involved, and everything would have worked out. But in this case there was a man involved, signora! How is it possible that you didn't think of me? Didn't I figure at all? (*Cap and Bells*, Act II, sc. 5)

In line with the culturally constructed lack of female agency, male policing is represented as a necessary process whereby male subjects, positioned in competition with each other in a system structured by the drive to possession, both monitor and engage with each other. When surveillance is inadequate, not only do rival male subjects successfully take over the highly prized use and exchange values represented by female sexuality. Female sexuality itself must be policed into passivity to enable the exchange process between male subjects to take place unhindered. Female identity is therefore constructed to be vulnerable, weak and in need of defence. Insufficient policing is consequently recognized as an evil, not only by male characters but, importantly, by female characters, who are portrayed as having internalized the values of a culture which in effect denies them any real agency.

Operating within the family unit which defines the legitimate boundaries of possession, male family members supervise those female members who, it is to be noted, are fertile. (Memmo's rather comprehensive list mentions fathers, uncles, brothers, brothers-in-law and male cousins who, as he goes on to enumerate, guard their daughter, niece, sister, sister-in-law and female cousin (*But It's Not Serious*, Act I, sc. 7).) Interestingly, he does not include husbands. This is perhaps in part because the wife's loss of her virginity and assumption of her new function of motherhood (in other words, the 'natural' passing from childhood into womanhood, according to the patriarchal code) actually remove her from an exchange system in which virginity is highly valued. Furthermore, far from cutting all ties, the male members of the wife's original family will continue to be responsible for monitoring both her and her treatment at the hands of her new husband (as we have seen both Paolino and Gesa indicate (*Man, Beast and Virtue* and *Liolà*). An earlier example from Boccaccio which illustrates this point is Day VII, Story 8, in which a husband who suspects his wife of adultery, having beaten her and cut off her hair, takes recourse to her brothers, who set off in order to punish her. When they arrive to find that she is in perfect health and with all her hair (she had managed to bribe her unfortunate maid to take her place), the brothers warn him that they will turn their attentions to him if he repeats the misaccusation.

However, as indicated in this story, and in the plays we have examined, not only do husbands play a significant role in policing the sexuality of their wives; the methods with which they and other males enforce their control are alarmingly violent. So far we have been examining overt references by Pirandellian characters, both male and female, to male policing of female sexuality, and in particular the way in which such policing is represented as an unquestioned necessity. I want now to move on to the use of violence as a means of effecting the policing of female sexuality, bearing in mind the particular ways in which this is brought about in the specifically dramatic context of the plays.

In the plays we are about to examine, stage directions, in conjunction with verbal reports, are an important means of indicating violence, whether or not the violence actually involves physical contact. For example, the Father in *Six Characters in Search of an Author* acts in a physically violent way towards the Mother, both by manhandling her (when he attempts to force her to remove her veil) and by non-tactile, gestural reinforcement of verbal aggression. Speech itself is an important vehicle for violent coercion. However, I intend to focus on physical violence and its detrimental effects on the recipient (as indicated by both stage directions and verbal reports), on the basis that this represents the visible, and potentially life-threatening, apotheosis of all types of violence; in short, the last resort when other methods of coercion have failed.

What is at stake here is the elucidation of methods of dramatic representation of the physical and symbolic violence which underlies the exchange of women; in other words, the male-dominated system of exchange which, at however deep and indiscernible a level, constitutes the basis of patriarchal culture. Despite my focus on the physical, it should be borne in mind that the physical derives from, and works in conjunction with, the symbolic (e.g. linguistic) violence inevitably engendered by a system which depends for its survival on an ongoing process of gender-specific domination and subordination. Nevertheless, the physical is in one sense clearly also symbolic, in that it is Woman as sign (of use or exchange value), and not the real, individual woman herself, which is the actual target of violent coercion (while it is, importantly, also real, individual women who are actually aggressed when this process erupts from the representational to inform the behaviour patterns of real-life society).

It is this point of transition, at which cultural symbol and the structures that underpin it move from the verbal to a more extreme, physical enforcement of their meaning, which is enacted in the dramatic representations of violent acts which we are about to examine. We shall look first at the stage directions and verbal indications which both describe and prescribe a range of physically violent actions resulting in various forms of submission. These are perpetrated by male characters on female characters and, occasionally, by female on female characters. In the latter case, female characters are constructed so as to internalize patriarchal values demanding the policing of fertile female relatives, usually daughters. Instances of female characters attempting to coerce male characters by violent means are rare and unsuccessful (for example, Tuzza's attempt to stab Liolà at the end of the play is laughingly thwarted by the hero). We shall then proceed to examine the portrayal of physical violence directed by male characters at each other as an effect of male rivalry and the policing of female sexuality.

Violence to female characters

A variety of dramatic devices in *Liolà* combine to portray the physical violence inflicted by Simone on his young wife, Mita, who, as her name suggests (it is linked to the adjective *'mite'*, meaning 'meek') is designed to respond with tears of submission. Even before any indications of physical abuse appear in the text, she is afraid even to move unless her husband commands it. With his arrival on stage, a series of violent actions clarifies his response to what he sees as the failure of female sexuality to fulfil its required function. (She has not borne him a male child, or indeed any child, in four years of marriage.) When Mita, immobilized by fear, does not move when he tells her to, the stage directions describe him as 'bearing down on her, forcing her to her feet, pulling and shaking her', as a result of which she leaves the stage 'mortified and crying' (Act I).

This act of violence involving physical contact is immediately followed by another which does not, when Simone 'kicks the chest on which he had been sitting', a kick which is clearly meant, by analogy, for Mita, who has just left. Later in the play, Simone gives a verbal indication that he has, in the past, struck Mita: 'Shut up, shut up', he says, 'or by Christ I'll make you feel the back of my hand again!' (Act II). Mita's aunt, Gesa, also refers to his violent treatment of her niece. Physical violence by one female character to another is represented in this play too, as Croce Azzara grabs her daughter Tuzza by the arms and drags her indoors (stage directions). After a lot of crying and shouting, the young girl emerges dishevelled and beaten but, unlike Mita at the hands of Simone, defiant and proud. The reason for the violence lies, once again, in what is perceived as a malfunctioning female sexuality. In this case, it takes the diametrically opposite form, namely the pregnancy of an unmarried girl (an event which literally 'devalues' her in the context of a system in which the exchange value of virginity is highly rated).

The same reason motivates Marianna's striking and beating of her young sixteen-year-old daughter Lillina when told of her pregnancy in *Think It Over, Giacomino*. This scene, described in the stage directions as very violent, shows attacks by both mother and father on Lillina and her lover, as she is accused of having ruined, and he of having stolen or wrongfully appropriated, her honour (in other words, her virginity/as yet unused reproductive powers). These two commodities (which are rendered synonymous only in patriarchal terms) determine her value, and the bargaining power of her father, in the marriage market. In this particular case, the father refuses to give her to Giacomino in marriage as the young man is poor and unemployed, preferring instead to disown his daughter as worthless.

The pregnancy of an unmarried daughter does not inevitably lead to the infliction of physical violence on an offending female sexuality. In this context, it is interesting to contrast the occurrence of such violence in the two plays we have just discussed with its absence in *The Pleasure of Honesty*. In this play, Maddelena's daughter Agata is pregnant by a man she cannot marry (he is already married). Although emotions run high in the search for a solution to a situation which is seen as particularly disastrous, there is no indication even of the possibility of physical violence on the part of the mother towards the daughter.

Various factors combine to contribute to this lack of violence; these relate to issues of class, topography and age. The class context of *The Pleasure of Honesty* is upper middle class. Maddelena Renni is a respectable 'signora' whose daughter, having had an affair with a marquess, will enter a marriage, initially of convenience, to a 'signore'. The first act of the play takes place in the 'elegant drawing room' of the Renni household, and the second and third acts in the 'magnificent drawing room' and 'richly furnished study' of the new conjugal home. The play is set in a town or city (the noun 'città' does not indicate a distinction between these two) in central Italy. By contrast, the class base of the physically violent mother–daughter dyads in *Liolà* and *Think It Over, Giacomino* is peasant and working class, respectively. Mother and daughter in the former play are peasant workers on a farm belonging to the mother's male cousin.[4] The setting of the play is rural (the countryside around Agrigento), in complete antithesis to the sophisticated, urban context of the Renni household.

Along similar lines, *Think It Over, Giacomino* takes place not in a sizeable town ('città'), but in a small provincial town ('una cittaduzza di provincia'). Mother and daughter in this play, as school cleaners, belong to the working class, the urban equivalent of the peasantry. In both this play and *Liolà*, the physical violence which is inflicted on the daughter by the mother takes place in a lower-class context, both urban and rural, while the mores of the upper middle class in a larger urban conglomeration do not countenance physical violence between women. In other words, the kind of frenzied, uncontrollable physical violence which involves beating, pulling of hair and general scrapping and manhandling does not belong to upper-middle-class female behaviour.

---

4. For an account of androcentricity and *machismo* in a variety of peasant communities, see Michaelson and Goldschmidt (1971).

(Even as far as physical violence between males is concerned, this class has its own, very different, code, as we shall see later.)

In conjunction with considerations of class and topography, a third factor influencing the presence or absence of physical violence by mother to daughter concerns the age of the daughter herself. Both Lillina and Tuzza are young (Lillina is sixteen years old, and the indications are that Tuzza is about the same age). Agata, on the other hand, is twenty-seven-years-old, an age which, as her mother makes clear, classifies her as no longer young in the context of a patriarchal system which prioritizes female reproductive capacity. Presence and absence of physical violence between female characters in these three plays is specific to class, place and age, thereby indicating differences in the ways in which females police other females for, and from, males, in the context of a system whose male-dominated values they have assumed as their own.

Another play which appears to bear this out is *Six Characters in Search of an Author*. When the Mother discovers her daughter, the Stepdaughter, in the embrace of the Father (the Mother's estranged husband, but not the Stepdaughter's biological father), she is horrified at what she perceives as a scene of incest. Her reaction is not to set about her daughter violently, but to detach her, with a cry, from the Father. Mother and daughter in this play belong to the middle class, judging from the profession of the Father which, although never mentioned, is such that he requires the services of a secretary (whom he also calls his subaltern). The Stepdaughter, furthermore, refers to herself at one point as belonging to a poor but respectable (middle-class) family. As far as location is concerned, we glean from the Father's narration of past events that the family was urban-based. (He tells how he sent the Son into the country as a baby to be wet-nursed by a peasant woman owing to the delicate health of the Mother.) Lastly, although the Stepdaughter is only eighteen years old, it is her earning power which supports her family unit, and she is not likely to be treated aggressively by those who are dependent on her. The non-violent policing of the daughter's sexuality by the mother in this play, then, is similar in several important respects to that in *The Pleasure of Honesty*.

It is now time to turn our attention to cases of physical violence by male characters to female characters. Following on from the Father's forceful removal of the Mother's veil, an action which she attempts, unsuccessfully, to resist, and from Simone's more extreme violence towards Mita, there are two plays in particular in which the violent aggression of a male character (once again a husband) plays a not insignificant role in the death of a female character (a wife). In these two plays, physical violence is significant not as a direct cause of death, but as an overt expression of underlying, and less visible, forms of coercion inflicted on the subordinate gender, a process which takes its toll on female sexuality in a variety of ways. At the end of *The Epilogue*, Giulia is heard to shoot herself offstage, as her lover comes on stage to join her husband. 'You have killed her,' the husband accuses the lover. The death of the object of their rivalry, of the mediating agent in the relationship between the two male characters, is immediately preceded by a violent confrontation between Andrea and his wife. During the process of this confrontation, his physical manhandling of her bears out the obduracy of his enforcement of the patriarchal rules which forbid any association between motherhood and female desire, particularly when the object of desire lies outside the marriage. Pulling and pushing her about roughly, he proclaims with equal violence that, as a result of her infidelity with his friend and colleague, she has forfeited the right to her children, a punishment which leads to her suicide.

Tonight We Improvise (1930) also ends with the death of a female character, Mommina, Verri's wife, after an unpleasantly violent scene during which he grasps his wife by the nape of the neck, biting her and tearing her hair. This is the physical manifestation of years of extreme policing by Verri of his wife (the particular severity of which is acknowledged by the reference of Doctor Hinkfuss, the Director, to the jealous nature of Verri's father, his role model, whose wife had died of a broken heart). The culmination of Verri's violent surveillance is Mommina's death, through heart failure, at the moment when she is indulging in the activity forbidden by her husband, namely singing. The particular form taken by this female death is that of physiological and psychological problems of the heart, and is reminiscent of Melina's case in *Belonging to One Person or to No-One*.

The death of both Melina and Mommina is the result of male policing and prohibition; however, Melina does not suffer physical violence at the hands of Tito and Carlino. Furthermore, the violence inflicted on Mommina is significantly and ominously transferred on to the 'actress' playing her part (a part which is itself played by a real actress), as she lies gasping at the end of the play because of 'genuine' heart problems. This is a prime example of a dramatic Pirandellian device which, while experimenting with aspects of traditional theatre on a formal level, still provides a vehicle for the transmission of traditional patriarchal values. Indeed, as a vehicle it is all the more effective in that this level of the dramatic representation (namely the outer play in the 'play inside the play' complex) in which it is the 'actress' who suffers, moves the representation, complete with ideological underpinning, one stage closer to real life.

Female characters other than wives are also at the receiving end of various types of physical violence at the hands of lovers or would-be husbands. In *Man, Beast and Virtue*, an exasperated lover-turned-pimp angrily shakes Mrs Perella. 'It is your martyrdom, my dear,' he informs her, as he prepares her for her husband's bed, reacting with impatience as she resists ineffectually, laughing and crying in turn: 'In the grip of a growing frenzy, he shakes her angrily and pulls her forcibly into an upright position, as if she were a puppet fallen to pieces in his hands' (Act II, sc. 5). A similar sort of manhandling takes place in *Sicilian Limes*, when the potential mother-in-law reveals tearfully that she has failed to police her now unworthy daughter satisfactorily. The would-be husband, in an angry outburst, falls on her, 'forcibly pulling one of her hands away from her face' as she prays for mercy, only to turn his attentions to the daughter when she appears: 'Immediately Micuccio leaves Aunt Marta and turns to her; he grabs her by the arm and pulls her in front of him.' The scene and the play end as more stage directions describe his action of pushing some money down the front of the weeping daughter's dress, as he physically reinforces his opinion of what she has become.

In *I Dream (But Perhaps Not)*, the violent on-stage strangling of the Young Married Lady by her lover, the Man In Dinner Jacket, is interrupted just in time by a knocking on the door, at which point the female character wakes up. She has been dreaming – or has she? The near-fatal violence to which she has been subjected is represented at one remove from reality by the narrative device of the dream. However, her expectation (and therefore that of the audience) which gives rise to the dream in the first place, namely of some extreme form of punishment for having broken the rules, is real enough. Nevertheless, the use of the dream of a female character as a context for the representation of serious physical violence to that character does have the superficially benign effect of placing the violence of the male character and, by inference, the punitive enforcement of patriarchy, at one remove from the realm of the possible. The actual threat of violence remains, of course, in the title's implication that this is perhaps not a dream, a possibility reinforced by the entry on stage of the Man himself after her awakening, and the ominously civilized tea-drinking scene which concludes the play.

The rape of Giulia in *The Grafting* is similarly represented at one remove from reality, although different dramatic techniques are brought into play. The act of violation is not performed on stage, or even off stage, but is reported to have taken place, being visible to the audience only in the physical state of the female character, who is described as deathly white, needing to be held up, her hair and clothes dishevelled and bleeding from the lip and from deep scratches on her neck (Act I, sc. 3). While this is doubtless in conformity with theatrical rules of decorum, which would have prohibited the portrayal of such an extreme act of sexual violence on stage, it also has the reassuring effect, again, of placing the act at one remove from the seen-to-be-real, and so from the possible.

The use of these dramatic devices, then, is indicative of an ideology attempting to cover its traces, camouflaging the more violent extremes of its punitive system, while at the same time ensuring both the expression and reinforcement of its patriarchal rules.

Violence to Male Characters

While fertile female characters (especially daughters and wives) are at the receiving end of varying kinds of physical violence, the strategies of both competition and policing also result in physical violence to male characters. There are, however, important differences in the ways in which male characters are assaulted in Pirandello's plays. The first of these concerns the gender of the aggressor; whereas in the case of violence to female characters, most assailants were of the opposite gender, male characters, by contrast, are physically attacked by characters of the same gender, with very few exceptions. In other words, it is the male characters who, overall, carry out the vast majority of acts of physical violence, towards each other as well as towards female characters. Of the few examples of physical female-to-male violence, none results in injury of any kind. In the most extreme of these examples, Tuzza's attempt to stab Liolà is foiled by the amused hero (*Liolà*, Act III). Other examples are Ignazia in *Tonight We Improvise*, who is in the habit of slapping her husband; Nada in *Cecé*, who slaps Cecé's face on one occasion; and the Stepdaughter, who pushes the Young Boy around in *Six Characters in Search of an Author*.

The second principal difference lies in the particular type of physical violence employed by male characters against each other. Whereas female characters are physically aggressed in various ways, usually without the use of weapons, most male-to-male violence involves the use of pistols, or occasionally a sword. As a consequence, when physical violence between male characters occurs, it leads more often than not to serious injury, if not death. By contrast, violence towards female characters covers a much wider spectrum, ranging from extreme, near-fatal violence to more general manhandling and pushing around which, in its lesser forms, appears insidiously to pervade body language, often seemingly unnoticed, unremarked upon and hence socially accepted.

Of the few instances of male-to-male violence where weapons are not used, only one is fatal. This is the death of Sirio, at the end of *Diana and Tuda*, which occurs when his older rival Giuncano, 'like a wild beast, leaping up behind him and grasping him by the throat with one hand, tears him down and falls to the ground with him'. In some other non-fatal examples, Melina's lovers, Tito and Carlino, 'like two wild beasts', grab each other by the throat, Tito having scratched and clawed

Carlino's hand as they carry her dead body in *Belonging to One Person or to No-One* (Act III); Verri, in a fury, tears Pomàrici, his fiancée's pianist, from his piano stool and throws him to the ground (*Tonight We Improvise*, Act III); and the Father grapples with the Son in *Six Characters in Search of an Author* (Act III).

In contrast to this body-to-body violence, the use of a pistol or revolver is more commonly found in these plays, sometimes in the controlled, ritualized form of the duel. In *The Rules of the Game*, an offstage, but unheard, duel takes place, using pistols and swords, as a result of which one of the male characters is reported to have been seriously wounded; Memmo Speranza in *But It's Not Serious* has recovered from a sword injury sustained in a duel with a girlfriend's brother; and Verri is reputed to have fought, and presumably inflicted either serious or fatal injuries, in at least three duels on account of his wife in *Tonight We Improvise*. Two examples of on-stage shooting which is not part of a ritual duel are, first, the shooting by Giorgio of Romeo at the end of *One Doesn't Know How*, when he learns that Romeo has cuckolded him; and second, *The Wives' Friend* ends with the fatal shooting of Fausto by his rival Francesco. In *Lazarus*, a shot is heard offstage as Diego Spina tries to kill his wife's lover, Arcadipane, a shot which grazes the latter's temples. A sword, on the other hand, is used to despatch Belcredi at the end of *Henry IV*, as 'Henry' takes Landolfo's sword and attacks his old rival, with a weapon determined by the twelfth-century context of the scene. Finally, shooting has already taken place between Tommaso and Neri before the opening of *A Doctor's Duty*, when Neri found Tommaso in bed with his wife.

In conjunction with this, it is of interest to note that all the murders in Pirandello's plays are committed by male characters. Of these nine murders, three are of female and six are of male characters. In the case of the female characters, as we have seen in the last section, murder is not necessarily caused by violence in its physical manifestation (for example, Melina, who dies of 'problems of the heart' for which Tito and Carlino are, as far as the psychological element at least is concerned, responsible). Similarly, the murder of Mommina is not due to physical violence (although such violence does shortly precede her death) but, again, to the emotional violence inflicted on her over the years by her husband. The Murdered Woman in *At The Exit*, on the other hand, is murdered by direct physical violence. In the case of the male characters, on the other hand, all six are murdered, or presumed to be about to die, as a result of serious injury by means of physical violence, whether this takes the form of shooting (4), stabbing (1) or just bare hands (1).[5] In other words,

---

5. These are: Neri in *The Doctor's Duty*, Guido in *The Rules of the Game* (although it is not clear whether he has been shot or stabbed), Fausto in *The Wives' Friend*, Romeo in *One Doesn't Know How*, Belcredi in *Henry IV* and Sirio in *Diana and Tuda*.

male characters tend to inflict physical, rather than psychological violence on each other, while female characters are subjected to psychological as well as physical forms of punishment.

Suicide

Not all deaths in the plays, of course, are the result of murder. Eleven other deaths occur as a result of self-inflicted physical violence, in other words, suicide. Like the murders and other forms of violence, these eleven suicides, together with the attempted suicides by Fulvia and Salter in *As Before, Better Than Before* and *As You Desire Me*, are mostly linked to issues of sexuality. (Two suicides by male characters, Pulino and Luca in *The Imbecile*, are, on the other hand, motivated by medical and political reasons.) I am going to leave aside, for the most part, the problematic question of ultimate responsibility for the suicides. In any case, it is not always easy to determine the degree of influence by one character on the decision of another to commit suicide. What is certain, however, is that most of the suicides and, in the last resort, all the murders and other forms of violent coercion we have examined, are all underpinned by, and symptomatic of, the processes of the patriarchal system within which they occur.

Taking a closer look at the suicides, both male and female characters choose this method of resolving their problems. (There are three suicides and two attempts on the part of female characters, and eight suicides and one attempt on the part of male characters.) As far as the female suicides are concerned, Giulia, in *The Epilogue*, shoots herself offstage after her husband has decided to deprive her of her children as a result of her infidelity, in a clear case of implementation of patriarchal rules by a female character. In *A Doctor's Duty*, Angelica is reported to have thrown herself out of the window to her death, during the shooting between her husband and her lover, and Ersilia, having recovered from one suicide attempt carried out before the opening of *Clothing the Naked*, again takes poison at its end. Fulvia, too, recovers from having tried to shoot herself before the opening of *As Before, Better Than Before*, but, unlike Ersilia, does not make a second attempt.

Of the eight male suicides, only four are described in detail; of these, three are by shooting and one by hanging. Only the suicide of the Young Boy in *Six Characters in Search of an Author* is (re-)enacted on stage. Three other male suicides take place as follows: Tommaso in *The Doctor's Duty* has shot himself before the beginning of the play; it is reported that Pulino has hanged himself; and Luca will shoot himself, for medical and political reasons, in *The Imbecile*. The manner of the other four suicides is not specified: the lover who has murdered the

Murdered Woman in *At the Exit* subsequently kills himself; and in *Each in Their Own Way* it is merely stated that three of Delia's lovers have committed suicide.

From a theatrical point of view it is, of course, true to say that it would be of little dramatic interest to represent deaths which occur from natural causes, and that death by violent means, and even physical violence itself, holds much more dramatic potential. However, what is important here is that the physical violence and the majority of deaths portrayed in the plays owe their existence, and even their particular form of representation, to the patriarchal context within which they take place.

Enclosure

In this final section we shall examine a form of male policing of female sexuality which involves the threat, if not necessarily the use, of physical violence, but which nevertheless represents an extreme type of coercion exercised exclusively on female characters. The work of Foucault on the development of the prison provides some useful insights here. Foucault points out that imprisonment, in constituting punishment via surveillance, and thereby affecting primarily the soul (although of course also involving the body), developed as a highly effective disciplinary method. The cultural institution of what may be termed 'enclosure', whereby men lock away women, is a punishment that, in the first instance, likewise 'acts in depth on the heart, the thoughts, the will, the inclinations' (Foucault, 1987, p. 16). Several of Pirandello's plays in fact show the virtual imprisonment of wives or daughters by husbands or fathers, effected in order to exclude other men, an enclosure which is on occasion simulated by the wearing of a veil when the female character is outside the home. This is the case of Mrs Ponza, whose husband keeps her locked up in *That's How It Is (If You Think So)* and who makes a brief, veiled appearance on stage at the end of the play. Although the fact that she wears a veil is meant to symbolize the hidden, unattainable nature of truth, with the inquisitive characters remaining thwarted as to her 'true' identity, the veil clearly also belongs to the discourse of repressed, enclosed female sexuality.

A discussion between the characters about Ponza's enclosure of his wife points to the topographical specificity of this form of male policing. Ponza's mother reveals that enclosure is the accepted norm in the smaller towns: 'You know – we women – we are used, in small places, to always staying at home', and explains it as 'the fullness of love – enclosed – that's it, yes, exclusive, in which the wife must live, without ever leaving it, and into which no other may enter' (Act I, sc. 4). The Ponza family have moved from a hamlet to the provincial capital where the play is set, and are being interrogated by the socially superior family of Ponza's employer and their friends. In an interesting surfacing of class difference, both male and female members of the latter group are horrified at what they perceive as his wife's imprisonment. The Prefect, on the other hand, believes it to be understandable in terms of the husband's jealousy, and thereby dismisses it as inconsequential. And even in Councillor Agazzi's household, the underlying position of female members, who are ultimately in male possession, is apparent in Agazzi's outrage at the insulting behaviour of his employee 'towards my household, towards my women' (Act I, sc. 3).

The normative aspect of female enclosure is encapsulated by proverbial wisdom, as indicated by Ciampa's motto 'Wife, olives and anchovies: the last two, under oil and brine; the wife, under lock and key' in *Cap and Bells*, a play set in a small town in Sicily. He produces the key as evidence, and when Beatrice points out that there is still the window to take into account, proceeds to explain the rules of enclosure in terms of a contract between man and wife:

> Nevertheless, it is the husband's obligation to lock the door . . . You think I am so terrible? Me? Come on! Why? When the conditions of the pact have been clearly established beforehand . . . – This is the window. (As for the door, I'm locking it). Appear at the window. But take care that nobody has to come and tell me: 'Ciampa, your wife is about to break her neck getting out by the window:' – I don't think there's anything so terrible about that. The man takes into consideration the woman who needs to get some air at the window; the woman takes into consideration the man whose obligation it is to lock the door. And that's all there is to it. (*Cap and Bells*, Act I, sc. 4)

There is, of course, a certain amount of ironic detachment in what Ciampa says here, and elsewhere in the play. This type of irony is a familiar Pirandellian trait in the (male) character/philosopher. This particular character is typically aware of, and therefore distances himself from, the process of role-playing which characterizes social behaviour. He even expounds his theory on this, using the term 'puppet' to denote social role. However, the fact remains that Ciampa does play out his role, rather than really questioning or attempting to subvert it. The fact that his enclosure of his wife fails to achieve its objective (she is having an affair with Beatrice's husband) does not prevent him, in the long run, from saving face as husband-puppet. He manages this by securing the enclosure (this time in a mental institution) of another female character, namely Beatrice herself, who has publicly exposed his failure to police his wife's sexuality. He therefore redeems himself in the eyes of society precisely by proving his ability to police female sexuality in this way.

An extreme case of enclosure is depicted in *Tonight We Improvise*, the 'inner' play of which is, again, set in Sicily. Mommina is:

imprisoned in the highest house in town. The door, all the windows and shutters, all were locked: one small window only was open, giving a view of the distant countryside and the distant sea. Of that town, high up on the hill, she could only see the roofs of houses, the belltowers of churches . . . tiles, tiles, nothing but tiles. Only in the evening could she appear at that window to get some air. (*Tonight We Improvise*, Act III)

The reference to the window, where she can be seen from the outside (by men other than her husband), but where she has to go in order, almost, not to suffocate, suggests airlessness and claustrophobia, and even the possibility of choking, all reminiscent of Ciampa's description of his wife's situation. Mommina's enclosure, however, is more severe than that of Nina Ciampa, in that Verri attempts to police her very thoughts and dreams and, unlike Nina, who appears not to suffer, Mommina eventually dies of heart problems which are related in great part to her treatment at the hands of her husband.

While reference is made to the particularly virulent jealousy of Verri which gives rise to his virtual imprisonment of his wife, it is only the degree of his jealousy which is questioned, rather than the emotion itself and the basic social structures giving rise to it. A biographical reason is given, in that Verri's father was a violently jealous man, without, however, suggesting any explanations (biographical or otherwise) for *his* jealous disposition. Exploration of this topic is therefore restricted to the domain of the individual, rather than the social, intimating the behaviour of the individual in this case to be exceptional and unusual, rather than conforming all too consistently to the demands of the underlying social structures. The fundamental lack of questioning of this issue is heightened all the more by the formal dramatic device involving the transference of heart 'problems' from Mommina (in the 'inner' play) to the actress playing her (in the 'outer' play), a device which itself helps to implicate the existence of male jealousy, and its effects, on a wider basis which extends well beyond mere individual exception.

A less extreme case of enclosure (which remains unquestioned) occurs in *The Licence* (1917). This time it is a father (rather than a husband) who forbids his daughters to leave the house. When the youngest daughter, the sixteen-year-old Rosinella, disobeys and visits D'Andrea, an investigating magistrate, in order to help her father's court case, she makes sure her face is almost entirely concealed by a black woollen shawl. Hearing that her father has arrived unexpectedly, she leaps to her feet in panic and explains that 'he doesn't want us to leave the house'. She is then shown a secret passageway which leads out of the building.

In *The Rules of the Game* (1918), Silia feels enclosed, not because her husband (who has left) coerces her with violence into staying indoors, but, by an apparent paradox, because he ensures that she is 'rich, in charge of my own life, free'. This, she says, is his revenge. In other words, it is precisely the fact that she owes everything to him, including her freedom, which actually pre-empts any genuine self-determination on her part. 'I am suffocating,' she complains. If she had any hope of changing the basis of her situation, she would 'stay put here, breathing only the coolness of this hope, without running to the window to see what there is for me out there' (Act I, sc. 1). The enclosure represented here therefore lacks the dimension of an imprisonment which is physically enforced by a male character like Ciampa or Verri, although the tangible aspects of such imprisonment are present in her description (the claustrophobia, her appearance at the window, the contrast between inside and outside).

The apparent paradox that Silia's enclosure is occasioned by her estranged husband's continued financial support remains undeveloped in any real social sense. It is, rather, part of the process of logic, of form, whereby Leone plays out his role of legal husband (the Italian title literally means 'The Game of Roles' or 'Role-Playing'). His obedience to the dictates of logic, to the rules of this particular game, leads to the dramatic dénouement; as Silia's legal husband he challenges a renowned swordsman to a duel for having offended her, and then argues that it is her lover who must actually fight it, since he, and not the husband, was present on the occasion of the offence. Centre-stage are the workings of logic, the play of empty roles, of form without content. It is in this context, then, that Leone's financial provision for his wife appears in the play, along with his statutory evening visits lasting precisely half an hour, whether or not any conversation takes place between the couple.

However, there are other important implications arising from this financial provision and its enclosing effects on Silia, implications which are not explored by the play. These have their origins in the socio-economic base which makes possible not only the enclosure of female characters as wives or daughters, but which ratifies the very existence of patriarchy itself, namely the economic dependency of women on men. It is Silia's continuing dependency on (the financial generosity of) her husband, particularly in the restrictive pre-divorce era, which determines his power to delimit her freedom, to ensure her enclosure. Any real chance of escape from the inside, from enclosure, and so from under the surveillance of male relatives, lies in moving into the outside world – the world of work.

–4–

Danger, Women at Work

VIRGODAMO: But the blessed young girls, they ruin themselves, they really do! Too many subjects to learn. An enormous overload of the intellect. And they lose, they really do lose, the flower, the fragrance, of femininity: that certain something which makes them so fascinating.

But It's Not Serious, Act I, sc. 1

Introduction: Inside vs Outside

The inside/outside dichotomy, explored at the end of the previous chapter under the phenomenon of enclosure, is of great relevance to the issue of women working. While some of Pirandello's working female characters clearly work outside the home, many of his plays also show dependent female characters waiting at home for the return of husbands or lovers. These male providers range far afield for reasons of work, or, as Beatrice in the middle-class play *Cap and Bells* (1918) complains, for other reasons. She is aware that her husband is having an affair, and is not satisfied with the fact that he treats her 'like a queen' at home. 'Prudence, sure! Respect, abundance, a well-stocked house,' she says bitterly. 'And outside, what does he get up to?' (Act I, sc. 1). Indeed, he is so busy in the world outside that he does not come home once during the entire course of the play. In other words, he never appears on stage, the dramatic setting which represents the couple's luxuriously furnished drawing-room.

Beatrice, on the other hand, is on stage in every scene but one (Act II, sc. 4). Even then she is obviously within earshot (i.e. at home), as indicated by her brother who calls out her name in order to summon her into the drawing-room, and so back on stage. The drawing-room provides a common setting for Pirandello's middle-class plays, and can be said to epitomize the social front of the inside/home facet of the living arrangements of this class. Writing about the bourgeois family, Montroni describes the central, and even rather dramatic, role of the drawing-room in the context of the development of domestic spaces specific to bourgeois family culture. 'The drawing-room,' he says, 'even when it is only small, displays ostentatiously the most tangible symbols of the myths and aspirations of this social group before a public consisting of relations, friends and acquaintances who frequent the home' (Montroni, 1988, p. 109, my translation).

In the rural context of *Liolà* (1917), which is set out of doors, and in whose peasant economy both male and female characters work, emphasis shifts from the inside/outside axis to that of stasis versus activity, or mobility, as an indicator of freedom of movement. The protagonist of the title, who represents the apotheosis of idealized masculinity, is named in accordance with the facility of movement which entitles him to go anywhere (his name means 'here or there'). This freedom is further associated with sexual potency, as Liolà similarly names his three little boys, whom he has fathered on his wanderings outside the village, 'Li' ('here'), 'O' ('or') and 'Là' ('there'). It is also Liolà, with his use of the age-old metaphor of woman-as-fertile-terrain, who is the mouthpiece for the stasis/mobility dichotomy taken to its logical extreme. He describes the farmer (men), who in order to grow a tree (father a child) must not simply stand there gazing at the land (woman), but must busily work it, hoeing, manuring and then planting the seed, while the land itself lies there, immobile and fertile, waiting to be worked. A similar metaphor used by Paolino in *Man, Beast and Virtue* (1919), likewise infers a static position for the woman, who in this case is represented by a piece of neglected but fertile land with a fruiting tree on it. On to this scene of immobility comes a man who eats the abandoned fruit, throws away the kernel and so inseminates the waiting land.

The absence of the inside/outside, home/work dichotomy in the agricultural context of *Liolà* also characterizes the non-agricultural, pre-industrial phase in the historical development of the woman's workplace. During this phase work was still carried out in the home (for example, in cottage industries). As a consequence, the home did not represent the diametric opposite to the workplace, an opposition which came into being with the arrival of wage-labour and industrialization. Hamilton, in her work *The Liberation of Women: A Study of Patriarchy and Capitalism*, formulates the process as follows: 'For with the separation of labour from the objective conditions of its realization came the concurrent separations – really the same separations looked at in different ways – between production and consumption, work and home, work and domestic chores, public and private' (Hamilton, 1980, p. 27). As a further consequence, childcare was not yet the obstacle to the working woman which it would later become. Hamilton again: 'Producing at home had, at least, left her in the same physical location as her children. Nursing a baby, supervising a young child, preparing meals had been part of the general labour' (ibid., p. 40). Indeed, in the context of the peasant economy, male children, as Liolà points out, are in themselves an economic asset to the family: 'As male children, when they get bigger, as you know, in the countryside, the more working hands there are, the richer we are' (Act I).

The inside/outside, private/public dichotomy is the rule, however, in the vast majority of Pirandello's plays that involve the urban middle (and occasionally upper) classes. While the male characters in these plays who are not of independent means work in a wide-ranging variety of professions, belonging mostly to the professional level of the tertiary sector, a considerable number of female characters are economically dependent on their husbands. They accordingly carry out the exclusive duties of wife and mother within the home environment, to the exclusion of any work-related activities outside the home (or in some extreme cases, as we saw at the end of the previous chapter, to the exclusion of even setting foot outside). In this class the inside/outside, home/work dichotomy has become fixed, with motherhood no longer 'part of the general labour'. In plays that represent working female characters, the inside/outside dichotomy reappears with various connotations, depending on the type of work involved.

The first section of this chapter will look at the various kinds of work carried out by female characters, work which differs distinctly from that carried out by their male counterparts. Attention will be paid to the context of class and marital/family status, in an attempt to clarify the ideological bases and assumptions which inform the dramatic representation of this fundamental aspect of patriarchy. In conjunction with this, the sphere of education will also be examined. This is followed by a second section dealing with the class-specific categories of non-working female characters, and the chapter concludes with an appraisal of the price paid by these female characters for their dependency. Use will be made in this chapter of figures collected and categorized for the census of 1911, 1921 and 1931, and for the annual statistics review of 1919–21, 1922–5 and 1927, by Istat, the Central Institute of Statistics in Italy. Whenever categories are broken down, I have included all the relevant sub-sections. Frequently, however, categories remain relatively general. Furthermore, it would be unrealistic to assume that any census figures represent a population in its entirety. In other words, as with all statistical data, the figures obtained are to be regarded in terms of trends rather than absolutes.

Female Characters At Work

Marriage, Family and Class

Most working female characters are unmarried. Indeed, the assumption that work and marriage are incompatible is one which informs several of the plays. *Finding Oneself* (1932), while portraying at length the concerns of a female character, the actress Donata, concludes with her recognition that she has to choose between marriage to the artist Eli and her own career. In an early play, *Sicilian Limes* (1911), the musician Micuccio visits his intended bride Sina, only to reject and humiliate her when he discovers that she has become a popular singer. In the fatal case of Mommina, she is not only forbidden to pursue a career as a singer, but is imprisoned and gradually driven to her death by her jealous husband in *Tonight We Improvise* (1930); meanwhile her unmarried sisters become famous (even though they do not sing as well as she does).

Another working female character, the artist's model Tuda, marries during the course of *Diana and Tuda* (1927). However the marriage, contrary to her desires, is in name only, and is purely a means for her husband, the sculptor Sirio, to ensure that she continues to work exclusively for him. Although his uncaring, exploitative attitude towards her is explained away in philosophical terms as an obsession with form over life, there is also an underlying implication that no genuine marriage can take place with Tuda precisely on account of the nature of her work. In other words, Sirio 'marries' her because she is a model, but it is not a real marriage precisely because that is what she is. Another relatively rare instance of a married working female character is Silvia in *All For the Best* (1920). Significantly, her decision to resume teaching is made to coincide in the narrative with the period of her adultery, a coincidence which points up the nature of the threat posed by the career female when she moves out of the confines of the home and into the world of work outside it.

As this last example shows, compulsory choice between marriage and career for female characters does not apply merely in the case of specific types of work which were considered, at the time, to have distinctly sexual connotations (in particular acting, singing, dancing and modelling). Furthermore, a choice between career and marriage would have been unthinkable, and is in fact absent, as far as working male characters are concerned. Micuccio, in *Sicilian Limes*, is therefore entitled to be a musician, while Sina is not, and the work of Eli as an artist in *Finding Oneself* (1932) goes unquestioned, whereas Donata's acting career is jeopardized by the prospect of their marriage. The nearest approximation to a conflict between marriage and career for a male character is the desertion of the husband by his wife on the grounds that he is always working. Professor Agliani's widow has left him for this reason in *All For the Best*, and Giulia's adultery in *The Epilogue* (1898) is explained (but not excused) by her husband's preoccupation with his work. Even in these two cases, it is the amount of time and energy devoted to work, and not the work itself, which poses the problem.

Certain female characters do not have to face this choice between marriage and work. In the shopkeeper sector of the lower middle class, the wife of the sweetmaker Bellavita, in the play of that name, works in the family business, namely in her husband's shop. Other such characters belong to the peasant and working classes. As indicated earlier, in the agricultural sector and during the pre-industrial, pre-wage labour phase of non-agricultural labour, the division between home and work did not exist in the same way. So, for instance, home and the workplace are identical for Mita in the peasant play *Liolà*. She is married to Simone, and as well as keeping house for him she works shelling almonds on his land, along with the unmarried female peasants. Just as the entire family, including wife and children, work in the peasant economy, so all the members of the working-class Cinquemani family, consisting of father, mother and daughter, are employed cleaning at the school where Toti teaches in *Think It Over, Giacomino* (1917). The Cinquemani family hierarchy itself is reproduced in the workplace: the father is the caretaker and the two women are cleaners working under his direction.

There is clearly no problem here about either mother or daughter working outside the home. The daughter stops working when she marries Professor Toti (who gives her shelter after she becomes pregnant by her impoverished lover Giacomino and is evicted from the parental home). As Toti points out, his marriage to her will give her status. By marrying him, she moves out of the working class and into the world of the leisured middle-class woman, to become a non-working wife and mother. The marriage is also, however, a positive social move for Toti. Having a leisured wife is a characteristic status symbol for the upper-middle-class male, in that she is evidence of his capacity as provider. In *Lazarus* (1929) the opposite process can actually be seen to take place, when the leisured wife of a landowner leaves him and proceeds to labour on the land. It seems, then, that class distinctions play an important part in determining the working or non-working status of the female character.

Moving on from the peasant and working classes to the lower-middle-class world of the landlady, issues of work and actual marriageability are very closely interlinked in *But It's Not Serious* (1919). Gasparina is both unsuccessful at her work and unmarried. Her lack of assertiveness hinders her efficient management of the boarding-house of which she is the landlady. She allows herself to be taken advantage of and even insulted, and ekes out a meagre, impoverished existence as the uncomplaining butt of ill-humour. It is, however, precisely on account of her qualities of gentleness and unassertiveness that she receives a proposal of marriage (if in name only) from the handsome hero. Gasparina is, in particular, sufficiently unattractive to make such a marriage a possibility in the first place. Memmo has also noted that she is thrifty enough not to be a drain on his resources, and self-sacrificing enough not to make any emotional demands. She has also proved her selflessness and demonstrated her nurturing skills by spending entire nights at his bedside while he recovers from an injury incurred in a duel with the brother of his current beloved.

In short, this is Memmo's way of avoiding a real marriage which, in his view, would by contrast entail considerable financial and emotional investment. His attitude is based on the assumption of bourgeois women as 'parasites, living a life of ease and luxury', a notion which prevailed in historical accounts of the early formation of the bourgeois class. Clark, for example, writes that 'the parasitic life of its women has been in fact one of the chief characteristics of the parvenu class' (Hamilton, 1980, p. 42; Clark, 1919, p. 296, quoted in Hamilton, 1980, p. 43). Memmo's outlook denotes a return to a pre-bourgeois type of womanhood, characterized by 'modesty, frugality, keeping at home, good housewifery and other economical virtues then in reputation' (John Evelyn, in Phillips, 1926, p. 70, quoted in Hamilton, 1980, p. 42). In conjunction with these considerations, Gasparina's stereotypically feminine qualities of gentleness and self-denial, which determine the unsuccessful nature of her working life, play an important part in guaranteeing her eligibility for marriage.

When Gasparina stops work and moves to the country estate which the marriage contract confers on her, a significant development takes place. In addition to the feminine attributes of character which she already possesses, she now acquires physical femininity. As a direct result of not working, she no longer looks older than her twenty-seven years. While early in the play much was made of her excessive physical ageing, with both Maestrina Terrasi and Memmo expressing disbelief at her declaration that she is only twenty-seven years old, by the end of the play, and after a period of time as a non-working, leisured wife, she has become healthier, younger-looking and positively attractive. The assumption, in other words, is that working is detrimental to physical femininity (as well as being incompatible with feminine character traits). When, added to this, Memmo discovers that she has managed to retain that most prized of feminine possessions, namely her virginity, he decides that the marriage can actually be consummated and become 'serious'.

The forging of links between femininity, marriageability and not working (or working unsuccessfully) is echoed in the portrayal of Gasparina's female lodger, the young teacher (Maestrina Terrasi). Unlike Gasparina, this female character is assertive and reprimands Gasparina for allowing herself to be ill-treated. 'We are both working women', she says, 'and don't have to account to anybody' (Act I, sc. 4). However, while Gasparina manages to snare, albeit unintentionally, the prize catch of a rich, handsome husband (a positive achievement in the terms of the play), Maestrina Terrasi is single. Her actual title, the diminutive form of 'maestra', indicates that she is still young and therefore marriageable. Noticeably, however, while there are no pejorative indications of any lack of femininity in her appearance, there are, at the same time, no flattering references either. She is, interestingly, the least developed character in the entire play and is the only one who is not described physically. It is only in relation to the portrayal of the other characters, in particular that of the male teacher Virgodamo (as we shall see later) and to Gasparina herself, that the delineation of Maestrina Terrasi takes on any shape at all.

One key factor which Gasparina, Maestrina Terrasi, the two prostitutes Loletta and Fanny, and indeed the great majority of other working female characters in Pirandello's plays have in common is that they are apparently without any family. The implication behind these family-less female characters who work is that they work out of necessity rather than choice. In other words, no female character would as a rule choose to work if a source of financial support were already available (in the form, for instance, of a husband, a father, another male relative, a widowed mother with inherited income or a family inheritance). Not only are they unmarried, but they appear to be without relatives of any kind. The exceptions to this appear to be class-specific, in that working and peasant-class female characters (who inevitably have an occupation) can, as we have seen, be either married or single. They are also part of a family (which, in the case of the peasant-based *Liolà*, is of the extended type, including aunts as well as illegitimate children).

The concept of a career providing not only an income, but also an opportunity for the personal development and fulfilment of the middle- or upper-class female character, is not really represented in these plays, which express the dominant view of a traditional femininity defined and circumscribed by home-based marital and maternal functions. Well before Pirandello wrote his first play, however, the feminist insistence on work outside the home as 'the primary condition for the development of the feminine personality' had already made itself heard in Italy. The League for the promotion of feminine interests, founded in Milan in 1881 by, among others, Anna Maria Mozzoni, had as one of its key aims the eradication of all types of discrimination against women in terms of professions and salaries (Ravera, 1978, p. 73).

In the rare cases when a female character is portrayed developing her identity through her career, as in the example of the actress Donata in *Finding Oneself* (1932), she is forced, as we have seen, to choose between her career and the traditional feminine roles of wife and potential mother. This is in direct contrast, for example, to the case of the newly-married male character Venzi in *The Wives' Friend* (1927). He decides to undertake legal work solely in order to occupy his mind, not to earn a living (he has independent means). Donata decides to pursue her career, but at great personal expense, as the man she loves disappears uncompromisingly out of her life. Furthermore, his behaviour is emphasized as not being in any way out of the ordinary (another male character likewise maintains that he would not allow any wife of his to work as an actress). While the climax of the plot is the choice which Donata makes, and Eli's negative reaction to it, it is automatically assumed that Venzi, on the other hand, may have both a career and a wife.

We have seen, then, that the majority of female characters who work are unmarried (with the exceptions of Silvia in *All For the Best* (1920) and Tuda in *Diana and Tuda* (1927), and certain working and peasant-class female characters). As far as family belonging is concerned, only a couple of working female characters have any family. (Sina in *Sicilian Limes* (1911), and the Stepdaughter in *Six Characters in Search of an Author* (1921) both have mothers, and the latter also has a young brother of twelve, a young sister of five, and an estranged stepbrother of twenty-three). The other working female characters appear to have no family at all.[1] Apart from the small number of married exceptions, then, working female characters significantly tend not to have any adult relatives.

Types of Work

It is no coincidence that many of these family-less working female characters who work outside the home are involved either in prostitution or in a type of work which, during the early twentieth century, also had dis-

---

1. The actress Delia and the character Amalia whom she plays, who is also an actress, in *Each in Their Own Way* (1924); the actress Donata in *Finding Oneself* (1932); the artist's models Tuda, Sara and Jonella in *Diana and Tuda* (1927); the dancer L'Ignota, whose lack of family is an issue in *As You Desire Me* (1930); the landlady Gasparina in *But It's Not Serious* (1919); the childminders Ersilia in *Clothing the Naked* (1923); perhaps understandably, as she is a visiting foreigner, Miss White in *Mrs Morli, One and Two,* (1922); and the prostitutes Nada in *Cecé* (1913), Loletta and Fanny in *But It's Not Serious*, Melina in *Belonging to One Person or to No-One* (1929) and La Spera in *The New Colony* (1928).

tinctly sexual connotations (namely acting, singing and modelling). What is more, as we saw in the case of the teacher Silvia in *All For the Best* (1920), even her non-sexually related career is made to coincide in the narrative (through the perceptions of the husband) with the period of her adultery. The underlying assumption appears to be that, unlike male characters, when female characters work outside the home, this automatically invokes their sexuality in some way. In other words, women inevitably work with, and are therefore exclusively defined by, their bodies. In the same vein, the historical view of the profession of acting, when pursued by women, was that the actresses merely '*play themselves*, a patriarchal premise that conveniently and skilfully removes women from any possibility of cultural creativity' (Ferris, 1990, p. xi). It is this basic assumption that she is 'playing herself' which informs not only Eli's objections to Donata's career in *Finding Oneself*, but also the prurient probings into her portrayal of love scenes on the stage.

It is now time to take a closer look at the types of work undertaken by female characters in Pirandello's plays. Both the primary and particularly the tertiary sector are represented by the various types of work performed by female characters in Pirandello's plays. (The secondary, industrial sector, which is not portrayed at all, did not develop significantly in Italy until the 1920s and 1930s, although an 'industrial spirit' has been identified in the period 1898 to 1913 (Hay, 1987, p. 100).) In the primary sector, the agricultural sphere is represented by female peasants, both married and unmarried, in *Liolà* (1917) and *The Jar* (1925). In this archetypally patrilineal system, it is male characters who are the landowning proprietors for whom both female and male peasants work (Uncle Simone in *Liolà* and Don Lolò Zirafa in *The Jar*). While the peasants working for Don Zirafa are not related to him (his title indicates that he belongs to the landowning nobility), Uncle Simone, on the other hand, is a peasant with his own land whose cousin and her daughter work for him. In this particular hierarchy, it is the older female relative, namely Simone's cousin, Aunt Croce, who appears as the next most powerful figure. This can be seen by her management of the almond-shelling and grape-picking sessions in which she dominates the young peasant girls. Figures for 1911 illustrate that only the minority of agricultural workers in Italy actually managed or worked family-owned land. These figures also show the male-dominated nature of the peasant workforce.[2]

The majority of female characters who work in Pirandello's plays do so in the tertiary public or service sector. It is particularly significant that they are located mostly at the lower range of occupations in this sec-

---

2. 1,108,728 out of 6,051,835 male peasants, and 606,532 out of 2,972,883 female peasants managed or worked family-owned land in Italy in 1911 (Istat figures, 1911).

tor. Only two teachers, Silvia in *All For the Best* (1920) and Maestrina Terrasi in *But It's Not Serious* (1919), and the writer Diana in *When One Is Somebody* (1933), can be said to belong to the upper range, namely that of the professions. The actresses (Donata in *Finding Oneself* (1932), Delia and Amelia in *Each in Their Own Way* (1924), and the First Actress in *Tonight We Improvise* (1930) and *Six Characters in Search of an Author* (1921)), singers (Sina in *Sicilian Limes* (1911) and Mommina's sisters in *Tonight We Improvise*) and models (Tuda, Sara and Jonella in *Diana and Tuda* (1927)), all belong to the arts-related occupations, which were, in the case of women, considered suggestive of sexual activity and therefore negatively valued.

The up and coming film culture in Pirandello's era demonstrates a parallel preoccupation with these socially stigmatized careers. Hay notes the link between acting and loss of reputation in Italian films such as *Love Everlasting* (1913). In this film, 'family circumstances compel [the heroine] to relinquish her innocence and Italy to become a stage actress with a questionable reputation in Paris' (a plot which is re-echoed, to give just one example, by Pirandello's *As You Desire Me* (1930), in which Ignota is forced to leave Italy to become a dancer with a questionable reputation in Berlin) (Hay, 1987, p. 119). Similarly in the film *Ballerinas* (1936), 'a ballerina is forced to choose between her career and her love for her middle-class boyfriend, a radio announcer and journalist' (ibid., p. 129). Once again, this plot can be found in Pirandello's *Finding Oneself* (1932), with the dilemma faced by the actress Donata who must choose between her acting career and her artist boyfriend Eli; and in *Sicilian Limes* (1911), with the singer Sina's loss of her prospective husband, himself a musician, once he finds out that she is pursuing this 'immoral' career.

The vast remainder of female characters in Pirandello work in semi-skilled and unskilled jobs (as domestics, maids, housekeepers, governesses, nurses, wet-nurses, child-minders, chaperones, landladies, school-cleaners), in the trades (as seamstresses) and in varying types of prostitution. Figures show that the domestic services in Italy were in fact female-dominated.[3] The ubiquitous maids and female housekeepers in the bourgeois plays would seem to bear out the characteristics of this category. However, male butlers and servants are by no means absent, particularly but not exclusively in bachelor households (for example that of Leone Gala in *The Rules of the Game* (1918), Lori in *All For the Best* (1920) and the upper class 'Henry' in *Henry IV* (1922)). Similarly

---

3. Figures for domestic services workers in Italy: 1901, 394,741 females : 79,879 males; 1911, 390,199 females : 92,810 males; 1921, 380,614 females : 65,017 males; 1931, 473,070 females : 66,883 males (Istat, 1911, 1921, 1931).

the trade of dressmaker, which we see being carried out by a female character in *Diana and Tuda* (1927), is predominantly a female occupation, perhaps for reasons of decorum. In 1921 more women were not only employed in this area, but also owned their own workshops.[4]

One burgeoning area of female employment is barely hinted at, in that female characters are mentioned only once as cashiers and typists, and then only hypothetically (in the case of Loletta and Fanny, who in this way attempt to conceal the fact that they are prostitutes in *But It's Not Serious* (1919)). Once again, the parallel with film is interesting. Hay comments on the enormous success in 1931 of the film *The Private Secretary*, 'one of the first Italian sound films to use as its central dramatic situation the experience of a woman seeking work in the city'. According to the film critic Rosario Assunto:

> [*The Private Secretary*] was born during the height of the transformation of the social order and system – what has been christened 'the world crisis of 1929', a time when every family felt a need to augment the income of its domestic budget. And young women closed their fashion albums, put away their embroidery, and began to study typing, stenography, and bookkeeping in order to get jobs in banks, in offices, and in businesses. (Hay, 1987, pp. 119–20)

Only two years after *But It's Not Serious*, figures already show this type of work to be very much a female domain in Italy (as indeed elsewhere), with 5,841 women as opposed to only 571 men working as typists, stenographers and copyists.[5] It would seem, then, that Pirandello's portrayal of working women was somewhat more backward-looking than that of his cinematic peers.

Overall, a very different picture emerges regarding working male characters in the plays. Most importantly, the vast majority of these characters are to be found predominating at the opposite end of the tertiary sector, namely in the upper, professional zone. Here they not only perform a much wider range of professions than their female counterparts, but also do so in significantly greater numbers. They can be seen working as teachers (Professor Toti in *Think It Over Giacomino* (1917), Professor Virgodamo in *But It's Not Serious* (1919), Paolino in *Man, Beast and Virtue* (1919), Cesarino in *As Before, Better Than Before* (1921) and Daula in *The Wives' Friend* (1927)); writers (Leonardo in *As Others See It* (1916), Nota in *Clothing the Naked* (1923), Salter in *As You Desire Me* (1930) and Somebody in *When One Is Somebody*

---

4. In 1921 in Italy more women (360,216) than men (119,089) were employed as dressmakers and owned their own workshops in greater numbers (692 women vs 220 men) (Istat, 1921).

5. Ibid.

(1933)); and journalists (Leonardo, D'Albis and Ducci in *As Others See It* and Cantavalle in *Clothing the Naked* (1923)).

The teaching profession is of interest not merely as regards the manner in which it is portrayed in the plays, but because of its bearing on the next section, in which we shall examine the representation of education as a whole. For the moment we can note, as we attempt to correlate Pirandello's representation of this profession with the historical situation during his lifetime (and bearing in mind that Pirandello himself pursued this profession under financial duress from 1897), that female teachers have always outnumbered male teachers overall.[6] However, it is important to bear in mind that the higher the level of education involved, the lower the proportion of female to male teachers.

Infant schools were both managed and staffed exclusively by women.[7] At the compulsory elementary level, female teachers (*maestre*) far outnumbered their male counterparts. This is further evidenced by figures for student enrolment at the *istituti magistrali*, state institutions set up in 1911 specifically to train elementary school teachers. For the year 1923–4, 36,283 female as opposed to only 2,522 male students enrolled in these institutions. Two-thirds of their teachers, however, were male.[8] The typical relation of male teacher/ female pupil at this level finds a place in *But It's Not Serious* (1919) in the characters Professor Virgodamo and his ex-pupil, Maestrina Terrasi, who is now an elementary school teacher. It is at this level that Pirandello taught Italian literature; his reactions to female student-teachers are documented by his biographer.[9]

While dominating at infant and elementary levels, it is in the middle schools where female teachers begin to give way to their male counterparts, and figure, if at all, predominantly as supply rather than regular teaching staff. At the lower range of middle school (the *scuole normali* and the *scuole complementari*) female teachers still outnumber male teachers.[10] However, the next stage sees male teachers taking over from female teachers in numerical terms. This is the gymnasium (*ginnasio*), the type of school where Professor Toti teaches for the first part of *Think It Over, Giacomino* (1917).[11] Lastly, census figures for teaching faculty at

6. Overall figures for teachers in Italy: 1901, 63,873 female : 39,557 male; 1911, 71,391 female : 44,430 male; 1921, 114,445 female : 46,826 male (Istat, 1911, 1921).

7. In 1921, for instance, there were 3,878 headmistresses and 8,529 teachers in infant schools, all of whom were female (Istat, 1919–21).

8. Istat (1922-5).

9. See Giudice (1963, p. 231).

10. 1917–8 saw 1,720 female : 1,147 male teachers in the *scuole normali*, and 1,469 female : 351 male teachers in the *scuole complementari* (Istat, 1919–21).

11. Figures for 1917–8 show only 622 female teachers as opposed to 2,574 males in the *ginnasio* (Istat, 1919–21).

university and other higher level educational institutions are not broken down in gender terms, as in the case of lower level education, suggesting that faculty were usually male.[12] It would appear, then, that the plays portray the actual position as regards gender-differentiation in terms of level of teaching in state institutions, but not in terms of numbers.

The other male teachers who appear in the plays work in the private sector as tutors, teaching either in their own homes or visiting the homes of their pupils. Paolino (*Man, Beast and Virtue*), Cesarino (*As Before, Better Than Before*) and Daula (*The Wives' Friend*) all fit into this category, as do certain characters who are mentioned, but who do not appear on stage (Professor Dalbuono, tutor in painting, and various professors of French, English and music in *The Grafting*). Figures for music teachers (represented in the plays by the male characters Cesarino and Daula) show how this area was in reality dominated by males rather than females.[13] The literary field (including writers, publishers, translators, interpreters, journalists and archeologists) is also recorded by the census to have been male-dominated, as the plays indeed suggest.[14] In addition to the areas of education, writing and journalism, male professionals can also be found in the plays as school directors, judges, notaries, lawyers, senators, district councillors, prefects, party leaders, doctors, pharmacists, newspaper directors, journalists, poets, bank managers, marine officials, sea-captains, customs officials, stage directors, philosophers, photographers, police commissioners and priests.

Taking a closer look at the legal profession, for example, the first figures showing any female participation in this field in Italy are for 1921, when 85 female professionals are registered, compared with 35,613 men (figures for 1901 and 1911 show only male professionals).[15] All Pirandello's legal characters are male (the four judges in *The Licence* (1918), Lello and Giorgio in *Mrs Morli, One and Two* (1922), the unnamed notary and lawyer in *The Festival of Our Lord of the Ship* (1924), Fausto and Francesco in *The Wives' Friend* (1927) and Contento in *Bellavita* (1928)). In the world of banking, *Cap and Bells* (1918) shows a male bank principal (figures for 1921 reveal higher positions to be held mainly by men, who occupy 3,550 such positions compared to 175 women).[16]

In terms of social attitudes regarding the performance arts, male characters who work in the field of acting (the actors in *Six Characters*

12. See Istat (1919–21, 1922–5, 1927).
13. Music teachers: 1909, 4,254 males : 1,018 females; 1911, 4,050 males : 1,171 females; 1921, 5,015 males : 2,194 females (Istat, 1911, 1921).
14. In the literary field: 1901, 2,569 men : 148 women; 1911, 3,832 men: 236 women; 1921, 5,104 men : 420 women (Istat, 1911, 1921).
15. Figures for male professionals only: 1901, 33,746; 1911, 37,545 (Istat, 1911).
16. Istat (1921).

in Search of an Author (1921), *Each in Their Own Way* (1924), and *Tonight We Improvise* (1930)) or music (Micuccio in *Sicilian Limes* (1911) and Mauri in *As Before, Better Than Before* (1921)) are not negatively valued, unlike their female counterparts, as the sexual connotations of these occupations simply do not apply in their case. In the realm of the fine arts, only male artists (Caravani in *Diana and Tuda* (1927), Eli in *Finding Oneself* (1932)) and male sculptors (Sirio and Giuncano in *Diana and Tuda*) are represented, while female characters merely work as their models (Tuda, Sara and Jonella). In reality, male models were in fact more numerous than their female counterparts. This trend was even on the increase. Census figures for 1901 in Italy show 38 male to 34 female models, while 1911 saw 71 male to 45 female models. In 1921, six years prior to the first performance of *Diana and Tuda*, the gap widened to 138 male to only 58 female models.[17]

The exclusive representation of the female model in the play therefore appears to reinforce a longstanding stereotype which, far from representing the historic situation, has always linked modelling with women rather than with men. At the outset of her study *The Artist's Model*, Borzello poses the question in the following way: 'Clearly the female nude model accounts for only a tiny proportion of the model-based art that has been produced through the centuries. How could she have come to stand for it all?' She goes on to elaborate on the implications of this stereotype: 'The male artist–female model relationship is seen as the norm, and other relationships either deviations (female artist–male model), too dull to consider (male artist–male model) or too threatening to the image of the artist as sexual hero (homosexual artist–male model)' (Borzello, 1982, pp. 6, 9).

As far as artists themselves were concerned, figures show that male painters, sculptors, stages designers, miniaturists and engravers heavily outnumbered their female equivalents (1901: 7,737 males to 426 females; 1911: 9,433 males to 693 females; 1921: 5,819 males to 669 females, with the sizeable drop in male artists in 1921 possibly due to fatalities during the Great War).[18] In this area, then, the play reiterates the cultural assumptions which align the male with artistic creativity and activity, while the female is associated with the body and passivity, even when these assumptions are not reflected by historical data. As suggested earlier, female (but not male) models bore the further burden of their work being socially stigmatized. Borzello describes the nude model as 'a site for irreconcilable notions about nudity in art (good) and nudity in

17. Istat (1911, 1921). Statistics for any socially stigmatized area should clearly be regarded with some caution.

18. Istat (1911, 1921). I am grateful to Clare Coupe for bringing Borzello's book to my attention.

life (bad)' (ibid., p. 73). From here it is but a short step to the association of the nude female body with immorality and hence prostitution: 'The link between models and immorality frequently becomes a link between modelling and prostitution; a connection established in the anecdotes of prostitutes modelling for artists by classical Greek writers' (ibid., p. 72).

At the lower, non-professional end of the tertiary service sector, including the trades, and semi-skilled and unskilled jobs, male characters are portrayed working as clerks, secretaries, typesetters, shopkeepers, manservants, jar-menders, sailors, muleteers, fishermen, gardeners, food vendors, ushers, guards, shop assistants, school caretakers and porters. At the lower end of the tertiary sector, then, large numbers of both male and female characters are to be found. However, here too a difference is apparent in that the female section is biased towards the home-based domestic and nurturing occupations. Even the trade of seamstress, the only non-domestic, non-nurturing trade represented, is pursued within the confines of the home of the client. This is illustrated by the scene in *Diana and Tuda* when Tuda is fitted for a dress and cloak at home. Only the fake occupations of the prostitutes Loletta and Fanny as typist and cashier in *But It's Not Serious* (1919) would involve working in a non-domestic environment. The male section, by contrast, contains mostly jobs which are very much oriented outside the home. Indeed, all types of work carried out by male characters, apart from manservants and gardeners, entail non-domestic working surroundings such as banks, offices and ships.

It has been shown that there is an interesting relation between Pirandello's representation of gender-based distinctions in the field of work and the historical situation regarding job distribution. The main observation to be made is that the plays tend to reinforce the dominant ideology in gender-differentiation in the sphere of work, even when this goes counter to the historical situation (as, for instance, in the case of the artist's model). As his 'Feminism' illustrates, Pirandello cannot be described as being sympathetic to the changing role of women in society, and to the demands for transformation in this particular social area which were being voiced throughout his lifetime. Although he raises important issues, such as the relationship between career and marriage for women, the combination of the two is never portrayed as a viable proposition, and his conclusions inevitably work to maintain the status quo.

Education

Female Characters and Education As we have seen, the teaching profession appears to be represented according to the trend of the time in that female teachers are shown teaching at a lower level in the educational system than male teachers (in the case of Maestrina Terrasi in *But It's Not Serious* (1919)). Similarly in the realm of traditional assumptions which tended to associate work outside the home with illicit sexual activity, Silvia's return to teaching, as noted earlier, is made to coincide with her adulterous affair in *All For the Best* (1920). Contrary to the historical situation, however, the plays show more male than female teachers. As well as looking at the portrayal of female and male teachers in relation to each other, it is of relevance to examine the dramatic representation of education itself, education being a necessary precondition to the pursuance by these characters not only of the profession of teaching, but of any profession at all.

References in the plays to the education of women are negative, and range from overt antagonism couched in biological arguments on the part of male characters to implicit indications of low levels of education in female characters, levels which are represented as the norm and which go unquestioned.[19] In *But It's Not Serious*, Professor Virgodamo launches an attack on the education of girls. His hostile remarks take place, significantly, in an entirely male setting (they are addressed to one male character and in the presence of another). They are, furthermore, strategically positioned, in that they not only follow a misogynistic interchange between himself and Grizzoffi, but also immediately precede the first entrance on stage of Maestrina Terrasi, the young female teacher.

Grizzoffi opens the misogynistic dialogue, in which he compares woman to a cigar, with the rhetorical question 'Are women more, or less, harmful than nicotine?' To which Virgodamo replies vehemently, 'Ah, much more! Women are terrible, especially at a certain age.' The conversation then turns to Virgodamo's career at a higher institution for girls, where he taught pedagogy. When Grizzoffi declares that he would never send any daughter of his to be taught by him, Virgodamo replies:

> And you would be perfectly justified! Not on account of me; but these blessed young girls, they ruin themselves, they really do! Too many subjects to learn. An enormous overload of the intellect. And they lose, they really do lose, the flower, the fragrance, of femininity: that certain something – which makes them so fascinating. (*But It's Not Serious*, Act I, sc. 1)

The dialogue which, until that point, had been confrontational, now concludes with agreement on this particular topic, as Grizzoffi confirms Virgodamo's negative view of the effects of education on girls. It is immediately after Grizzoffi's final remark that the female teacher her-

19. For an illuminating account of the biological argument in relation to the education of women, see Sayers (1982).

self makes her first appearance. Like Pietra in 'Feminism', the absence of this female character from a discussion in which she is very much implicated, and would presumably have much to say, is underscored by her actual physical proximity. The unusual fact that she puts her head out from behind a curtain, rather than a door, in order to appear on stage, implies that she could easily have overheard the highly relevant end of the conversation and joined in. This conspicuous omission underscores her exclusion from the male-dominated debate.

In fact, the portrayal of this female teacher is not at all positive. This is largely on account of the overall inconsequentiality and indifference with which it is drawn. In contrast to the characterization of Professor Virgodamo, there is a striking omission of information about her, particularly as regards her work. Unlike Professor Virgodamo, whose pupil she once was, Maestrina Terrasi's teaching job is completely glossed over, never forming the basis of discussion. Virgodamo's subject, on the other hand, is pedagogy, the science of teaching itself, and is the topic of a prolonged dialogue, during the course of which he maintains that girls should not be educated in the first place. In other words, the details of her work, for which the Professor himself has, however reluctantly, trained her, are deemed irrelevant and remain undisclosed, let alone discussed. Furthermore, as the difference in their titles indicates, the Professor teaches, or rather has taught, at a higher level than she does (he has now retired from training female student teachers, while she teaches young children).

The received notion of biological incompatibility between femininity and intellectual (and by implication, educational) activities is reiterated in *All For the Best* (1920). When Lori reminisces about his deceased wife, Silvia the teacher, he recalls how she 'wanted to dominate using her intelligence'. He goes on to say: 'But when a woman is beautiful . . . you only look at her eyes, her mouth . . . at how she looks. And you smile at those lips which are speaking, without paying attention to what they say' (Act III). It appears that Silvia colluded with this process, herself reinforcing the stereotypical incompatibility between intellect and feminine beauty: 'She would notice at once, and it would irritate her; but afterwards – being a woman – she would smile with the same smile of whoever was looking at her lips.' As we saw earlier, it was not possible for the beautiful Silvia to pursue her career without involving her sexuality in some way, and Lori recalls that it was at the time when she resumed teaching that she must have begun her affair with Manfroni.

On a more covert level, several instances of unquestioned, implicitly low levels of education in female characters serve to reproduce the status quo in this aspect of patriarchy. In *Belonging to One Person or to*

No-One (1929), Melina, pleading to keep her child and insisting that she would still have sufficient time to cater to the needs of Tito and Carlino, argues that 'looking after you as I do, tending to your laundry and your clothes, I have a lot of spare time – so much so that, as you know, I have learnt to read and write all by myself' (Act II). The fact that she has become literate through her own efforts is clearly a positive feature. However, the fact that she was illiterate in the first place is not. What is more, the former illiteracy of this ex-prostitute, who now provides a variety of personal services exclusively to Tito and Carlino, serves to highlight the superior level of their education, which is sufficient to enable them to be employed by the state as secretaries.

In a similar vein, knowledge of Latin emerges as an exclusively male domain in *Each in Their Own Way* (1924). When the two elegant young men and Diego Cinci come across the two young ladies ('Giovani Signore') in Lady Livia Palegari's salon, one of the male characters breaks into Latin, quoting Cicero. Although one of the female characters recognizes it as Latin ('Pardon?' she asks 'Are you speaking in Latin?'), it is obvious that neither of them understands the quotation. The second young man explains that his companion is citing Cicero, adding that he still remembers this author from his schooldays, and when the other female character asks what it means, he gives a translation. His knowledge of Latin, together with his use of the term *liceo*, suggests that he used to attend the classical (rather than the scientific) type of upper middle school (*scuola media superiore*), the institution which prepares pupils for university over a five-year period. It seems likely that these two female characters have not had this level of education, or indeed studied at an *istituto magistrale*, for example, where they would have learnt Latin. Figures for female attendance at *licei* for the year 1923–4 show that male students were indeed much more numerous (13,534 males to 3,175 females).[20]

Despite the fact that female students were not absent from the *licei* (indeed a small number (7) of these schools existed solely for women), no such educational reference ever occurs in the case of female characters, who are represented, here as in the previous play, in such a way as to provide an uneducated foil to the erudition of their male companions on stage.[21] This process continues as the three male characters then proceed to hold a seminar on the implications of Cicero's concept of conscience, leaving the female characters stranded intellectually and unable to contribute anything other than inanities. Furthermore, this philosophical discussion contrasts strongly with the nature of the preceding

20. Istat (1922–5).
21. Ibid.

communication between the two female characters, a conversation revolving, rather stereotypically, exclusively around affairs of the heart, as one quizzes the other on how she thinks her lover looked when she saw him last.

Two female characters who, by contrast, have received an education, are the wealthy, middle-class Laura and Giulietta in *The Grafting* (1921). However, this has not taken place in the public context of a school, but in the private context of home tuition, during the course of which they have been taught English, French, music and, in the case of Laura, painting. This education, which is not preparatory either to university or to the world of work, has been very much an acquisition of finishing-school accomplishments and, as their mother points out, consists of activities which cease upon marriage. At this point, she says, these achievements become merely ornamental, as wifely and maternal duties take over. It is notable, moreover, that Laura, who is married but childless, and has continued to paint, is raped while she is outside pursuing this activity.

Child Characters and Education Further to the above representations of limitation or absence of education in relation to female characters, it is interesting to note that when allusions to the education of child characters occur, these characters are inevitably male. The gymnasium where Professor Toti teaches in *Think It Over, Giacomino* (1917) (in other words, the two-year section of the upper middle school which links the lower middle school with the *liceo classico* attended by the young man in *Each In Their Own Way* (1924)) appears to have only male pupils. All references to these pupils are in the masculine. Although the recurring generic masculine plurals (*alunni* and *scolari*) may include female children, whenever the singular form occurs (that is, the form which is indicative of gender in the case of both these words), it is always in the masculine (*alunno* and *scolaro*). Other words used to denote these pupils are also always in the masculine (*giovinotto, ragazzi, ragazzini* and *fanciulli*); Giacomino himself was once Toti's *scolaro*.

However, according to educational statistics for that period, state-owned schools of this type were attended by both male and female pupils, even if male children predominated.[22] It seems likely, then, that the presence of female pupils in this play is being misrepresented and indeed suppressed. Moreover, in Toti's view the pupils in his school have made the environment unsavoury with 'all the foul language which [they] (*alunni*) imprint on the walls and benches'. This, he says, has

22. In the year 1916–7, 39,832 males as opposed to 11,567 females attended the *ginnasio* (Istat, 1919–22).

played a part in the young female cleaner at the school, Lillina, falling pregnant. The implication here is once again that the pupils are all male. In terms of the plot and of audience interest, the actual gender of these pupils is clearly rather insignificant. However, it is imperceptible detail such as this which plays an important part in the covert reinforcement of the status quo.

In a similar vein, all three of Professor Paolino's private pupils are male in *Man, Beast and Virtue* (1919). Belli and Giglio are learning history, geography, Latin and Greek, and the eleven-year old Nonò, Latin (all subjects in preparation, possibly, for the *liceo classico*, and contrasting with those taken by Laura and Giulietta in *The Grafting* (1921)). In *Bellavita* (1928) a discussion takes place about sending the young Michelino to Naples for a better education, whilst in *Lazarus* (1929), it is a male child, Lucio, who is educated in a seminary from the age of six, and later goes on to university. In *The Life I Gave You* (1924), Donna Anna's son left home in order to study engineering in Liège and Nice. However, for the young male children of the peasant Liolà just as for the working-class Lillina when she was a child, there is no question of an education. As Liolà points out, as soon as his sons are old enough they will help to increase the family's wealth by working on the land, and Lillina's parents similarly put her to work as a cleaner from an early age. This brings us to the issue of class in relation to education.

Class and Education   While Liolà's young boys will be groomed for working on the land, their middle-class counterparts, as we have seen, will be learning a variety of academic subjects in preparation for the *liceo* and possibly university. Several descriptions of older male students indicate that education is indeed related to wealth and a middle- or upper-class belonging. In *The Festival of Our Lord of the Ship* (1924), two young men appear on stage described as follows: 'of gentlemanly appearance (possibly students)', while the pair of young men quoting Cicero from their schooldays at the *liceo* in *Each in Their Own Way* (1924) are 'very elegant' (in other words, expensively dressed). Class distinctions within male gender are thus maintained by the educational system. This is also evidenced by instances when male domestics are ridiculed precisely for their lack of education by their more educated male employers. In a manner reminiscent of the virtual exclusion of the two young 'ladies' from the intellectual discussion of the three male characters in *Each in Their Own Way* (1924), 'Henry' in *Henry IV* (1922) and Laudisi in *That's How It Is (If You Think So)* (1918) run philosophical circles around their bewildered manservants.

Lack of education, then, places not only female, but also certain male characters, in a subordinate position, resulting in an implicit alignment of middle-class female with lower-class male characters on account of their shared low-level education. Female domestics, too, are the butt of their educated male employers' criticism; one example is Lisa, the maid in the Carpani household in *Mrs Morli, One And Two*, who is portrayed as being unable to remember the names of visitors correctly, and explains that her employer chastises her for this. In an interesting class (but not gender) reversal, it is the male gardener in *The Grafting* (1921) who educates the middle-class Laura on the 'natural' facts of life. With a lesson on the forceful manual grafting of (female) plants in order to produce fruit, this female character, who is pregnant as the result of a rape, 'learns' to naturalize the experience and, by means of this allegory, to accept and even love the fruit of her rapist's labours.

We can conclude that education is represented in the plays as a privilege which is both class and gender related; a privilege which is, in other words, available to the middle and upper classes, rather than to the lower classes, and to male, rather than to female, characters, the higher the level of education involved. These issues of class and gender are inseparable: a character from the normally subordinate female gender may, by virtue of belonging to the dominant middle or upper class, achieve higher levels of education than a male character from a lower class. An example of this is the contrast between the male peasant children's impending lack of education in *Liolà*, and the private tuition (albeit in 'ornamental' accomplishments) enjoyed by the middle-class female characters in *The Grafting*. However, female characters are not, as we have seen, represented in the plays as being on an equal footing educationally and intellectually with male characters of their own class. A particularly interesting non-dramatic representation of an intellectual female character will be discussed in the Appendix.

Leisured Female Characters

Marriage, Family and Class

As we have seen, the great majority of working female characters portrayed in Pirandello's plays are single and without families. The exceptions either belong to the impoverished lower class, in which the entire family works, or appear as middle-class female characters without families. In the latter case, an enforced choice between work and marriage frequently becomes a crucial plot issue in itself. By contrast, all non-working female characters are either married or living with their families. These are the leisured middle- and upper-class female characters who, with the aforementioned exceptions, are financially secure without having to work.

This is in direct contrast to their peasant- and working-class equivalents, who have to work whatever their marital and familial circumstances.

Most of Pirandello's leisured female characters are economically dependent on their husbands, while the few who are unmarried live in their parents' home. Others are widowed, or have lost their fathers, and live on inherited income, or, in the case of the former, may be supported by their working sons. In the final section we shall be exploring the implications in the plays of the actual price of such dependency, a price which is measured in terms of female identity and self-determination. Let us now take a closer look at the different types of economic dependency outlined above, together with the occupations of those male characters who are providing financial security for their female dependents.

Table 1 gives details of major leisured female characters (wife – w, wife and mother – wm, daughter – d, mother – m) together with the occupation of the husband, father or son, when known:

Table 1 Female Dependants and Their Male Providers

Character	Play	Occupation of husband/father/son
Giulia (wm)	*The Epilogue*	Land Manager
Anna (wm)	*A Doctor's Duty*	Land Contractor
Amalia (wm)	*That's How It Is (If You*	District Councillor
Dina (d)	*Think So)*	" "
Mrs Ponza (w/d)	" "	Prefectural Secretary
Mrs Frola (m)	" "	" "
Rosinella (d)	*The Licence*	Unemployed
(sister)	" "	" "
Beatrice (w)	*Cap and Bells*	Bank Principal
Nina (w)	" "	Clerk
Silia (w)	*The Rules of the Game*	Independent Means
Mrs Perella (wm)	*Man, Beast and Virtue*	Sea Captain
Palma (d)	*All For the Best*	Senator
(w)	" "	Independent Means
Laura (w)	*The Grafting*	Unknown
Evelina (wm)	*Mrs Morli, One and Two*	Lawyer
Lucia (w)	" "	Lawyer
Lucia (wm)	*The Life I Gave You*	Businessman
The Wife (wm)	*The Festival of Our Lord of the Ship*	Unknown
Serafina (d)	" "	" "
The Wife (w)	" "	Notary
The Wife (w)	" "	Lawyer
Elena (w)	*The Wives' Friend*	Independent Means/ Lawyer

Anna (w)	" "	Lawyer
Rosa (w)	" "	State Deputy
Erminia (wm)	" "	State Councillor
Marta (d)	" "	State Councillor
Mrs Contento	*Bellavita*	Lawyer
Young Married Lady	*I Dream (But Perhaps Not)*	Unknown
Giovanna (wm)	*When One Is Somebody*	Writer
Valentina (d)	" "	" "
Natascia (w)	" "	Editor
Ginevra (w)	*One Doesn't Know How*	Marine Official
Countess Bice (w)	" "	Independent Means
Murdered Woman (w)	*At the Exit*	Unknown
The Wife (w)	*The Man With the Flower in His Mouth*	Unknown
Livia (d)	*As Others See It*	Unknown

One other, aged female character could be included in this table, were it not for her decision to become a beggar, rather than recognize Rocco (the child of a rape) as her son and accept the home and financial support he offers her. This is Maragrazia, in the peasant play *The Other Son*, who finds herself destitute in her final years. She is too old to work (she is over seventy), and her two other sons have emigrated to America without trace.

A few other female characters have lost their male providers (whose occupations while alive remain unknown in most cases), and appear to survive on inherited income:

Table 2 Female Characters of Independent Means

Character	Play
Maddalena (wm)	*The Pleasure of Honesty*
Agata (d)	" "
Francesca (wm)	*The Grafting*
Mrs Barbetti (wm)	*All For the Best*
Marchioness Matilde (wm)	*Henry IV*
Frida (d)	" "
Donna Anna (wm)	*The Life I Gave You*
Donna Livia (wm)	*Each in Their Own Way*
Mother (m)	*The Fable of the Changeling*

There are two notable exceptions to the trend shown in Table 2, namely two cases of widowed female characters, both mothers, who are economically dependent on other female characters, namely their daughters. They are Marta, the mother of Sina the singer in *Sicilian Limes*, and the Mother of the Stepdaughter in *Six Characters in Search of an Author*. Interestingly, both of the occupations pursued by these daughters are negatively portrayed, in that they are associated with the selling of sexual favours. This is particularly the case as regards the Stepdaughter, who works as a prostitute, but Sina's career as popular singer is also perceived as taking place in the context of sexual services.

A survey of the occupations followed by male providers in Table 1 shows that they belong mostly to the professional middle classes in the upper echelons of the tertiary sector. A few male providers, some of them from the titled upper class, appear to live on independent means and do not need to work. Of the deceased providers indicated in Table 2, the first two can be presumed to have belonged to at least the professional middle classes, given the apparent lack of financial problems of their widows and children, while the titles of some of the other widows ('marchioness' and 'lady') indicate that they were from the upper class and therefore probably had independent means. These two tables illustrate, not surprisingly, that the non-working status of a female character is directly related to her class affiliation. No female characters from the peasant or working class appear in these tables. As we shall see in the next two sections, however, this leisured, non-working status is not without pernicious side-effects.

Stasis vs Mobility

In the section on working female characters, we noted that even when these characters do work, the type of work that the majority of them do means that they are still located very much in and around the domestic, home environment. (The exceptions to this are the sexually connotative occupations of acting, modelling, singing, dancing and, of course, prostitution.) The location of the non-working female character inside the home is even more marked. Extreme cases were examined in the section dealing with the enclosure of female characters (wives and daughters) as an element of male policing. It was suggested that one effective means of escape from such policing, as well as from all the other negative effects of patriarchy on women, was to be found in the economic sphere. In other words, by calling a halt to economic dependence on male providers and entering the public, outside world of work (a solution for which Italian feminists of the time were fighting). For the non-working female characters under scrutiny in this section, the stifling effects of being 'inside' are still apparent. In connection with those extreme cases of enclosure which have already been examined, I now wish to develop the notion of stasis specifically in relation to non-working female characters. The aim will be to contrast this with the paramount mobility of male characters, a mobility which, in the majority of cases, is closely linked to their work.

Several plays show female characters waiting at home for the return of the male provider (in most cases husbands or fathers). In the plays already examined for various types of enclosure, examples of such characters are Mrs Ponza (*That's How It Is (If You Think So)* 1918), Beatrice and Nina (*Cap and Bells,* 1918), Mommina (*Tonight We Improvise,* 1930), Silia (*The Rules of the Game,* 1919) and Rosinella (*The Licence,* 1918). All of these characters are wives except for Rosinella, who is a daughter. At the beginning of this chapter we noted that the location 'home' is often represented dramatically by the stage itself, a considerable number of plays being set in the family home, and particularly in the drawing-room, that area of the home where all visitors to the real-life middle- and upper-class household would duly be shown by the maid or manservant. On the other hand, peasant plays such as *Liolà* (1917), *The Jar* (1917), and *The Other Son* (1925) are set outside, with the action often taking place while all the characters are actually working.

We began this chapter with the particularly striking example of Beatrice in *Cap and Bells* (1918). She is at home (in other words, on stage or within earshot) during the entire play, while her husband does not come home once (he never appears on stage). Similarly we find Giulia looking out of the window of her home at the beginning of *The Epilogue* (1898). Crochet work in hand, she awaits the return of both husband and lover from a work-related trip they have taken to another town. She remains 'inside' (on stage) throughout the play, while the male characters come and go from the outside world of work. The only time she leaves the room (the stage) is to go to yet another room (off-stage) at the end of the play, and then only in order to shoot herself (a shot which is heard on stage).

The Man With the Flower in His Mouth (1926) shows a husband (the Man) complaining that his wife wants him to stay inside the home with her. He describes her desire for him to 'enjoy the perfect order of all the rooms, the gleaming furniture', thereby acknowledging the home to be typically her territory, rather than his. Her head appears tentatively from time to time, as she follows him into his (outside) territory in a vain attempt to lure him back inside. Two more plays indicate an association of the female dependant with the 'inside'. There is no evidence to suggest that either Agata or her mother leave the home during the course of *The Pleasure of Honesty*. And the Young Married Lady in *I Dream (But*

Perhaps Not) remains in her drawing-room (or, in her dream, bedroom), while her lover comes and goes (in both rooms). What is more, both conversations with the lover centre on the expensive jewellery she is expecting to be given, thereby highlighting her economic dependency on men from the 'outside'.

Of course, not all non-working female characters are portrayed in the situation of stasis outlined above. Alongside those who do not leave the home, there are some who do. In these cases, however, they often go out merely in order to visit the homes of others. In other words, they move to yet another private, 'inside' location. For example, Amalia and Dina Agazzi in *That's How It Is (If You Think So)* (1918) visit Mrs Frola in the next apartment and also go to inspect the outside of Mrs Ponza's home; Silia in *The Rules of the Game* calls on her estranged husband in his home; Mrs Perella goes to the home of her son's tutor (who is also her lover) to tell him she is pregnant (a visit which he in fact considers unwise); Matilde and her daughter Frida visit 'Henry' in his 'castle' (in this unusual case involving issues of madness, it is the male character who, for once, remains firmly 'inside'); Nina is brought by her husband to the home of his employer in *Cap and Bells*; Marta, in *The Wives' Friend*, specializes in setting up the homes of other female characters; and Bice and Ginevra visit each other's homes in *One Doesn't Know How*. Under unusual circumstances, female characters occasionally leave their homes to visit male characters in their workplace. For example, Lidia in *As Others See It* goes to see her estranged husband at the newspaper office where he is a journalist, and Rosinella disobeys her father and leaves their home to call on the judge who will be trying his case in *The Licence*. Finally, by contrast, the childless Laura, in *The Grafting*, goes out not in order to pay a social visit, but to paint, and is promptly raped.

On the other hand, instances of female characters who actually travel outside their home towns, or even to other countries, are uncommon. The exceptions are those female characters working in the socially-stigmatized professions (the actresses Delia and Donata have travelled or will travel with their theatre companies in *Each in Their Own Way* (1924) and *Finding Oneself* (1932), respectively; Sina in *Sicilian Limes* (1911) has left Sicily to become a popular singer in northern Italy; and the models Tuda and Jonella in *Diana and Tuda* (1927) travel to find work). The few other cases of far-ranging travel on the part of female characters usually denote circumstances of an unusual nature. For example, Mrs Morli, who has two husbands (one legal and one common-law) travels between Florence and Rome in order to be with both of them and their respective children, during the course of *Mrs Morli, One And Two* (1922) (while Miss White, in the same play, has come to Italy from

England to work as a nanny in the Morli household). In *The Life I Gave You* (1924), the pregnant Lidia travels from Nice to Tuscany, having left her husband in the hope of joining her lover. And the Unknown Woman in *As You Desire Me* (1930), whose life history is nothing if not uncommon, has left Italy for Berlin as a result of having been raped during the war, and travels back again, during the course of the play, in order to try to ascertain her real identity.

For male characters, however, mobility outside home, town and country is the norm, rather than the exception, and is almost invariably work or, as we saw earlier, study-oriented (one exception being Maurizio's holiday travels not merely to the 'ordinary' destinations of Paris or Cairo, but to the Congo, 'the land of rubber and bananas', in *The Pleasure of Honesty* (1918)). In *The Epilogue* (1898), Giulia's husband and lover, who are working together, return from a trip to what appears to be the provincial capital, where they have spent two nights in a hotel. Lucia's husband, in *The Life I Gave You* (1924), has left their home in Nice for Paris, on business. She complains that he is not only obsessed with his work (a criticism which she holds in common with both Giulia and, in *All For the Best* (1920), Mrs Barbetti), but that he is also a womanizer.

Several examples of work-related male mobility in fact reveal a clear link with adultery on the part of the husband (a link which is, as we have seen, precisely what is feared by male characters as an inevitable consequence of female characters working, or, in extreme cases, merely leaving the home). While both Beatrice and Nina remain indoors, the latter under lock and key, Beatrice's husband commits adultery with Nina, the wife of his employee, in the rooms adjoining his workplace in *Cap and Bells* (1918). During the course of the play both he and Ciampa also travel overnight to Palermo from their small town in the interior of Sicily for various reasons connected with work, and it is on the husband's return, when he calls on his mistress before coming home, that his adultery is exposed. As this play, *The Epilogue* (1898), *Man, Beast and Virtue* (1919) and *One Doesn't Know How* (1935), all demonstrate, it is actually the husband's absence from the home which facilitates and even encourages the wife's adultery.

In the last of these plays, Ginevra, whose husband Giorgio is away at sea for eight months at a time as a marine official, commits adultery once with her friend's husband, Romeo. A double standard is in force, as Giorgio shoots Romeo when he finds out, despite the fact that he himself has had various affairs while away from home. Romeo has pointed this out earlier: 'And even you, Giorgio, good man that you are, are well aware of all you do, even the little deceits, which aren't sins, during the long absences . . . .' To this Giorgio replies laughingly, 'Oh, I've never concealed them from my wife; I'd have to consider her stupid otherwise, in not supposing, since I'm far away for so long, that . . .', and adds, 'women are different'. Among other arguments, then, he uses his work-related mobility to actually justify his adultery. In *Man, Beast and Virtue* (1919), Captain Perella, another sea-faring and therefore far-ranging male character, has gone so far as to set up an entire second family in Naples. Once again, the only recourse portrayed as presenting itself to the wife, in her husband's absence, is shown to lie not in possible work interests which she might wish to pursue, but in adultery, and, in this case, motherhood (in the form of a second child). So, while husbands leave their homes to travel far and wide in their work and, by extension, in their sexual lives, their non-working wives remain at home and, even from within this supposedly desexualized, private world, play out patriarchy's worst fears.

Emigration is another aspect of work-related mobility which, in these plays, appears to be the prerogative only of male characters.[23] Ferrante Morli returns to Italy from America in *Mrs Morli, One and Two* (1922), having left his young wife and child fourteen years previously after his business collapsed. The brother of Someone in *When One Is Somebody* (1933) is similarly reported to have emigrated to America, where he is making a successful living. Two of Maragrazia's sons left for Santa Fé in America many years previously in *The Other Son* (1925), and Tino Ligreci, a young peasant who has just finished military service, is about to emigrate there too, leaving behind, as the old peasant Jaco Spina complains, only 'old men, women and children'. Another male character is reputed to have returned to Italy from Java, where he has made his fortune, according to the Young Married Lady's lover at the end of *I Dream (But Perhaps Not)* (1929). This female character, while spending her time indoors reclining, day-dreaming and drinking tea with visitors, turns the mobility of her lovers to her advantage, as they travel in search of wealth with which to satisfy her expensive tastes (a dangerous game of exploitation, as her dream acknowledges). The overall incidence of male mobility, then, is much higher than in the case of female characters, who are represented as tending to remain at home, or in their home town, unless unusual circumstances dictate otherwise. The dream of the Young Married Lady, in which one of her lovers tries to strangle her, is indicative, among other things, of the fact that the economic dependence of female on male characters is a relationship which holds problems for both genders, but especially for the female.

23. Until 1927, when the Fascists suppressed the General Commissariat for Emigration and the emigration fund, government policy had, apart from the war years, supported emigration in an effort to counter unemployment. In his account, Glass refers only to men who sought work abroad. They were joined by their families, until this was prohibited in July 1928 (Glass, 1967, pp. 221–4).

The Price of Dependency

Dependent adult characters, examined in the context of marriage and the family within which they live out their dependency, are predominantly female in these plays, a trend that mirrors the pattern of the particular historical period in which they were written. Many more women than men were recorded as being maintained by family income, despite the fact that men outnumbered women.[24] Some representations of non-working female characters show them to be leading relatively unproblematic lives of financial security and leisure. In particular, two daughters, namely Dina, the daughter of a district councillor in *That's How It Is (If You Think So)* (1918), and Marta, the daughter of a state councillor in *The Wives' Friend* (1927), appear to have untroubled, carefree, if rather vacuous, existences. However, similarly troublefree portrayals of wives (and wives who are also mothers) seem to be more rare. For instance, even the mothers of these two daughters are each portrayed in such a way as to either deny them the same apparent peace of mind (Marta's mother is described as stiff, and barely opening her eyes), or to insinuate that they are living vicariously through their husbands (in the case of Dina's mother, who gives herself airs on account of her husband's position).

This type of vicarious living, whereby a female character does not work to fulfil her own potential, but acquires a 'false' status through the occupation of her husband, is one of various indications in the plays of the price to be paid for financial dependency. This price is most apparent in its limiting effects on feminine identity and self-determination. One such limitation, enforced on the physical as well as the non-physical plane, has been examined under the section on enclosure at the end of the previous chapter. We shall now turn to other ways in which financial dependency can be seen to work to the detriment of the dependent character, confining our attention to characters who are old enough to work.

The vicarious living out of a husband's high status by his non-working wife receives an unsympathetic portrayal in *That's How It Is (If You Think So)* (1918). Amalia Agazzi is described as 'behaving with ostentatious importance, on account of the position occupied by her husband in society'. Both she and her daughter busy themselves gossiping and investigating other people's private affairs. Laudisi remarks that this is

24. Out of a population of 17 million men and 16.8 million women in 1901, 6,983,605 women as opposed to 1,015,857 men were dependants, and in 1911, a population of 18.6 million men and 18.3 million women contained 8,075,556 female as opposed to 1,210,798 male dependants. (In 1901, 719,931 of the male dependants and 1,054,400 of the female dependants were aged under 15; figures for 1911 are 866,279 male and 1,225,915 female dependants aged under 15) (Istat, 1911).

precisely 'because you have nothing to do'. (He then, however, proceeds to mastermind the investigation of the Ponza family himself, and there is in the last resort no indication that he does anything else either.) While the leisured Amalia and Dina Agazzi are by no means alone in occupying themselves with gossiping (an activity which translates itself, in the case of Laudisi, into the more laudable pursuit of the quest for truth), there is a suggestion here that when women, as opposed to men, are idle, they spend their time worthlessly. In other words, it is for their underlying dependency that Laudisi's criticism (albeit challenged with wit by Dina), together with the negative portrayal of Amalia, makes both these female characters pay.

A more damning portrayal of a female character, who, like Amalia, lives through her husband's identity, rather than her own, is that of Giovanna, wife of 'Somebody' in *When One Is Somebody* (1933). While he has forged a powerful identity for himself with his successful occupation as a writer, she is described as the 'statuesque, shapely, but rigid personification of her husband's official glory'. This description contrasts sharply with that of Giaffredi, the minister of state who accompanies her on to the stage. He is characterized as 'authoritative but smiling, someone of recognized superiority who cannot countenance not being obeyed; accustomed to moving in the high spheres of finance and politics'. Along with Someone's wife, both son and daughter are also depicted as being little more than living extensions of their famous father. Economic dependency can therefore lead to the lives of both female and male dependants being lived in the shadow of the provider.

Absence of identity and lack of self-determination characterize the leisured Silia, estranged wife of Leone Gala in *The Rules of the Game* (1919). Although living apart for the last three years, and despite the fact that his wife has a lover, her husband continues to support her in what appears to be a comfortable life-style. Silia is aware that he has made her 'rich' and 'free', and concludes, interestingly, that in fact 'this has been his revenge'. She exclaims to her uncomprehending lover: 'But what good is it if I am never myself!', and then proceeds to explain why she is not, as her lover maintains, free. 'Him! I always see him, who has given it to me, this liberty, as if it were a trifle, going off to live on his own, and showing me for three years that it doesn't exist, this famous liberty, because, however I avail myself of it, I will always be enslaved' (Act I, sc. 1). In her frustration she wills her husband dead, and even conspires with her lover to try to manipulate Leone into fighting a duel with the formidable aristocrat, Miglioriti. The fact that the frustration of this dependent female character is voiced at all can be interpreted in one sense as the representation of a feminine position. However, as is so often the case in Pirandello, this position makes a fleeting appearance only to be recuperated for the purposes of the overriding patriarchal ideology. This process can be seen at work in the way in which narrative closure is brought about. Silia's frustration finds an outlet which is neither radical nor successful. She employs the stereotypically feminine device of pitting one man against the other, thereby continuing her dependency on men. This is a game which Leone easily wins. He outwits Silia, and it is her lover who in the end is forced to fight, receiving a fatal wound as a result. Leone is the play's voice of reason, the character with whom the audience empathizes. His repeated references to his wife as a child, together with her malevolent and ineffectual plot on his life, all conspire to create a portrayal of this female character which is ultimately negative.

Silia's financial dependency and resulting lack of self-determination mean that she has no power in the relationship with her husband. Beatrice likewise struggles ineffectively, not only against her husband, but also against his employee, Ciampa, in *Cap and Bells* (1918). When she schemes to reveal her husband's adultery, and so change her situation of powerlessness, she discovers that she not only has her husband to contend with. She, too, fails in a struggle of wits, and ends up conceding not a lover, but her sanity. The powerlessness inherent in this type of financial dependency, as manifested by these two different types of marital relationship, can therefore be seen to extend to other interlinking relationships, such as that between the wife and her husband's colluding employee.

Another type of relationship over which the dependent female character has no control, is that between herself and her child. In *The Epilogue* (1898), Giulia is forbidden by her husband ever to see her children again when he learns of her adultery. She accepts his verdict and shoots herself in the ultimate expression of powerlessness. Melina, in *Belonging to One Person or to No-One* (1929), is similarly portrayed as not having the power to keep her child, and dies broken-hearted as a result. Although the two male characters on whom she is financially and emotionally dependent withdraw only their emotional support (they disapprove of her keeping a child whose paternity is uncertain), this is sufficient to drive her to her death. Once again, the female character is portrayed in self-destructive mode and in collusion with values which ensure her dependency and impotence. Death is therefore represented in these plays as the ultimate but seemingly inevitable price to be paid by the dependent female character.

The point of view of the male character on whom the female character is dependent, on the other hand, is expressed in instances of the topos of woman as financial drain on the male provider. This negative stereotype, which developed alongside the gendered division between male production and female consumption, is evoked by certain remarks.[25] Totina comments that 'it is one of the greatest satisfactions, for us women, to make men pay' (*Tonight We Improvise*, 1930, Int. sc. 1). *But It's Not Serious* (1919) is based on this stereotype. Memmo is so wary of both the financial and emotional demands he believes a wife would make on him, that he goes to the inordinate lengths of arranging for himself a marriage in name only, in order to pre-empt such a situation. His choice of Gasparina is based on her exceptional thriftiness and frugality, as well as on her physical unattractiveness, and reinforces the received truth that wives, as a rule, are a drain on their husband's resources.

The Young Married Lady in *I Dream (But Perhaps Not)* (1929) is an extreme representation of this feared stereotype. She is portrayed actively encouraging her lovers, of which there are at least two, to buy expensive jewellery for her. The first lover, who appears on stage, has won some money gambling and is eager to spend it on her, while the second lover, to whom he unwittingly refers, has just returned from Java a wealthy man. Dramatic irony is played out at the visiting lover's expense, as his entrance is immediately preceded by a scene in which the Young Married Lady examines a pearl necklace sent to her by her second lover, a necklace which the first lover had consequently been unable to purchase for her. The underlying guilt which she feels towards this lover, and which presumably gives rise to the dream in which he tries to strangle her, is not apparent as she later listens to his regrets at not having been able to buy the necklace for her.

Furthermore, her suggestively erotic pleasure in handling the necklace (she 'admires it, smiles, presses it with both hands to her breast and half closes her eyes') links erotic with economic desire, as she deceives and drains men both financially and, by implication, sexually. As her dream of being strangled by her first lover would seem to indicate, the punishment for this is a violent death. Her 'murder' is reminiscent of that of the Murdered Woman (*At the Exit* (1916)), whose insatiable sexual appetite and draining of her lover's sexual resources would, as her husband predicts, result in her murder. In the case of the Young Married Lady, then, the playing out of what appears on the surface as the mildly

25. Hamilton, writing about the transition from the feudal to the bourgeois family, says: 'Women, furthermore, in popular mythology, if not in reality, are seen as the prime agents of . . . consumption, whether modest or conspicuous, and men as the chief producers. The feudal family was a self-sufficient economic unit . . . The point to be made is that production and consumption were coterminous, inter-related and both embedded in the economy of the household. . . The identification of men with production and women with consumption awaited the emergence of capitalism. Even then, at first it only properly fitted the bourgeoisie. For working-class women were swept into the proletariat along with their children' (Hamilton, 1980, pp. 24–5).

negative topos of the economically (and sexually) demanding, 'spend-thrift' woman, culminates in a potentially violent resolution for the offending female dependant.

All the female characters so far described in this section have been financially dependent on male providers, and are also represented as paying some sort of price for their dependency. One of these characters, however, was not always in such a disadvantaged position. This is Giulia, in *The Epilogue* (1898), whose marriage began with her as the wealthy partner, and her husband as the dependant. As he acknowledges, he was penniless when she eloped with him, against the will of her brothers. He then worked hard, using her money, and admits that, 'If I have made myself rich, the merit is yours.' However, his use of 'myself', rather than 'us', indicates how the financial situation has reversed over the years. Her money has disappeared; now it is he who is the wealthy one and in a position to order her summarily out of the house.

One female character who, exceptionally, retains a position of financial superiority over her husband, is Livia in *As Others See It* (1916). However, she is only able to do so by virtue of being the daughter of a wealthy and influential father. In this marriage, it is she who holds the power, and her husband who is dependent and submissive. He not only accepts full responsibility for his adultery, which has resulted in the birth of a child, but is also portrayed as suitably humble, penitent and full of gratitude to his wife for allowing him to continue living in the marital home, albeit separately. Leonardo works as a journalist and novelist in an unsuccessful attempt to maintain his second family, and is heavily in debt. However, Livia is not portrayed entirely sympathetically, and is in fact made to pay a price for her dominance. The play opens with a scene in which she comes to her husband's office to warn him of the imminent arrival of her father. D'Albis, her husband's colleague, tries unsuccessfully to persuade her to forgive Leonardo and pay his debts. His failure leads him to describe her afterwards in negative terms, which suggest that she is not all that a woman should be, and which imply, by extension, that she is frigid (a particularly relevant detail given the central issue of her childlessness discussed earlier): 'She's an awful woman, my dear chap . . . with those eyes . . . *cold* . . . hard' (Act I, my italics). This assessment is given credibility by D'Albis's earlier philosophizing, a discourse which always enjoys high status in the plays.

What is more, by the end of the play she has even managed to achieve her one all-consuming desire, namely to be a mother. As she herself has no children (she is, after all, frigid), she does this by using the persuasiveness of her wealth and position in order to take her husband's young daughter away from her mother, who is left weeping as the final curtain falls. This ending directs audience sympathy, once again, away from the powerful wife. While Leonardo, then, is a rare example of a dependent husband, and is appropriately portrayed, the female provider does not enjoy the same positive status as her male equivalents in terms of representation. In other words, this play shows that there is a price to be paid for independence too.[26]

26. In a preface which Pirandello added to the 1917 edition of the play after its poor reception at the première, he in fact refers to the novelty and originality of Livia, but concludes by commenting that she does not cut a particularly pleasant figure. He also refers to the way in which a leading actress would (and indeed did) opt for the part of Elena, for whom there would be more audience sympathy, rather than for that of Livia, the play's actual female protagonist (see also Ragusa, 1980, p. 65). I am indebted to Jennifer Lorch for drawing both of these references to my attention.

PART II

–5–

Reconstructing the Family:
The Power of Speech in *Six Characters in Search of an Author*

MOTHER: You know how to speak, I don't.
Six Characters in Search of an Author, Act I

Introduction: Family Matters

In this part we take a closer look at the family, that particular constellation of socio-economic relationships which structures interpersonal existence within patriarchy. As a microcosm of the Western nation-state, the family unit organizes its members along hierarchical power lines, with the father at its head, thereby preparing them for relations of authority and subordination beyond the family. The role of the family in reproducing appropriately conditioned members of an authority-based patriarchal society, and the consequences of this role for the position of women within the family, was expertly theorized by Horkheimer, writing as part of the Critical Theory School in 1936. His essay *Authority and the Family* draws together a variety of issues relevant to a thorough-going consideration of the function of the family, and welds them into a useful theoretical framework. This framework provides the necessary context for the following twin analyses of *Six Characters in Search of an Author*, a play which focuses in great part, as we shall see, on the family as a crucial social unit. There now follows a detailed outline of the salient points of this seminal essay which are of particular relevance to our purpose.

Horkheimer prefaces his comments on the family with an essential statement of the importance of authority as a theoretical concept: 'authority proves ever more clearly to be a dominant category in the historian's apparatus of concepts' (Horkheimer, 1972, p. 68). He establishes that, although it may take on different forms, depending on the period in question, authority itself is a trans-historical hallmark of any society:

all . . . forms of society are marked by the superordination or subordination of classes. . . Amid all the radical differences between human types from different periods of history, all have in common that their essential characteristics are determined by the power-relationships proper to society at any given time. (ibid., pp. 68–9)

In a foreshadowing of feminism's motto 'the personal is political', he emphasizes that '[T]he class system within which the individual's outward life runs its course is reflected not only in his mind, his ideas, his basic concepts and judgments, but also in his inmost life, in his preferences and desires' (ibid., pp. 69, 91). Important arguments on the historically-determined pros and cons of authority and attitudes towards it, culminating in 'the deification of naked authority as such' on the part of bourgeois thought (ibid., p. 72), lead us into the relationship of the individual to authority, or power-relationships, in the state, through the mediating institution of the family.

One of the historically variable factors which affects the precise nature of this relationship is the particular means of production in force. Horkheimer's section on the family begins:

> The relation of individuals to authority is determined by the special character of the work process in modern times and gives rise, in turn, to a lasting collaboration of social institutions in producing and consolidating the character types which correspond to the relationship. (ibid., pp. 97–8)

One such institution is the family:

> The family, as one of the most important formative agencies, sees to it that the kind of human character emerges which social life requires, and gives this human being in great measure the indispensable adaptability for a specific authority-oriented conduct on which the existence of the bourgeois order largely depends. (ibid., p. 98)

'Christianity', he points out, 'had, of course, recognized long ago the family's task of educating men to live under authority in society.' He then quotes from works of St Augustine (a) and a work on Lutheranism (b), both of which clearly define the relationship between the patriarchal family, male domination and the state (a relationship which is clearly transhistorical, given the different periods to which these quotations apply):

> a) . . . that domestic peace has a relation to civic peace – in other words, that the well-ordered concord of domestic obedience and domestic rule has a relation to the well-ordered concord of civil obedience and civil rule. And therefore it follows, further, that the father of the family ought to frame his

domestic rule in accordance with the law of the city, so that the household may be in harmony with the civic order. (ibid., p. 99)[1]

b) . . . the very essence of Lutheranism, which looks upon the physical superiority of man as the expression of a superior relationship willed by God, and a stable order as the chief end of all social organizations. The house-father represents the law, and possesses unlimited power over others; he is the breadwinner, the pastor, and the priest of his household. (ibid., p. 100)[2]

The conclusion, then, is that '[i]n this kind of familial situation, with its determinative influence on the child's education, we find anticipated in large measure the structure of authority as it existed outside the family' (ibid.).

We are now in a position to move, along the trajectory of authority, from the public, outside world of the patriarchal state into the private, inside world of the patriarchal family (a direction, as we have just seen, which in reality leads both ways, dialectically). At this point we can already perceive the power hierarchy within the family, an order of superordination (or domination) and subordination which is determined by gender and, in the bourgeois consumer, as opposed to the productive, family community, also by money-earning capability. This hierarchy does not derive, as Horkheimer points out, from any natural or religious truth (although this is how it is represented), but is related to economic factors such as earning-power:

the fact that in the average bourgeois family the husband possesses the money, which is power in the form of substance, and determines how it is to be spent, makes wife, sons, and daughters even in modern times 'his,', puts their lives in large measure into his hands, and forces them to submit to his orders and guidance. (ibid., p. 105)

The subordination of women is located specifically in the context of this hierarchical organization of the patriarchal family. Following the line of argument used by Engels, who believed that 'The overthrow of mother-right was the world historical defeat of the female sex', Horkheimer holds the patriarchal system responsible for 'introduc[ing] mankind to class conflict and to the rupture between public and familial life, while within the family the principle of naked authority came to be applied' (ibid., p. 118). It is this 'principle of naked authority', in other words, hierarchized power-relations, which was absent under matriarchy, and which, under patriarchy, placed women in the position of being subordinate to men. Within the private, patriarchal family unit

1. Saint Augustine, *The City of God*, Book 19, chapter 16, translated by M. Dods, 1950, p. 695 (Horkheimer, 1972, p. 99, n. 39).
2. E. Troeltsch, *The Social Teaching of the Christian Churches*, translated by O. Wyon, 1931, p. 546 (ibid., p. 100, n. 41).

which functions to reproduce the authority principle as a means of ordering relations at the public level of patriarchal society, the role of the woman (as wife and mother) is to assist in this reproduction. One way in which she does this is simply by virtue of her dependency on her husband, which works to ensure *his* obedience to the authority of the public, patriarchal system. His own 'sense of economic and social responsibility for wife and child' deters him, in turn, from countering this all-embracing authority.

Woman's primary, and indeed all-exclusive role, as we saw in earlier chapters, is posited as lying within the confines of the family. In the context of the bourgeois consumer household (as opposed to the productive household), her function is accordingly reduced to that of reproducer of patrilineality, and of labour and military manpower. Horkheimer's quotation of Müller-Lyer's 1911 list of functions of the family appears to sum up the position of the wife and mother within it:

> the management of the household, the reproduction, rearing, and education of children, the control of population growth and of genetic lines, the development of sociableness, the care of the sick and elderly, the accumulation and hereditary transmission of capital and other property . . . (ibid., pp. 101–2)

It is important to bear in mind that, although basic correlates obviously apply, the subordination of women is variable in kind and degree according to class. As this second section concentrates on the play *Six Characters in Search of an Author*, we are therefore concerned in these two chapters with the bourgeois, professional middle class to which the Characters belong. They do so either as salary-earners (in the case of the Father and, until his death years before the beginning of the play, his rival and former secretary) or as dependants (the other five Characters). At the time of the play, in other words the period which the Characters relive on stage, the four now-destitute dependants of the dead man are relying on the Stepdaughter's income as a prostitute. Her chance encounter in the brothel with the Father, and the ensuing near-incestuous consummation which is pre-empted by the intervention of the horrified Mother, provides one of the central traumas which the Characters are compelled to re-enact.

The play appealed to Marinetti, who hailed it as a Futurist masterpiece after its first performance in Rome in 1921.[3] One cardinal Futurist aim

3. Marinetti (1968 [1924], p. 146). An earlier version of the remainder of this chapter appears in *The Yearbook of the British Pirandello Society*, nos 8 and 9, 1988–9, pp. 32–50, under the title '"Tu sai parlare: io no . . ": Reconstructing the Family in Pirandello's *Sei personaggi in cerca d'autore*'. This article grew out of a talk given to members of the Italian Department at the University of Kent in March 1987, and was read at the British Pirandello Society's Conference on 13 November 1988 at the University of Bristol. I should like to thank students and faculty members at both events for their comments.

was to break with tradition and with the past, and there is no doubt that, on the level of dramatic form, the play breaks new ground, in true *avant-garde* fashion. It is, however, true to say that the same archetypally traditional ideological stance which actually underpins the Futurist movement, also informs the play, particularly as far as family and gender relations are concerned. In this respect too, then, the play can be described as Futurist, in that it is fundamentally in tune with mainstream Futurism's patriarchal base (Marinetti even went so far as to glorify 'contempt for women', along with war and militarism, in his manifesto of 1909).[4]

Pirandello thus appears to fall into the Futurist paradox of, on the one hand, espousing *anti-passatismo*, while, on the other, perpetuating the traditional family/gender roles of the past. Nowhere is this encapsulated more succinctly than in the title of the play. Its reference to six characters and an author successfully foregrounds the literary/formal aspect, a favourite tenet of the *avant-garde* and contemporary Formalist theory. However, the play itself is not, as the egalitarian nature of the title misleadingly implies, about six characters who are equal in status, but about six members of a family structure with its own internal hierarchy. In effect, the dynamics of the play centre, if anything, less on the Character-producer, Character-actor or even Character-Character exchanges, than on the increasingly intense and absorbing interplay between the Characters *as family members*, an interplay with which the former exchanges become enmeshed.

It is this interplay between the characters as family members on which I intend to focus, in an attempt to make more 'visible' the traditional family/gender hierarchy which the play, while prioritizing issues of form, in fact subtends. The first obvious point to note in this connection is that the six Characters have no identity or existence outside their family roles, and four of them are named accordingly: Father (*Padre*), Mother (*Madre*), Stepdaughter (*Figliastra*), and Son (*Figlio*). The significance of the names Young Boy (*Giovinetto*) and Little Girl (*Bambina*) will be discussed shortly. Two proper, first names are mentioned purely incidentally (the Mother is called Amalia and the Little Girl, Rosetta). The family role of each character is therefore her/his defining feature, over and above any other identity. As the Father says of the Mother: 'She is not a woman, she is a mother.' Here the woman is differentiated from the role of mother and is, in effect, negated by it. In other words, and as we saw in chapter 1, womanhood *is* motherhood.

---

4. '9. We wish to glorify war – the only hygiene in the world – militarism, patriotism, the destructive gesture of libertarians, fine ideas for which one dies and contempt for women' (Marinetti, 1968 [1909], p. 10, my translation). For Futurism's less visible women's contributions, see, for instance, C. Salaris, *Le futuriste: donne e letteratura d'avanguardia in Italia* (1982).

The second point is that, perhaps in an attempt to fulfil the Futurist desire 'to fight against moralism', the subversive incest motif is introduced (Marinetti, 1968, p. 10). However, it is presented in such a way as to simultaneously construct and deconstruct itself. As has been pointed out, incest between father and daughter is actually sidestepped as a possibility from the start because the daughter is not the real daughter of the Father, but the Stepdaughter. And in the case of the Mother and the Son, the distant attitude of the latter empties the relationship of any sexual content (although the Little Girl's drowning is directly linked to the Mother being in the Son's bedroom) (Stone, 1980, p. 46).

The third major point is raised by the actual naming of the Stepdaughter, which is indicative of the traditionally patrilineal/patriarchal thrust of the play, rather than of any truly subversive, *avant-garde* direction. She is named/identified in relation to the Father, whose stepdaughter she is, rather than in relation to the Mother, whose real daughter she is, and in which case she could have been called Daughter. (Her real father, whom we shall call the Other Man, does not appear in the play.) The significance of how the six Characters are named becomes clear when we examine the precise nature of the family structure to which they belong. This consists, in effect, of an extended family (Ex) which is made up of two families, one which we shall call legitimate (L), on account of the status of the child (the Son), and the other, correspondingly, illegitimate (IL), as Figure 1 illustrates.

As the Stepdaughter clearly belongs to Family IL, the illegitimate family (the Other Man, the Mother, the Young Boy and the Little Girl), it is noteworthy that she is named in relation to Family L, the legitimate family (the Father, the Mother, and the Son), to which her only link, in fact, is her Mother. Her brother and sister, on the other hand, are not named in relation to any parent or family, be it Stepson and Stepdaughter (in relation to the Father and Family L, as in their elder sister's case), or Son and Daughter (in relation to the Mother and Family L, or the Mother, the Other Man and Family IL). In other words, none of the children of Family IL is named in relation to that Family. (Although this may be so as to avoid possible confusion, such an explanation would not account for the actual nature of the naming process.)

The ideological thrust of the play, in effect, is its support not just of the family, but, specifically, the legitimate nuclear family, as a positively valued social structure. If we look at how the play progresses, at the beginning both Family L and Family IL, except for the Other Man, are present together as an extended family made up of the six Characters: the Father, the Mother and the Son (who is their legitimate son), the Stepdaughter (who is the Mother's daughter by the Other Man) and the Young Boy and the Little Girl (who are both the Mother's by the Other

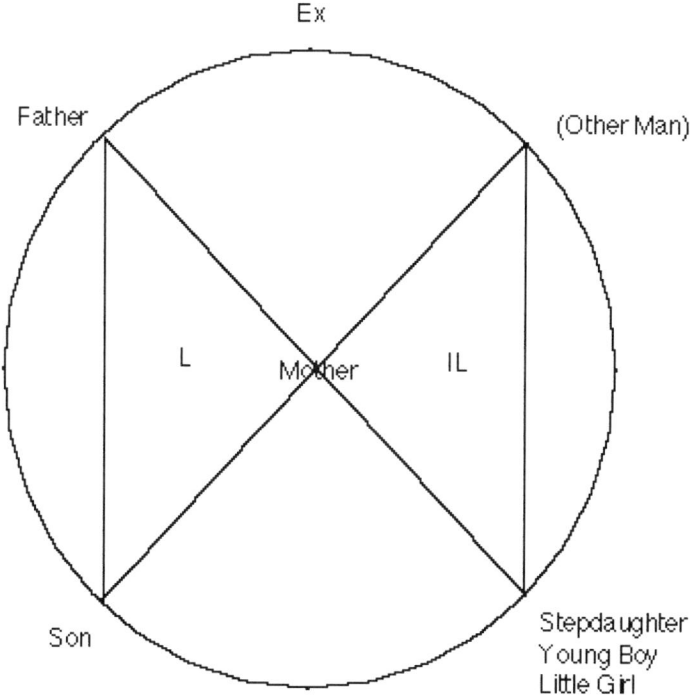

Figure 1 Family Structure in *Six Characters in Search of an Author*

Man). At the end of the play, we are left with legitimate, nuclear Family L: the Father, the Mother and the Son. In other words, the extended family has been 'purged' of its illegitimate members (the Little Girl drowns, the Young Boy shoots himself and the Stepdaughter runs off the stage and out through the auditorium) – a purging which is re-enacted, theoretically, each time the six Characters manage to find a stage.

If we take a closer look at the nature of the demise of the two younger children of the illegitimate family, we see how social class enters the picture to link up with gender. Their father, the Other Man, was inferior to the Father of the legitimate family: he was his 'subordinate' ('a poor man, my subordinate, my secretary . . . humble', Act I), and his son, the Young Boy, is said to be like him ('He really resembles his father! Humble; doesn't speak', Act I). When we also consider that in patriarchy, it is the male child who has most to gain, and furthermore is on the active side of the traditional active-male/passive-female dichotomy, it is significant that the Young Boy, the socially inferior Other Man's illegitimate, and thus doubly socially doomed son, shoots himself (a sort of real man's/honourable death, an escape from a society where his birth has placed him at an ineluctable disadvantage). The illegitimate Little Girl, on the other hand, dies by accident, passively. Or, seen on a different level, her death is due to the Mother's negligence/her intimated incestuous involvement with her legitimate male child, with whom she is desperately trying to communicate at the moment of the Little Girl's death. The neglect of the daughter in favour of the son also raises the problematic issue of the mother-daughter relationship within patriarchy, which is characterized at a deep level by an ambivalent attitude of mothers towards daughters.[5]

The purging of the three illegitimate children is structurally prefigured by the death of the head of the illegitimate family, the Other Man, before the beginning of the play. As a plot detail, his absence provides the narrative device which precipitates the plot of the drama the six Characters are compelled to re-enact: it causes the destitution of Family IL, who turn to the Father of Family L for financial help. They are thwarted by hostile encounters between the legitimate Son and the illegitimate Stepdaughter, leading to the Mother taking on work, in the form of sewing, from Madama Pace and the latter's employment of the Stepdaughter as a prostitute, and culminating in the Stepdaughter's climactic encounter with the Father in Madama Pace's brothel. The absence of the Other Man thus allows narrative space for the 'shocking' incest motif to be introduced.

It also allows the conflict characterizing relations between the Father and the Stepdaughter to take place, a conflict which is essentially that between the heads of two families. For the Stepdaughter has effectively taken over from the Other Man as *socio-economic head of Family IL*. She has acquired this status by being the main breadwinner of the family (there are, significantly, references to the Mother's inadequacy in this sphere, and the Young Boy and Little Girl are too young to work). The way in which she earns money for Family IL is signified by her presence in Madama Pace's brothel, and it is here, at her workplace, that her dramatic encounter with the head of Family L takes place, an encounter which signals the culmination of her subversively competitive role. On yet another level, this can be seen to signal the Father's prohibition/ denial of the (Step)Daughter's sexual desire.

Thus Family IL itself may not, in the ideological context of the play, continue to exist: it is illegitimate, has no male head, or even voice, and is, in effect, predominantly female, the only adults/speaking members

5. See p.27.

being women. Hence the Little Girl drowns, and the Young Boy shoots himself, significantly at the precise time when Mother and legitimate Son are together. And the Stepdaughter, as the concluding stage directions indicate, runs out of the theatre after repeatedly looking at Father, Mother and Son, the legitimate family, who are left on stage:

> She stops for a moment on the first step *to look at the other three*, and bursts out in stridulous laughter, then throws herself down the stairway; she runs across the gangway in between the seats; she stops once more and laughs again, *looking at the three left up on stage*; she disappears from the auditorium and again, from the foyer, her laughter is heard. Shortly afterwards the curtain falls. (*Six Characters in Search of an Author*, Act III)

There is no space for her in Family L. The departure of the last remaining illegitimate child, accompanied by stridulous (not triumphant) laughter, thus signals, inevitably, the end of the play, as the final stage of the purging of the extended family is completed.

As indicated earlier, the terms 'legitimate' and 'illegitimate' used to define Family L (Father, Mother, Son) and Family IL (Mother, Stepdaughter, Young Boy, Little Girl) describe the status of the children involved. This status of course derives from whether the parents are married or not. In the case of the Son in Family L, he was born to the married couple, the Father and Mother (and then sent out to be wet-nursed in the countryside, an apparently not uncommon practice in the urban middle classes) (Clark, 1984, p. 163). They later separated to enable the Mother to cohabit with the Other Man, by whom she had three illegitimate children.

Illegitimacy is as a rule negatively regarded in patrilineal culture (with the exception of particularly pro-natalist periods, usually around wartime, when even unmarried mothers are aided by state legislation in an attempt to increase the birth-rate, and propaganda works to temporarily counter the morality of peacetime).[6] It was not in fact until thirty years after Pirandello's death that illegitimacy ceased to be socially stigmatized. Golini, writing about illegitimacy and the first Italian orphanages of the thirteenth century, cites 1967 as the turning point, when a law for special adoption was introduced and marked 'the arrival point of a cultural movement directed towards the vindication of every child's right to an environment suited to its psycho-physical development'. It was not until 1975 that 'the reform of family law allowed for the near-total disappearance of abandoned children', at which time 'illegitimacy

---

6. The foundation of the Opera Nazionale per Maternità ed Infanzia on 10 December 1925 included support for unmarried mothers (Caldwell, 1986, pp. 112, 132; Glass, 1967, pp. 242–3).

and abandonment which marked the lives of millions of people – and which was common to all of Europe – was cancelled out after more than seven centuries' (Golini, 1988, p. 361). In 1921, when *Six Characters in Search of an Author* was performed, illegitimacy was therefore still socially marked as a 'marginal phenomenon which affected women of low social class' (ibid., p. 362). Figures for the periods 1911–20 and 1921–30 show that slightly over 95 per cent of births were legitimate, with the small minority of illegitimate births forming the exception and consequently being open to stigmatization (ibid., p. 362).

The purging of the three illegitimate children which is enacted in the play on a covert level, in other words, by means of a process which is not foregrounded, and which happens almost as if by chance, is therefore to be seen very much in the light of the prevailing morality of the time. The cohabitation of unmarried partners was similarly a minority phenomenon and, during the period when the play was written (and indeed until 1970, the year of the first divorce law), was probably accounted for by the sole possibility of legal separation once a marriage had failed.[7]

In addition to prioritizing marriage and legitimacy, the play also works to privilege the nuclear family (Family L) as opposed to the extended family (Family Ex). The term 'nuclear' refers to a family composed of one married couple with or without children; 'extended' refers to a family consisting of one married couple cohabiting with one or more relatives who may be ascendent (in the case of the vertical extended family) or collateral (in the horizontal extended family).[8] In our case, the nuclear family (L) is made up of a married couple and child (the Father, the Mother and the Son). The extended family (Ex), which is of the horizontal type, is made up of one married couple and four collateral relatives (the Son, the Stepdaughter, the Young Boy and the Little Girl). It is the Stepdaughter who is responsible for the actual composition of the six Characters into the particular familial form represented by the extended family unit which appears, however incohesively, at the beginning of the play. She has attempted to create the extended family unit via the amalgamation of her illegitimate family (IL) with the nuclear family (L), by asking the Father, breadwinner and head of Family L, for financial support.

---

7. Figures for cohabiting couples compared to married couples in 1931 are low, ranging from 1.5% in Piedmont and Valle d'Aosta to 5.4% in Venice and Zara. Figures for legal separations during the period 1911–20 are 1,005, and for 1921–30, 1,375, rising dramatically to 20,190 divorces in 1971 [Golini, 1988, p.360]. This increase remains significant even in the light of rising population figures (1931, 41 million; 1971, 54.1 million) [S. Clerice and A. Di Pierro, 1991, p.75].

8. Definitions taken from Laslett (1977) in Golini's account (1988, p. 330).

This does not meet with success, the reason given being the hostility of the Son towards her. He is represented in terms of character as sullen and antagonistic. However, viewed from the particular perspective of familial organization and structure outlined above, his reaction to the Stepdaughter, and indeed his behaviour throughout the play, can be seen to be motivated by ideological factors. As the only legitimate child, he presumably has most to lose, and nothing to gain, from a fusion of the two families L and IL into an extended family unit. The members of Family IL, on the other hand, have most to gain, having been left destitute by the death of the Other Man. It is the apparently coincidental, but in terms of family ideology, pivotal encounter of the Stepdaughter during the course of her enforced role as head of household (i.e. supporting her family (IL) by working as a prostitute) with the head of nuclear, legitimate Family L, which sets in motion a process culminating in the demise of the extended family unit, together with that of the illegitimate Family IL.

The nuclear family was, and still is, the characteristic familial arrangement in the urban middle class. Writing about the lower middle classes, which began to proliferate during the latter part of the nine-teenth century, Montroni comments that 'in metropolitan areas, the nuclearization of the family was rather precocious', as far as profession-als and white-collar workers in particular (at least up until the First World War) were concerned. The family structure among artisans, traders and shopkeepers, on the other hand, was more flexible, being dependent on the needs of what was usually a family business in which all the family worked (Montroni, 1988, pp. 131–2). This is reminiscent of, and indeed continues, the practice in pre-wage labour society, where-by home and workplace were not yet separated. The private/domestic vs public/work divide characterizing modern capitalism, with the concomi-tant rise of the nuclear family, and resulting in the polarization of female and male roles within it, was not yet present.

Noting the urban vs rural divide which influenced family structure, Clark points out that 'the nuclear family reigned supreme, at least outside the sharecropping areas' (Clark, 1984, p. 162). In effect, while the nuclear family represented the norm in urban areas (in the case of the profession-al sector to which the Father presumably belongs), extended families were to be found more commonly in agricultural households. As we saw in the peasant play *Liolà*, illegitimacy and non-nuclear familial arrange-ments are not negatively viewed, at least in the case of Liolà, who lives with his three illegitimate children and his aunt. He voices the peasant position regarding children, legitimate or otherwise, which is that more hands mean more money. (The same licence was not applicable in the case of the unmarried female peasants who actually gave birth to these children, and to whom pejorative references are made.)

The urban middle-class belonging of *Six Characters in Search of an Author* is therefore a vital element in any consideration of the play's move from an extended to a nuclear family structure, a move which, accompanied by the expulsion of illegitimate offspring from the narrative in various ways, signals that the ideological thrust of the play is to preserve the traditional family structure characterizing the bourgeois middle-class household of the period. By positing a possible alternative, represented by the designs of the Stepdaughter (who attempts to create an extended family unit), only to ultimately dismantle it, the play may be reinforcing traditional family values in a response to growing contemporary anxieties about what was perceived as their decline.

Marriage rates were in fact falling (Glass registers 'a steady decline from 11.5 per 1,000 of the total population in 1921 to 7.6 in 1925 and to 7.5 in 1926' (Glass, 1967, p. 261)). There is some doubt, however, as to the extent to which the traditional family was in fact under threat. Clark maintains that, despite contemporary concern, the family as a basic social unit was never really in danger, given the hostile reactions to attempts to introduce divorce laws from the 1880s onwards. He notes that, as early as 1881, an unsuccessful attempt was made by Villa, a Minister of Justice, to bring in a divorce law enabling separated couples to remarry. A petition opposing this was organized by the Catholic Church, and raised 637,000 signatures, a figure which rose to 700,000 in 1893. A phenomenal 3.5 million opposed a similar bill by Zanardelli in 1902 (Clark, 1984, p. 81).

Nevertheless, changes were taking place in the earlier part of the twentieth century, changes which caused alarm in certain quarters. Factors such as growing urbanization and rates of emigration (which brought with them a decline in the nation's birth-rate), the changing role of women, more of whom were seeking wider ranges of employment outside the home, and the increasingly feared voice of a growing women's movement, were all perceived as working counter to the strengthening nationalistic urge to place Italy on the world map. The drive to prepare Italy for war on all levels was already visible in the politico-military journal *Preparation* which ran from 1909 to 1921, and for which Pirandello himself wrote. This culminated in pro-marriage, pro-family and, above all, pro-natalist legislation and propaganda under Fascism, particularly from 1927 onwards (the year of Mussolini's Ascension Day speech) (Glass, 1967, p. 219; Caldwell, 1986, p. 116). Fascism's fundamentally pro-natalist policies included anti-urbanization, land reclamation schemes and legislation which made emigration more difficult (Glass, 1967, pp. 221–31). One measure of particular interest was the bachelor tax penalizing unmarried men, a tax which the two young bachelors, Tito and Carlino, complain about in *Belonging to One Person or to No-One* (1929). The tax was initiated to take effect from 1927, and significantly increased in 1929, in order to provide revenue for government schemes concerned with maternity and child welfare (ibid., pp. 236–7).

The socio-political climate during which *Six Characters in Search of an Author* was written, then, can be seen quite clearly to have influenced the ideological direction of the play as far as the family is concerned. The play reinforces particular traditional values which appear increasingly to be under threat from a variety of sources at a period in Italian history when population concerns were beginning to come to the forefront, notably in the context of a 'war and peace politics' (Horkheimer, 1972, p. 81). Together with the traditional structure of the nuclear family, the play also works to maintain the hierarchy of gender positionings within the family which this structure entails. It is this hierarchy which provides the focus for the analysis that follows. The remainder of this chapter examines how the play constructs a gender hierarchy within the family in terms of access to speech. In other words, speech is taken as an important vehicle of empowerment. The final chapter will evaluate this hierarchy in terms of gesture in an attempt to clarify the functioning of a politics of the body in the play.

Speech and gesture are in one sense at opposite extremes as far as connotations of power are concerned. Importance has always been traditionally accorded to the Word, to the power of speech itself. From earliest times, 'Word' has been taken to be synonymous with 'logos', or reason, while in Christian theology either term is used to refer to Jesus Christ (OED). As a consequence power has been assumed by those sections of society which use the Word, in both spoken and written forms, as an instrument of domination over the uneducated and illiterate. The terms 'illiterate' and 'well-spoken', while appearing to refer exclusively to the use of written and spoken language, in fact also have diametrically opposed class connotations. In specific social contexts, gender and race connotations may also maintain. As far as gender is concerned, Lacan's structural re-reading of Freud, while continuing to uphold the phallocentrism of the system it describes, offers relevant insights into the psychoanalytical workings of actual entry into language in the context of the family in patriarchy. Entry into language is different for each gender, with the nature of the female's entry being more complex, and necessarily less complete, than that of the male. Rose summarizes the issue as follows:

> [T]he specificity of feminine sexuality in the more recent discussion has explicitly become the issue of women's relationship to language. In so far as it is the order of language which structures sexuality around the male term, or the privileging of that term which shows sexuality to be constructed within language, so this raises the issue of women's relationship to that language and that sexuality simultaneously. (Rose, 1986, p. 78)

No equivalent study, however, appears to have been undertaken regarding entry into gestural signification and symbolization, and any sexual difference involved in entry into that particular 'language'. The historically privileged position of the Word has established the primacy of speech over gesture as a communicative channel. Furthermore, gesture has been accorded a low status not only in its role of mere accessory to speech, but also in its connotation of the female, in its function of expressing emotion. One of the traditional patriarchal commonplaces is the association of female with emotion and of male with reason. In operation here is the system of opposites which lies at the heart of Western philosophy, and which is currently under debate both within and between postmodernism and feminism. In his section on the relationship between sex difference and other differences, Maclean says: 'From the earliest times, and in the most far-flung cultures, the notion of female has in some sense been opposed to that of male, and aligned with other opposites' (Maclean, 1985, p. 2). Quoting Lloyd's (1971) analysis of the use of polarity in early Greek thought, he goes on: 'The earliest stage in the use of polarity . . . is represented by the related opposites attributed by Aristotle to the Pythagoreans in *Metaphysics* A.3 (986a 21ff):

male	female
limit	unlimited
odd	even
one	plurality
right	left
square	oblong
at rest	moving
straight	curved
light	darkness
good	evil

Here there is no classification of the different sorts of opposites; nor is the alignment of male-limit-odd-one-right, etc. justified by reasoning or empirical evidence' (Maclean, 1985, pp. 2–3) (see also G. Lloyd, 1984). The following opposites can now, centuries later, be added to this list, the binary oppositional structure of which at present still maintains its hold on Western culture:

Male	Female
active	passive
culture	nature
social	biological

public	private
outside	inside
reason	emotion/instinct
mind	body
speech	gesture

This chapter continues with an analysis of speech in *Six Characters in Search of an Author*. The interplay between the six Characters will be examined mainly from the perspective of gender and within the ideological framework dictating the reconstitution of the legitimate, nuclear family. Attention will be focused in particular on how hierarchical relations governing the three families are constructed by the narrative in terms of access to speech.

Methodology

The methodology of this analysis consists of the application of some categories of turn-taking. These categories, which will be applied exclusively to utterances by the six family members, are as follows:

(a) TURN SIZE
(b) TURN FREQUENCY
(c) TURN DURATION
(d) TURN CONTINUITY
(e) TURN USURPATION AND TURN LOSS

Before proceeding with this analysis, a few introductory comments need to be made. These concern, first, the status of this type of linguistic analysis; and, second, the implications of using the dramatic text (the play in its written form), rather than the performance text (the play in performance), a distinction drawn by Elam (1980, p. 3).

First, some of the above categories can be found in socio-linguistic attempts to evaluate gender, class and colour difference in 'real' (as opposed to literary) speech. However, these attempts have been criticized on several counts. One criticism has been that the data involved may well be relatively easy to quantify, but not to interpret, often because of insufficient context. (Cameron makes this point in relation to establishing whether a conversation is logical or not (Cameron, 1985, pp. 39–40).) This is illustrated by the following questions which can be addressed to the five categories:

1. Should frequent, lengthy turns be regarded as indicators of dominance, in other words, as attempts to establish/maintain power, OR as attempts by a subordinate to gain/increase power?

2. Does a high proportion of short turns mean that the speaker already possesses power, and does not need to prolong what she/he has to say OR that only brief attempts to acquire power are permissible by a speaker who is subordinate?
3. Is silence a sign of dominance (i.e. there is no need to speak), OR of subordination (e.g. fear of speaking)?
4. Is fragmentation, namely breaks in speech caused by the speaker gesturing, pausing, laughing, singing, etc., an indicator of a negatively fragmented subject, OR of a speaker using classical oratorical skills of delivery in order to persuade?
5. Are interruptions indicators of dominance, namely attempts to establish/maintain power? Looked at another way, is an interruption by another speaker necessarily disruptive and antagonistic in nature, OR can certain interruptions be seen as attempts to help the original speaker? Research on women's conversations shows that interruptions abound, but that these are frequently supportive, running in parallel to, rather than in conflict with, the original speaker (Maltz and Borker, 1982).

These problems are effectively removed by the use of literary, rather than 'real', speech as data. A literary text, analysed in its entirety, may be said to constitute a complete set of data which provides, as it were, its own context, thereby facilitating interpretation. The *Six Characters*, as has been shown above, provides/is a con/text of ideologically-determined narrative specifics. It is this exigency which governs the nature, and thence interpretation, of turn-taking in the play. At the same time, however, dramatic dialogue clearly simulates 'real' conversation in its basic characteristics. Sacks et al. conclude their analysis of conversational turn-taking with the observation: 'It appears likely that conversation should be considered the basic form of speech exchange system, with other systems on the array representing a variety of transformations of conversation's turn-taking systems' (Sacks et al., 1974, p. 730). The particular aim of the present study is to delineate the features of turn-taking as a covert structure contributing to the narrative construction of, or progression towards, a set of traditionally nuclear and hierarchical familial positions which are fundamental in circumscribing the woman's position, in particular the position of the Mother, Stepdaughter and Little Girl: in other words, as an illustration of the textual mechanics of patriarchy in a specifically dramatic context.

This leads to another reservation made by Cameron, this time regarding the dangers of cultural stereotyping in the evaluation of 'real' linguistic features. She notes that socio-linguistic analyses of gender difference tend to ignore the fact that such stereotyping is not inherent in linguistic phenomena themselves, but in the way these phenomena are perceived and valued. One might therefore wish to argue that more care should be taken, once it has been established that difference exists, not to perpetuate the traditional evaluation of the different as negative deviance from a norm. Rather, difference should be evaluated positively by jettisoning the traditional 'false' dichotomy of the binary norm-deviance opposition and aiming at a set of equally valid differences.

The evaluation of difference in literary, as opposed to 'real', speech data, is clearly affected by the additional fictional dimension, which works to define precise limits within which the evaluation may be made. The obvious problem arises that evaluation is usually already present in the fabric of the text: it is clearly impossible to evaluate difference positively in a text which is structured around a norm-negative deviance axis – in other words, in a text which, like *Six Characters*, is largely produced in consonance with, rather than counter to, the predominating patriarchal ideology (or which is, in semiotic terms, 'closed'). It is, then, worthwhile recording that, while this study recognizes the need to break free from this norm-negative deviance framework for 'real speech' analysis, this is clearly not possible here, given the ideological thrust of Pirandello's play.

This brings us to the second introductory comment on methodology, which concerns the dramatic text itself. As Elam points out, any analysis of a play must take into account the fact that the written text of a play (the dramatic text) differs from the play in performance (the performance text). The staging of a play inevitably introduces a set of variables which are not fully present, or exist only implicitly, in the dramatic text. Thus while there is only one dramatic text, an infinite number of performance texts can be derived from it, each one taking its characteristics from the particular producer, stage manager, actors and actresses, audience, etc. involved in its performance. The dramatic text, on the other hand, while containing in embryo all possible performance texts, represents a relatively stable matrix. I would not wish to deny that, for the purposes of a turn-taking analysis, a performance text would add other valuable dimensions, such as that of overlapping (of the beginning of one turn over the end of that of the previous speaker). None the less the dramatic text, with all its limitations, provides fertile ground for a turn-taking analysis.

In the context of speech-act theory, the turn-taking categories dealt with here are based on easily quantifiable criteria dealing primarily with the formal properties of the utterance (and approximating to Austin's *locutionary act*, or Searle's *utterance act* (Austin, 1962; Searle, 1969)). The next, and less easily quantifiable set of criteria to be applied would be, first, that relating to *illocutionary acts* (acts performed *in* saying something to somebody, particularly relevant to drama, where action takes place by means of speech, as Pirandello himself argues in his essay on 'spoken action').[9] The second set of criteria would be that of *perlocutionary acts* (acts performed *by means of* saying something to somebody, discernible by means of the effect on the addressee) (Elam, 1980, p. 158; Searle, 1969, pp. 24–5).

The findings of the present study, when interpreted in the context of the narrative reconstruction of the legitimate nuclear family, reveal a hierarchy of turn-taking, and consequently of speakers, which would be complemented, rather than contradicted, by subsequent illocutionary and perlocutionary speech-act analyses. Bearing in mind the major determining factor, for the interpretation of turn-taking features, of the ideological base of Pirandello's play which, despite tantalizing hints at subversive possibilities (the extended family; the illegitimate family with a woman at its head; father-daughter, mother-son incest), supports a traditional legitimate nuclear family hierarchy, we are now ready to take a closer look at the turn-taking categories.

Analysis

The turn-taking categories are restricted to the speech of the six family members, whether addressed to each other or to the other characters. It should be borne in mind that the entire family is always present on stage, and that *not speaking* is thus foregrounded as significant (a feature which perhaps emerges with greater force in a performance text than in the dramatic text). The speech turn itself is positively valued: first, in the context of the play's overt narrative objective, namely the search by the six Characters for an author and their varying attempts to persuade the Director to fulfil this role; second, the play's covert ideological progression provides/necessitates a highly valorized, power-based speech system within which a Character's degree of access to speech turns is an index to her/his position in the family/gender hierarchy. All three family hierarchies will be evaluated. This will be done by calculating, mostly in terms of percentages, each Character's contribution to the turn production of the families she/he belongs to, as subdivided into the five turn-taking categories. When a Character does not belong to a particular family (for example, the Father is not part of Family IL), the contribution/positioning of that Character is represented by ×.

---

9. Pirandello, 'L'azione parlata' (1899), in Pirandello (1965, 1015–8).

Turn Size

The total turn size, in lines, of each of the six family members, was counted. Of a total of 914 lines spoken by the six members, the Father has the most, the Mother least, and the Young Boy and Little Girl none. (See Table 3.)

Table 3 Turn Size

	Line total	Lines	per	act	ExF	LF	ILF
Father	456	283	90	83	49.9%	77.4%	×
Stepdaughter	325	126	106	93	35.6%	×	85.1%
Son	76	37	—	39	8.3%	12.9%	×
Mother	57	25	19	13	6.2%	9.7%	14.9%
Young Boy	—	—	—	—	—	×	—
Little Girl	—	—	—	—	—	×	—

Turn Frequency

The total number of turns of each of the six family members was counted. Of a total of 323 turns for the six members, the Father speaks most frequently, the Mother and Son least, and the Young Boy and Little Girl not at all. (See Table 4.)

Table 4 Turn Frequency

	Turns	Turns	per	act	ExF	LF	ILF
Father	152	78	46	28	47%	69.4%	×
Stepdaughter	104	38	50	16	32.2%	×	75.4%
Mother	34	19	7	8	10.5%	15.5%	24.6%
Son	33	11	—	22	10.2%	15.1%	×
Young Boy	—	—	—	—	—	×	—
Little Girl	—	—	—	—	—	×	—

In the context of the turn as high in value, the hierarchical order in each of the three families as regards overall turn size is as follows:

Family Ex: Father, Stepdaughter, Son, Mother, Young Boy/Little Girl
Family L: Father, Son, Mother
Family IL: Stepdaughter, Mother, Young Boy/Little Girl

The order for overall turn frequency is the same, except that in Family L and Ex, the Mother has just one more turn than the Son.

The hierarchy in these two turn categories is instrumental in constructing the dominant position of the Father as male head both of the extended family of six members, and of the legitimate, nuclear family of three within it. Both the Son and the Mother have a correspondingly small turn size and frequency in these families, while the two youngest members, the Young Boy and the Little Girl, never speak, and as children have least power. The gradual demise of all three of Family IL's children, and the consequent strengthening of Family L, is accompanied by a pattern of turn size, which shows the legitimate Son to be the only speaking member whose turn size and turn frequency do not diminish by the end of the play. In fact, his turns in the last act are double those in Act I, and exceed those of the Stepdaughter in Act III (in terms of frequency, that is, if not in terms of size). He is now second in line after the Father in Act III, again in terms of frequency, not size.

The Stepdaughter has a high proportion of Family Ex's lines, and thus ranks alongside the Father, rather than with the Son and the Mother, who have a low proportion. Indeed, compared with the Father as head of Family L, she, as head of Family IL, has a higher proportion of that family's lines and turns. Her relatively large turn size and high turn frequency is one of the indices of her temporary potency, which reaches a peak in Acts II and III in the sense that her lines, despite diminishing in number, exceed those of all other members, even the Father. This holds true in terms of turn frequency for Act II, but not Act III, where she is overtaken by both the legitimate son and the Father.

Implications

Socio-economic Heads of families have the greatest overall turn size and highest turn frequency of their family. When two heads are part of another family (as Father and Stepdaughter in Family Ex), both have a considerably larger turn size and higher turn frequency than the rest of the family.

Gender The male head of Family L actually has a lower proportion of the family's overall turn size and frequency than the female head of IL (77.4% vs 85.1%, and 69.4% vs 75.4%). However, when both are part of the same family (Ex) the male has a greater turn size than the female (49.9% vs 35.6%, and 47% vs 32.2%). The Mother, who is the link between all three families, has her greatest turn size and highest turn frequency in Family IL, under a female head (14.9% vs 9.7%L and 6.2%Ex; 24.6% vs 15.5%L and 10.5%Ex). However, in relation to the female head of Family IL, the Mother has a low turn size and frequency, showing that gender alone is not the issue.

Turn Duration

Shortest Turns The proportion of shortest turns (½ lines or less) in relation to the total number of a member's turns was calculated. The Father has the lowest proportion, the Mother the highest. (See Table 5.)

Table 5 Turn Duration

	Short turns	%
Father	30/152	19.7
Stepdaughter	22/104	21.2
Son	9/33	27.3
Mother	14/34	41.2

Longest Turns Comparing the longest turns of the family members, the Father has the longest, and the Mother the shortest:

Father	24½ lines
Stepdaughter	14 lines
Son	12 lines
Mother	8 lines

On the basis that short turns are negatively valued, while long turns are positively valued, the hierarchical order in each of the three families is as follows:

Family Ex: Father, Stepdaughter, Son, Mother
Family L: Father, Son, Mother
Family IL: Stepdaughter, Mother

This turn category thus constructs the same hierarchies, in terms of heads of families and of gender, as the categories of size and frequency.

Turn Continuity

Unfragmented Turns The number of unfragmented turns of ten lines or more spoken by each member of the family was counted, and then the total number of lines which these turns add up to. The Father has the highest number of unfragmented turns of ten lines or more, and the Mother has none. (See Table 6.)

Table 6 Unfragmented Turns

	Unfragmented turns	Lines
Father	9	130
Stepdaughter	4	49
Son	1	12
Mother	—	—

Fragmented Turns The proportion of turns fragmented by the speaker her/himself in relation to the total number of the speaker's turns was calculated. Such fragmentation was inferred from gestures, pauses, etc. as indicated by the dramatic text. The Stepdaughter has the highest proportion of fragmented turns, and the Son has the lowest. (See Table 7.)

Table 7 Fragmented Turns

	Fragmented turns	%
Stepdaughter	23/104	29.8
Father	33/152	21.3
Mother	5/34	14.7
Son	4/33	12.1

Breaks in Fragmented Turns The number of breaks in these fragmented turns were counted. The Stepdaughter's turns have a considerably higher number of breaks than those of the other members. (See Table 8.)

Table 8 Turn Breaks

	Breaks	Turns
Stepdaughter	10	1
	8	2
Father	4	2
Mother	4	1
Son	3	1

The analysis and evaluation of this category of turn continuity is more problematic than that of turn size, frequency and duration. First, if the speaker has only short turns, then fragmentation is not a relevant criterion: there is nothing to fragment (the speech of that Character is already fragmented down to the smallest unit). Second, while unfragmented turns can be accorded high value, the converse is not necessarily the case. In other words, fragmentation need not necessarily signal a negatively fragmented speaking subject, but may indicate the presence of rhetorical techniques such as those described by classical writers on oratory. In this case, fragmentation on the part of the speaking subject would show (1) that the speaker actually has something to fragment, and is thus already in a relatively powerful position; (2) that the speaker is attempting to increase this power. The success or otherwise of this attempt could be determined (1) by the reaction of the other characters on the stage, in other words, the perlocutionary effect of speech-act theory, and (2) by the ultimate position of the speaker at the moment of closure and resolution, i.e. in the case of the *Six Characters*, as the narrative moves towards the reconstruction of the legitimate family by purging Family Ex of its illegitimate members (the three children: the Stepdaughter, Young Boy and Little Girl).

The greatest obstacle to this reconstruction is the head of Family IL, the Stepdaughter, who is the only one of the three to be involved in the turn-taking process. The relatively high incidence of fragmentation in her turns is indicative of her struggle. What emerges in relation to the Stepdaughter as regards the success or otherwise of her fragmentation technique, is that (1) as far as the reaction of other characters on the stage is concerned, she does manage at times to capture their attention and interest, but that (2) this is ultimately ineffectual in the light of the play's closure.

In chapter 2 we examined the song-and-dance routine of the Stepdaughter in the context of male appropriation of logos, manifested in dramatic terms in this play in the form of sustained, reasoned argumentation on the part of the Father. The spectacle of the Stepdaughter's intervention of singing and dancing disrupts, and indeed halts, narrative progress. Although such an intervention might be interpreted positively as a subversion of a logos-oriented narrative, the fact remains that she loses the argument. At most she temporarily interrupts the dominant discourse of logic with her own, negatively valued discourse of the body. The comparatively high incidence of fragmentation in her speech turns is similarly negative in its effect. She is represented as being unable to sustain a reasoned argument, in other words, she is excluded from the type of discourse which is prioritized not only by this play, but also by the vast majority of Pirandello's other plays. Other female characters in the plays who are similarly placed are, for example, Liolà's three groupies, Ciuzza, Luzza and Nela, who flutter around the hero never uttering more than short obsequious phrases, and with whom Liolà toys boastfully in *Liolà* (when he is not discoursing, with peasant wisdom, on the secrets of virility).

The Stepdaughter's speech turns are characterized, not only by a high level of fragmentation and exhibitionist physical display, but also by hysterical laughter and tears. In the particular mode of communication assigned to her, she appears to represent the opposite extreme to Pietra in 'Feminism'. Pietra, a self-confessed feminist, is positioned so as barely to speak at all. She is placed outside the discussion on feminism between the two male characters in such a way that she cannot hear what they say, and therefore does not speak herself (or, as we shall see in the Appendix, she can in fact hear, but nevertheless does not speak). Furthermore she cannot see and is not seen, except for the one occasion on which she stands up.

Both extremes, namely Pietra's deafness, blindness and mutedness, and the Stepdaughter's highly fragmented, emotionally-charged and at times hysterical communication, are brought together by Ardener's theory of muted groups, introduced in the 1960s as a methodological tool useful for the analysis of women's speech (E. Ardener, 1975, p. 20; see also Spivak, 1988). The basic premise of this theory is that, in a society organized along hierarchical lines, only the dominant modes of expression are actually heard. The so-called 'mutedness' and 'invisibility' of subordinate groups, among which can be counted the female gender, in fact corresponds to actual deafness and blindness on the part of the dominant group towards the voice of their subordinates. To listen to and see a subordinate group would indicate recognition of a power relationship, and would acknowledge a certain status for that group in the relationship. Mutedness, then, does not imply actual silence on the part of the group in question, but refers, rather, to an inability of that group to communicate meaning. This inability to express thoughts adequately in the appropriate form is translated by the activity of displacement into non-dominant modes of communication which are negatively perceived and even discounted. Examples of this are hysterical and apparently meaningless outbursts, or fragmented and apparently incoherent discourses.[10] These negatively valued forms of expression then become irrevocably associated with the group which makes use of them, and the circle is complete.

In this context, both the Stepdaughter and Pietra are subordinated and marginalized by their styles of communication, if in completely different ways. The final twist, of course, is that the source of their marginal-

10. For a discussion of these and other forms of hysteria in Pirandello's female characters, see Günsberg (1992).

ization by the text is the actual threat posed to the dominant ideology by the positions which they each represent: Pietra, as a (disturbingly masculine) feminist, and the Stepdaughter, first, as female money-earning head of an illegitimate household (money earned, moreover, through prostitution), second, as instigator of an attempt to create an unorthodox extended family unit, and third, as sexual attraction/threat. The element of fragmentation which plays an important part in characterizing the Stepdaughter's speech therefore has far-reaching implications for our present category. In the context of these arguments on the evaluation of turn fragmentation and continuity, the following hierarchies can be distinguished:

Unfragmented turns:
Family Ex: Father, Stepdaughter, Son, Mother
Family L: Father, Son, Mother
Family IL: Stepdaughter, Mother

This section, in which unfragmented turns are highly valued, thus produces hierarchies which are in line with those in the categories of turn size, frequency and duration.

Fragmented turns and turn breaks:
Family Ex: Stepdaughter, Father, Mother, Son
Family L: Father, Mother, Son
Family IL: Stepdaughter, Mother

Fragmented turns betoken an above-average need to retain attention (a need which, as we have just seen, is experienced by the subordinate gender). They are consequently indicative of a conflictual situation. This section shows those with most power, namely the two heads of families, to be engaged most actively in conflict. Of the two heads, the Stepdaughter, in these terms, struggles most: despite having a lower turn size and frequency than the Father, her turns are more fragmented than his. Conflict is also the key to the next, and last, category of turns.

Turn Usurpation and Turn Loss

Turn Usurpation Interruptions by one family member of another member's turn, leading to at least temporary turn usurpation, were counted. Indications of interruption are stage directions in the dramatic text, such as 'interrupting', 'suddenly', etc. The Father interrupts the greatest number of times, closely followed by the Stepdaughter, and the Mother interrupts least:

Interruptions

Father	10
Stepdaughter	9
Son	3
Mother	1

Numerically, the two heads of families usurp more turns than the other family members.

Turn Loss Turn loss due to turn usurpation by another member of the family was counted. Numerically, the Mother and Father lose most turns, and the Son least:

Agent of turn loss

Son	1 (Father 1)
Stepdaughter	6 (Father 6)
Mother	8 (Stepdaughter 4, Father 3, Son 1)
Father	8 (Stepdaughter 5, Son 2, Mother 1)

Each family head (Father and Stepdaughter) is interrupted most by the other, showing that this is a major area of conflict. The Mother is inter-rupted most by the two heads of family. She is the biggest loser in terms of proportional turn loss, losing almost a quarter of her turns:

Proportion of turn loss

Son	3%
Father	5.3%
Stepdaughter	5.8%
Mother	23.5%

Linked to this is a case of what amounts to turn-refusal on the mother's part, when she subordinates herself to the Father by saying 'You know how to speak, I don't.'

The hierarchical pattern created by these five turn-taking categories can be regarded as one of the channels through which the narrative, and specifically the dramatic narrative, constructs the ideological position, in socio-economic and gender terms, of the six family members. The reconstruction of the legitimate nuclear family, at the expense of the three illegitimate children, including the female head of Family IL and, in another sense, at the expense of the abject and downtrodden Mother of all the three families, can clearly be seen in other aspects of the dramatic narrative too. The stage directions, for instance, have already been mentioned in connection with identifying turn continuity, usurpation and loss. An examination of the stage directions alone, with no attention to what the family members actually say, or, in the case of the Young Boy and Little Girl, do not say, shows that body language is yet another channel through which power relations are communicated, particularly in a 'visual' text. This is the subject of the final chapter.

Behind the Veil: Body Politics in *Six Characters in Search of an Author*[1]

DIRECTOR: You are reason, and your wife is instinct.
Six Characters in Search of an Author, Act I

Introduction: Body Politics

The language of the body, no less than verbal communication, is an important vehicle for the establishment and maintenance of power relations. In this chapter, we examine the mechanics of body language in its textual representations. The main purpose of the discussion is to demonstrate that, like the turn-taking procedures analysed in the previous chapter, Pirandello's representations of the non-verbal work to reinforce the traditional family/gender hierarchy. Once again the text is scrutinized as one form of cultural re/production of gender relations.

Although the term 'body language' is relatively recent, it would of course be absurd to say that awareness of non-verbal communication itself has not always existed. What has developed is the recognition of this as a code, a language with its own structures of both an overt and a covert nature. It is the latter, covert structures in particular which have been at the centre of modern analytical studies, whose aim is to expose them as vehicles for the transmission of dominant ideological values. Conscious, deliberate use of the body, on the other hand, such as that informing the communicative technique of persuasion, was already proscribed in Classical treatises on oratory. Here it appears in the section on delivery (*actio* or *pronuntiatio*), the fifth rhetorical skill (along with *inventio*, *dispositio*, *elocutio* and *memoria*). To this end, a particular pose or stance (*corporis motum*), for example adopting an expression of

1. An outline of this chapter was given at a conference on Pirandello's Two Trilogies: The 'Theatre within the Theatre', The Myths and Their Fortune in the English-Speaking World, held at University College, Dublin, 3–5 May 1991, published in *Le due trilogie pirandelliane: il 'teatro nel teatro', i 'miti' e la loro fortuna nel mondo anglofono*, ed. John C. Barnes, Palermo, Palumbo, 1993, pp. 41–52.

bitterness (*acri aspectu*), was advocated at appropriate points in the speech. Quintilian speaks of *actio decora* as part of the combination of oratorical skills which impresses the hearer.

It is the post-Freudian era, with its interest in the unconscious, which heralds a significant stage in the study of the implications behind non-verbal (as well as verbal) acts. In the words of Sapir, a linguist with anthropological interests writing in 1927, 'another field for the development of unconscious cultural patterns is that of gesture . . . an elaborate and secret code that is written nowhere, known by none, and understood by all'. He continues:

> And this code is by no means referable to simple organic responses. On the contrary, it is as finely certain and artificial, as definitely a creation of social tradition, as language or religion or industrial technology . . . the unwritten code of gestural messages and responses, is the anonymous work of an elaborate social tradition. (Sapir, 1958, pp. 114–42)

Sapir's use of the term 'certain', in relation to the code of gestures, prefigures the semiotic notion of 'closed' with reference to a particular system in the transmission of meanings. The major elements of semiotics already apparent in this passage, especially his concept of a socially-determined, covert code, are central to subsequent attempts to identify and delineate semiotic systems of gesture, notably in the anthropological fields of proxemics (Hall) and kinesics (Birdwhistell). Hall's science of proxemics deals with the spatial aspect of body language, while Birdwhistell's kinesics aims at a notational system to facilitate analysis of body language.

Turning now from everyday non-verbal communication to its cultural/textual representation in various forms, such as art, literature, film and theatre, it is clear that, as an ingredient of the text, body language has always played an important part. This has perhaps been more obvious in the visual and performance arts. For instance, as far as Eastern theatre is concerned, gesture has always been of primary importance. Even in the theatre of the West, the relevance of gesture was recognized early on, as Juvenal's comments on the use of gesture in the Atellanae testify. Writing about Roman theatre, Brilliant says:

> In addition to their rhetorical training, Roman taste in the theater heightened their appreciation of the expressive power in gestures. The articulate theater of Classical Drama had been replaced in favor by the gesticulate productions of the mime which, although it had originated in Greece, had the heyday of its popularity at Rome . . . [so that] complete substitution of the visible for the audible theater took place in the pantomime which was the delight of the Imperial Period. (Brilliant, 1963, pp. 9–10)

In our century, body language in theatre has featured on a theoretical level in the work of Prague Structuralists such as Veltruský, in Brecht's ideas on the social implications of *gestus*, and in the exploration of a semiotic approach by, among others, Elam, Pavis and Serpieri. At the level of performance, Brecht's theory found practical expression in his dramatic output, while directors such as Schechner and Stern have deliberately taken kinesics into account in their productions.

The following study of body politics in Pirandello's play will examine the specific relationship between non-verbal communication and gender-related power; in other words, the actual mechanics underlying difference-related structures of dominance and subordination. In terms of body language, these structures are to be seen as a comparatively unconscious but nevertheless indisputable means of communication, and thence potential power nexus, operating on a covert, rather than on an overt, level.

The Dramatic Text

The text which provides the focus of this chapter is, once again, Pirandello's dramatic text *Six Characters in Search of An Author*, and in particular its stage directions. In the sphere of dramatic production, this section of the written text is reserved for instructions regarding body movements, facial expressions, moods, voice inflections, etc. If they are sufficiently detailed, stage directions offer another, specifically dramatic, channel for the transmission of hierarchical values. This is indeed the case as far as this play is concerned. The stage directions are remarkably meticulous, perhaps more so than in any other of Pirandello's plays, and provide a parallel narrative of their own, to the extent that gender and family relations can be clearly traced without recourse to what the characters actually say.

One reason for the comparatively extensive nature of the stage directions concerning body language for this play could be to allow for the fact that the four adult Characters may wear masks. The face plays an important part in the body language of the actor/actress. Veltruský calls it 'one of the constant components of the stage figure' and refers to 'its inherent semiotic quality which is very strong, both in its variable and in its constant features' (Veltruský, 1976, p. 107). As these masks conceal the face, only leaving holes for eyes, nose and mouth, and allow for no facial mobility, the gestures of the Characters presumably have to be correspondingly exaggerated in order to compensate, to ensure that their body language is sufficiently clear. (In his use of masks, Pirandello draws on the tradition of the *commedia dell'arte* in which, however, actors but not actresses were masked. The actress was not yet accorded the same status as the actor, and was considered to be 'merely playing herself' (Ferris, 1990, pp. 42-6). *Commedia dell'arte* in turn drew on the practice of Greek classical drama, where actors wore masks, partly in order to help them play women's parts, there being no actresses at that time.) The stiff, heavy material, 'of almost statuesque volume', used for the clothes to be worn by the Characters similarly inhibits freedom of movement.

Information regarding the body language of the players is not restricted to the stage directions, but is also to be found in the dialogue itself. For example, the Director's instructions to the Stage Manager throughout the play obviously elicit certain movements on the part of the latter. Another example is description by one Character of the movements of another, such as the Son's description of the Little Girl's fall into the basin, as well as his own movements as he tries to save her, or the Father's reference to his own action of taking the Stepdaughter's hat at the moment at which the action is actually being carried out. For the purpose of this study, however, attention will be paid only to the instructions for physical movement contained in the stage directions, and not to indications in the dialogue.

The relationship between gestural and verbal discourse in theatre is in itself an interesting one. Certain types of theatre, such as Eastern theatre, dispense with verbal discourse altogether. In theatre that uses both gesture and speech, the relation between them may be either *contradictory* or *concordant*. A contradictory relation can lead to a variety of effects, such as comedy, or Brechtian alienation to encourage distancing and critical thought, rather than identification and automatic empathy, on the part of the audience. A concordant relation typifies Western bourgeois realist theatre, which aims to represent 'reality' in a mirror-like way, with the audience as the fourth wall, identifying and empathizing unquestioningly. In the words of Pavis, 'The aesthetics of bourgeois drama insists most strongly on the fusion of text and gesture, as if it sought to cement through this fusion all the elements of performance into an illusion of nature' (by 'text' Pavis means 'speech') (Pavis, 1981, p. 84). In certain respects the audience of *Six Characters in Search of an Author* cannot be considered merely in terms of the fourth wall of realist drama. For instance, the audience enters the theatre to find the curtain up, and the stage unlit, without wings or scenery. This immediately draws attention to the stage for what it really is, namely a stage, and not an illusory other place, as would have been the case had the audience arrived to find the curtain down as a prelude to the revelation, at its raising, of the illusory other place. On one level, the play continues to highlight its own theatrical form and to challenge the realist mode. However, it does not do so in the sphere of gesture. The relationship between gesture and speech is one of concordance and not one of contradiction. In this area, then, the play continues the realist tradition.

The actual status of gesture relative to speech is another aspect of the concordant or contradictory relationship between them. In the case of contradiction, gesture and speech have equal status, as one derives meaning in opposition to the other. In a concordant relationship, however, such as that characterizing realist theatre, speech predominates with gesture as an accessory. Pavis notes, 'In European realist theater, gesture is subordinated to (or at best integrated into) speech' (Pavis, 1981, p. 88). He draws attention to the attempt by the kinesicist, Birdwhistell, to redress the balance in favour of gesture which, Birdwhistell argues, should be regarded as having a broader function than that of mere modifier of verbal discourse. When gesture and speech are compared in terms of their function, in other words, that of the illocutionary act (the act performed in saying something to somebody), then the status of gesture is on a level with that of speech, in that gesture too can perform such an act. Austin says, 'we can for example warn or order or appoint or give or protest or apologize by non-verbal means and these are illocutionary acts' (Austin, 1962, quoted in Elam, 1980, p. 119). As for perlocutionary acts (acts performed by means of saying something to somebody, discernible by means of the effect on the addressee), it is by means of gesture alone that the effect of an extreme act of this sort can frequently be discerned. The status of gesture as a significant channel of communication on its own is therefore indisputable.

The role of gesture in theatre, even in theatre of the realist tradition, is of great importance. For a start, it is the sheer physicality of gesture which ensures the actual 'materiality' of the dramatic performance. As Elam puts it, 'Gesture . . . *materializes* the dramatic subject and his world by asserting their identity with an actual body and an actual space' (Elam, 1980, p. 74). For Brušák, gesture is a visual sign belonging to 'the action space', with other visual signs (scenic articles, costumes and make-up) belonging to 'the scene', as opposed to acoustic signs, namely dialogue, music and sound effects (Brušák, 1976). Pavis refers to the 'enunciatory materiality' of theatrical discourse (Pavis, 1981, p. 87).

The most significant type of gesture in theatrical terms is the kinesic marker:

> there is a group of gestures that deserve a special status in verbal and gestural communication: the kinesic markers: 'Indicating position, temporality, special emphasis, subject, object, and so forth, the markers, like many gestures, are often so closely bound to linguistic behavior as to seem like extensions of it' (Birdwhistell) (189). In the theater, the role of these markers is

> even more obvious than in daily communication: the actor must locate his
> text in the concrete stage situation, he must make his discourse believable,
> make us believe that it is dictated by circumstances, stress the tension
> between discourse and corporal iconicity. (ibid., p. 83, n. 7)

This marker 'makes 'statements about the *context* of the message situation' (Birdwhistell, 1971, p. 117). Such signals serve, in the first instance, to *draw attention to* and so designate the protagonist in an interaction sequence, placing him *in relation* to others present and to the communicative situation' (Elam, 1980, p. 72).

The interactive aspect of theatre made manifest by the kinesic marker, or deixis, points to the social dimension, and consequently to the gender representation, inherent in this particular cultural form. Unless a play only has one character, action is centred on several characters in relation to each other. In order for the audience to understand the interaction, the gestural component must be related in some way to the everyday gestural code with which the audience is familiar. As Elam says, 'What, in summary, is peculiar to theatrical movement, distinguishing it from the kinesic system at large? It is clear that many of the syntactic and indexical functions of gesture in our theatre are founded on those prevailing in society, whereby they become recognizable and thus "expressive"' (ibid., p. 77). Similarly Pavis argues 'that all gesturality is connected with a certain social and cultural group, that it possesses certain codifying principles and that one must be in possession of this code – even if it remains very general and constructed – in order to "read" theatrical gesture correctly' (Pavis, 1981, p. 86).

The social element of gesture was much emphasized by Brecht. His notion of 'gest', referring to both gesture and language, denotes 'particular attitudes adopted by the speaker towards other men', while 'social gest is the gest relevant to society, the gest that allows conclusions to be drawn about the social circumstances' (Brecht, 1986, pp. 104–5). A later definition clarifies the position of gesture in social gest: 'The realm of attitudes adopted by the characters towards one another is what we call the realm of gest. *Physical attitude, tone of voice and facial expression* are all determined by a social gest: the characters are cursing, flattering, instructing one another and so on' (ibid., p. 198, my italics). Brecht, of course, used gesture in a particular way, by making it (and speech) work to produce the alienation effect which he considered essential to a critical, social awareness on the part of the audience. What is relevant to this study is the fact that Brecht, too, emphasizes the link between social context and the particular form of cultural production represented by theatre. Brecht is fully aware of this link, and bases his dramatic theory and production on it.

Despite various techniques foregrounding the dramatic form of *Six Characters in Search of an Author*, and creating a certain degree of alienation effect, Pirandello does not extend this to the gestural level of the play. There is no attempt to play with gesture, which retains its traditional realist relationship of concordance with the verbal level. Nevertheless, the actual link between gesture and social context remains; it is inherent, in the same way that the verbal discourse of the play reflects the social codes of the time. It is clear that theatre, as a cultural form, is produced within the social context specific to its time and that, in order to be recognizable, it re/produces various of its society's codes, such as that pertaining to gesture.

Social codes are an important means for reinforcing the hierarchical structures of the society in question, in areas such as gender, race and class. It follows that gesture in mainstream theatre re/produces the hierarchies of gender, race and class pertaining to the society of the time. As far as traditional, non-subversive drama is concerned, the re/production happens as a matter of course, whether or not the dramatist is aware of the process. In this chapter we shall look at the mechanics of the process whereby gender relations are re/produced on a gestural level in Pirandello's *Six Characters in Search of an Author*. In so doing, it is important to bear in mind the wider cultural context, discussed in the introduction to the previous chapter, which has traditionally devalued gesture, alongside emotion/instinct, the body, nature, and the feminine, while prioritizing and empowering speech, reason, the mind, culture and the masculine.

Methodology

Returning to the distinction between the dramatic (written) text and the performance text(s) discussed in the previous chapter, in basing the analysis of body politics on the stage directions, it is clearly, once again, the dramatic, and not the performance, text which is the object of study. One important implication of using the dramatic, and not one or several performance texts, is that, strictly speaking, it is of course not body language itself which is being analysed, but written descriptions of it. This means that not every single gesture which goes to make up each movement will appear in the description. As Veltruský says, 'Whether a movement is determined by the dialogue or by the author's notes, the actor is given considerable leeway in his choice of the specific means by which to carry out the movement, since only its global sense, never exactly transposable from language into the action of the muscles, is imposed on him' (Veltruský, 1976, p. 101). For our purposes, the movement itself suffices; the precise physiological means by which it is carried out is not of interest. It is in effect the 'leeway' to which Veltruský refers which contributes to the infinite number of possible performance texts, as well as creating a need for a standard notational system whereby physical movement may be transposed to facilitate analysis. There has been much discussion of the problems raised by such systems, but this need not concern us here, as we are not dealing with performance texts.

In a similar vein, body language described in the dramatic text occurs in separate movements; each time a movement is called for, it alone is described in the stage directions. There is no 'gestural text', which would include every single gesture in the play, running alongside the verbal text. In this sense, body language in the dramatic text occurs in discrete units, whereas in performance texts it would be continuous. In kinesic terms, body language in the dramatic text which is the object of this analysis is digital in nature, whereas in performance texts it is analogic. The gaps in between the digits, or discrete units, of body language described in the stage direction of the dramatic text are, in the performance texts which are derived from it, filled with gestures that do not form part of these units. These gestures, which Miller calls 'interstitial communiqués', help to ensure the continuum of the performance text (Miller, 1979, p. 359). It is important to bear in mind the existence of these gestures, even though they are not described in the dramatic text and do not therefore appear in this analysis.

Kinesics and proxemics, as has been suggested above, offer some useful methodological tools for the analysis of body language in theatre, even when this involves the dramatic, and not the performance, text. Broadly speaking, kinesics deals with the gesture itself, in other words, *what* the person does. Proxemics, on the other hand, is concerned with the spatial dimension, namely, *where* the gesture takes place. These two areas are separate for the purposes of analysis, but in reality they obviously overlap. For instance, the gesture of one person touching another may be analysed in terms of what the action is (i.e. touching, which can be characterized as, for example, ceremonial, affectionate, aggressive, patronizing or embarrassing, etc.) as well as in terms of where the action takes place (i.e. informal space, which may be particularly significant, depending on the relationship involved). Account will be taken, then, of the spatial dynamic, as well as of the characteristics of the physical action performed, in the context of the relationship between the characters as regards gender, family role, age, etc.

Proxemics divides spatial relations into three major areas: fixed-feature space, semi-fixed-feature space and informal space. Fixed-feature space refers to the 'material manifestations as well as the hidden, internalized designs that govern behavior as man moves about on this earth. Buildings are one expression of fixed-feature patterns, but buildings are also grouped together in characteristic ways as well as being divided internally according to culturally determined designs' (Hall, 1966, p. 97). Semi-fixed-feature space refers to movable objects, such as furniture. Informal space covers personal space, in particular 'the distances maintained in encounters with others' (ibid., 1966, p. 105). Hall divides informal space into four categories of distance: intimate, personal, social and public. Each of these categories is divided into close phase and far phase according to the precise distance involved:

intimate distance – close phase – 0 inches
intimate distance – far phase – 6 to 18 inches
personal distance – close phase – 1½ to 2½ feet
personal distance – far phase – 2½ to 4 feet
social distance – close phase – 4 to 7 feet
social distance – far phase – 7 to 12 feet
public distance – close phase – 12 to 25 feet
public distance – far phase – 25 feet or more

These categories are based on 'observations and interviews with non-contact, middle-class, healthy adults, mainly natives of the northeastern seaboard of the United States', and Hall points out that 'these generalizations are not representative of human behavior in general – or even of American behavior in general – but only of the group included in the sample. Negroes and Spanish Americans as well as persons who come from southern European cultures have very different proxemic patterns' (ibid., p. 110). Since Pirandello comes from a southern European culture, albeit from the middle class, Hall's qualification will have to be taken into account. In the absence of a similar study based on early twentieth-century Sicilian proxemic patterns, the best solution seems to be to accept the four basic categories of American proxemics, which are in themselves presumably cross-cultural as far as the West is concerned, while abandoning the precise distances.

In practice, one of the important distinctions which emerges in looking at the stage directions for the play is that between gestures of non-touching and touching, both of which occur somewhere within intimate distance. There is therefore sufficient material for an analysis of the dramatic text without having to give exact measurements, something which would be more feasible in an analysis of the performance text. There again, the particular theatre company would itself have to be Sicilian in order to replicate this area of the play accordingly. Here we are once again in the realm of the leeway given to the actor/actress performing the dramatic text, a performance which might itself vary from night to night. This illustrates the problems involved in analysing the performance text(s) as opposed to the dramatic text. However, the dramatic text yields enough information to establish the dynamics of the gender hierarchy in the play.

Elam provides a useful summary of proxemics in relation to the theatre, within which we will locate our analysis:

> fixed-feature space involves, broadly, static architectural configurations. In the theatre it will relate chiefly to the playhouse itself and, in formal theatres (opera houses, proscenium-arch theatres, etc.), to the shapes and dimensions of stage and auditorium. Semi-fixed feature space concerns such movable but non-dynamic objects as furniture, and so in theatrical terms involves the set, auxiliary factors like the lighting and, in informal theatrical spaces, stage and auditorium arrangements. The third proxemic mode, informal space, has as its units the ever-shifting relations of proximity and distance between individuals, thus applying, in the theatre, to actor-actor, actor-spectator and spectator-spectator interplay. . . In the typical Western bourgeois theatre, then, the informal and semi-fixed feature systems exist under the dominion of the fixed-feature. (Elam, 1980, p. 63)

In these terms, *Six Characters in Search of an Author*, as suggested in chapter 5, draws attention to its own theatricality. Fixed-feature space in its traditional stage-auditorium division is highlighted by the fact that the curtain is up and the stage is bare when the audience arrives, by the complete vacation of the stage after what thereby becomes the first act, and by the accidental dropping of the curtain before act three. The fact that the six Characters enter, and the Stepdaughter leaves, via the auditorium instead of via the stage wings also plays with the stage-auditorium division, as well as with the traditional actor-spectator interplay belonging to informal space. Semi-fixed-feature space is made an issue by the meticulous way in which props and lighting are discussed in the attempt by the Characters and the Director to recreate, for instance, the atmosphere in Madama Pace's boudoir. For our purposes, the most interesting area is that of informal space, in other words, the interplay between the Characters.

Kinesics is particularly relevant, as we have seen, in the area of deixis/pointing. There are five areas of deixis, referring to people, space, time, function and object. Each area is divided into proximal deixis (movement towards the speaker) and distal deixis (movement away from the speaker). The following system, based on Elam (1980, p. 186), will be adopted:

Person deixis   – proximal, towards the speaker 'I' (singular)
                                              'we' (plural)

	the listener 'you' (singular)
	'you' (plural)
	– distal, towards a third person 'he/she' (singular)
	'them' (plural)
Spatial deixis	– proximal, towards the context 'here'
	– distal, towards an elsewhere 'there'
Temporal deixis	– proximal, towards the context time 'now'
	– distal, towards another time 'then'
Functional deixis	– proximal, towards the current activity
	– distal, towards an absent activity
Object deixis	– proximal, towards the present object
	'this' (singular)
	'these' (plural)
	– distal, towards an absent object 'that' (singular)
	'those' (plural)

The distribution of the various types of deictic gesture among the male and female Characters/family members will be examined.

The basic unit of kinesic analysis is the kineme, a unit meaningless in itself. Birdwhistell says, 'these are building blocks with *structural meaning*. As these units are combined into orderly structures of behavior in the interactive sequence they contribute to social meaning' (Birdwhistell, 1971, p. 99). Kinemes combine to give kinemorphemes (a morpheme being a 'minimal meaningful unit' (Ducrot and Todorov, 1981, p. 200). Kinemorphemes in turn combine to give kinemorphs 'which may be analogically related to words' (Birdwhistell, 1971, p. 101). The final process in the production of social meaning is the syntactic combination of kinemorphs into complex kinemorphic constructions akin to sentences. Continuing Birdwhistell's parallel with linguistics, it is at the significative level of words and sentences, the equivalents of gestural kinemorphs and complex kinemorphic constructions, that the instructions for body language in the stage directions of Pirandello's play will be analysed. In this sense the various types of deictic gesture outlined above will be dealt with as kinemorphs or as complex kinemorphic constructions, depending on how they appear in the instructions to the Characters.

Analysis

The gestures as detailed by the stage directions for *Six Characters in Search of an Author* fall into two categories. The first contains independent gestures which do not accompany an utterance (G), whereas the second contains frame gestures which do (GU).[2] Independent gestures are divided into gestures which involve touching another person (GT) and gestures which do not (G). Frame gestures are also divided into gestures which involve touching another person (GUT), and gestures which do not, namely gestures (GU), and gestures which are specifically deictic/dramatic in nature (GUD). The reader is referred to Table 9. (Instructions relating to the vocal expression of the utterance, such as timing, volume, intonation, speed, etc., have been excluded because they are considered to relate more to the utterance than to body movement. Some aspects of these verbal modifiers have, furthermore, already been discussed in the previous chapter.)

Table 9 Types of Gesture

Independent gestures	G
	GT
Frame gestures	GU
	GUT
	GUD

Before proceeding to an analysis of each of these groups in turn, it may be helpful to begin with an overview of all the groups as set out in Table 10. The figures refer to the number of gestures in each group as indicated in the stage directions.

Table 10 The Characters and Their Gestures: An Overview

	G	GT	GU	GUT	GUD	Total
Father	3	1	28	8	42	82
Stepd	24	1	34	13	42	114
Son	6	—	10	2	7	25
Mother	18	—	10	3	4	35

2. The term 'frame', used here to denote a gesture which accompanies speech, is borrowed from Greimas and Courtes (1983). Veltruský talks about 'accessory movements' in this context. I have borrowed the latter's term 'independent' to denote gestures which do not accompany speech. However, his 'independent movements' refer to movement which is determined by the dialogue or by the stage directions (which he calls 'author's notes'), whereas my analysis restricts the term to movements indicated solely by the stage directions (Veltruský, 1976, pp. 100–3).

Overview

As shown by Table 10, the Stepdaughter has the most gestural instructions overall, followed by the Father and then, after a considerable numerical drop, by the Mother and the Son. This is significant when compared to the numbers of speech turns and line totals for each Character (see Tables 3 and 4, p. 155). As illustrated by Table 11, although the Stepdaughter does not have as many speech turns and lines as the Father, she is allocated more gestures than he is. The Mother similarly has less speech turns and lines than the Son, but does have ten gestures.

Table 11 Gestures and Speech Turns of the Characters

	Gestures	Speech turns	Line total
A			
Father	2 (83)	1 (152)	1 (456)
Stepd	1 (114)	2 (104)	2 (325)
B			
Son	4 (25)	3 (34)	3 (76)
Mother	3 (35)	4 (33)	4 (57)

(The first figure in each column shows the order of the Characters in each category, as indicated by the figures in brackets.)

There is, interestingly, no correspondence between gestures and utterances in quantitative terms. The Character with the most utterances (in terms of both turns and lines), the Father, who might have been expected to have the most gestures, does not in fact do so. Similarly, the Character with the least utterances, the Mother, does not have the lowest number of gestures. As far as the order of gesture allocation to the Characters is concerned, then, there is no correspondence with the order of utterance allocation. This lack of correspondence is both power- and gender-specific, in that the Father, who leads in the sphere of utterance, is superseded in the non-verbal channel of communication by the Stepdaughter. This is mirrored, if not quite so dramatically, by the position of the Mother, who is last of all in terms of utterance, but not in terms of the non-verbal, a position which might have been held by the Son, who has, if not conspicuously more turns than she (he has one more), more lines (19). It seems that the female Characters are associated with non-verbal communication to a greater extent than their male counterparts in each of the two pairs into which the allocation of gesture and utterance divides the Characters (Father-Stepdaughter, Mother-Son).

These two pairs (marked A and B in Table 11), are separated by a notable quantitative difference in both verbal and non-verbal allocations, with Father and Stepdaughter dominating Mother and Son. This corresponds to the fact that the major conflict zone in the play is that between the Father and the Stepdaughter. In chapter 5, I suggested that this conflict is of a socio-economic nature, being that between two bread-winning heads of family (the Father is the head of the legitimate family, consisting of Father, Mother and Son, and the Stepdaughter is the head of the illegitimate family, consisting of Stepdaughter, Mother, Young Boy and Little Girl). The locus of the conflict is the scene of the Stepdaughter's bread-winning activity, her workplace, namely Madama Pace's boudoir. The reason for the conflict, in socio-economic and gender terms, is the Stepdaughter's forbidden role as breadwinner and head of family, as expressed by the forbidden nature of her profession.

In this central conflict between two heads of family, then, the Father, male breadwinner and head of family, supersedes the Stepdaughter, female breadwinner and head of family, in terms of utterance. It is she, however, who uses non-verbal communication more than anyone else in the play, including him. The Mother and Son pair, who also have a conflictual relationship with incestuous overtones (see chapter 5), are in a less powerful position in family terms, neither of them being heads of family. Their verbal and non-verbal contributions are therefore correspondingly smaller in number. However, here too it is the woman who is allocated more of the non-verbal, if only marginally so.

For the Mother, the most important gestural category is that of pure gesturality itself, independent gesture (G/GT). This can be seen in Table 12, which shows the categories in order of importance for each Character.

Table 12 The Characters and Their Gestural Differences

Father	GUD	GU	GUT	G/GT
Stepd	GUD	GU	G/GT	GUT
Son	GU	GUD	G	GUT
Mother	G	GU	GUD	GUT

In the Mother's case, independent gestures (G) form a half of all her gestural output (18/35), while for the Father, at the other end of the scale, they make up a mere 5 per cent (4/82). It is at the lower end of the hierarchy of the four Characters, then, that the highest incidence of independent gesture is to be found, allotted to the Mother, with the lowest incidence occurring at the top of the hierarchy, allotted to the Father. This overview indicates that the nature of the allocation of gestures in the play is power-related and gender-specific and, in this context, low in status and associated more with the female than the male Characters.

There now follows a more detailed account of this process as each category of gestures is examined, either individually or in combination with others. When qualitative rather than quantitative aspects of body language are being considered (in other words, the actions and emotions which are expressed by gesture, as opposed to the number of times the gestures appear), then the examination clearly cuts across several gestural categories. For example, laughter may appear as an independent gesture (G), as is the case when the Stepdaughter laughs in the middle of the Father's speech, but does not say anything (Act I); or as gesture accompanying an utterance (GU), when she laughs after having spoken (Act I). However, the analysis will initially be structured around the categories, and then move on to cross-category survey of the characteristic features of each Character's body language. For practical purposes, then, categories G and GT, the independent gestures, will be dealt with together, as will categories GT and GUT, the gestures of touching. Categories GU and GUD will be described separately.

Independent Gestures G/GT

The independent gestures, as suggested above, can be described as pure gesturality, in other words, body language which does not qualify speech, but communicates independently. Independent gestures have been distinguished from frame gestures in that they are not linked to speech, and therefore do not occur immediately before, after or during an utterance by the gesturer.

In this category, the Mother has three times as many gestures as the Son (Mother 18, Son 6), and the Stepdaughter has more than six times as many as the Father (Stepdaughter 25, Father 4). Between them, then, the two female Characters have more than four times the number of independent gestures than the men (43 vs 10).

The expressive side of these independent gestures varies considerably from Character to Character. The major feature is that the Mother and Stepdaughter are significantly more expressive of extremes of emotion than either Father or Son. Of the Mother's 18 gestures, 10 express painful emotions: groaning (2), shaking all over with groans (1), bursting into tears (1), hiding her face in her hands (1), anxiety – horror – misery (1), getting up in order to attack Madama Pace (1), rising up in terror and anguish (1), squirming with discomfort (1), and struggling to prevent the Father lifting her veil (1). Another five gestures are associated with abortive movements on her part towards the Son: raising her arms *instinctively* ('levare le braccia *istintivamente*', my italics), opening her arms, stretching out her arms towards him, approaching him, and following him. Of the remaining two gestural instructions, one involves her climbing on to the stage at the beginning of the play, and waiting passively, and with the other gesture she agrees with what the Stepdaughter is saying, by nodding her head. The vast majority of the Mother's independent gestures, then, express some sort of negative, and mostly intense, emotion.

In the case of the Stepdaughter, the emotions expressed by her independent gestures are at the other end of the emotional spectrum. Although she is upset (Acts I, II and III) and bursts into tears (Act III), this occurs in association with what she is saying at the time. As far as her independent gestures are concerned, these are characterized by laughter, at times incontrollable and with hysterical overtones. Seven of her 25 gestures involve laughing, and 2 involve smiling, while 1 shows her trying hard not to laugh; another 2 gestures involve singing and dancing. As suggested in chapter 5, her singing and dancing occurs after she has successfully usurped a speech turn from the Father. Significantly, instead of using the turn to communicate rationally and so argue her case, she wastes it by using it inappropriately for 'meaningless' physical and sexual exhibitionism. Like the Mother, she gestures her agreement with another Character by nodding her head and, in the opposite case, by wagging her finger.

The Son's use of independent gestures is characterized by withdrawal. He shows his dissent from the other Characters, and his desire to disassociate himself from them, by keeping his distance and even trying to leave the stage. Four of his six gestures are of this kind (he remains below, sullen; he keeps his distance; he moves slowly along the footlights; he remains still, facing the stairway leading away from the stage). The remaining two gestures show him running towards the sound of the pistol-shot with the Mother, and appearing on stage at the end of the play. As the narrative progresses, it becomes clear that he does harbour strong emotions, such as resentment, but instead of expressing them, he chooses withdrawal. His independent gestures, then, re/produce the traditional masculine repression of and withdrawal from unwanted emotion, as required by the dictates of patriarchal culture. This withdrawal is a major feature of his stage presence: although he is always present on stage, he speaks little and reluctantly. Notably, although he is present throughout Act II, he does and says nothing at all.

The Father's independent gestures are relatively unmarked emotionally, in three of the four instances. Of these three, one involves his final appearance on the stage at the end of the play and the other two describe the gestures and smiles he shares with the Stepdaughter as they watch the actors and actresses performing the boudoir scene. With the fourth gesture (GT), the Father forcibly lifts the Mother's veil. This act of violence will be dealt with in the next section.

Gestures of Touching GT/GUT

The gestures of touching are significant in that they are the gestures which take place in the nearest phase of proxemic space, namely the close phase (0 inches) of intimate distance. All the six Characters, and Madama Pace, are at some point involved in this type of gesture, even if only as recipients, as in the case of the Young Boy and the Little Girl.

Major points out that 'Despite the acknowledged importance of touch, it is the least researched and least understood area of nonverbal communication' (Major, 1981, p. 15). She goes on to discuss the problems with research on touch:

> Another problem with research on touch is conceptual. Probably more than most forms of nonverbal communication, touch is ambiguous. Touch is used to communicate such varied emotions as extreme aggression, comfort, and intimate love. The message communicated by touch is a function of a number of variables including its *duration, intensity, location, intentionality, the nature of the relationship in which it occurs,* and *the context in which it occurs.* Existing research on touching behavior has typically failed to take into account important contextual and relationship factors. (ibid., p. 16)

This is reminiscent of the problem concerning the evaluation of gender, class and colour difference in everyday conversation discussed in the previous chapter on turn-taking. There the problem was resolved by the fact that a literary rather than an everyday text was being used, thereby providing the necessary information regarding context. The same is true of the evaluation of touching in this chapter, in that the contextual and relationship factors, as determined by the narrativity of the dramatic text, clarify the particular emotions communicated by acts of touching. The stage directions are very explicit, and there is certainly no problem of ambiguity between touching as extreme aggression and touching as comfort.

It is the latter class of emotion which has normally been associated with touching, according to Henley, who says:

> But most of the writers who have been quick to publish on the subject . . . have focused on its use in the communication of intimacy (particularly sexual intimacy), and have overlooked an important aspect of touch in a hierarchy-ridden society: *the use of touch (especially between the sexes) to maintain the social hierarchy.* (Henley, 1977, p. 95)

Similarly Major: 'Traditionally, touch has been seen as synonymous with affection and warmth' (Major, 1981, p. 21). The rules governing touch, which is apparently neutral in intent, but which may actually be communicating a non-neutral message on a covert rather than an overt level, would be, in the words of Sapir quoted earlier, 'written nowhere, known by none, and understood by all', and form part of 'the unwritten code of gestural messages and responses', the result of 'the anonymous work of an elaborate social tradition'.

An important step towards decoding this elaborate social tradition, and one which departed from the traditional association of touching predominantly with positive emotions, was taken when 'Henley (1973, 1977) theorized that touch, as well as other forms of nonverbal communication, also communicates a different message – one of status, power and dominance' (Major, 1981, p. 22). Henley draws attention to gestures of touch as 'status reminders' (Henley, 1973, p. 421), as 'shorthand for coercive force' (Henley, 1977, p. 121), and to touching as 'a sign of power' (Henley, 1973, p. 424) which, when 'used reciprocally . . . indicates solidarity; when nonreciprocal, it indicates status' (ibid., p. 430). The vast majority of gestures of touching in Pirandello's play do not fit the definition of overtly neutral touch as dealt with by Henley and Major, and are obvious in their intent, apart from a couple of interesting exceptions. However, the conclusions which Henley and Major draw regarding touch patterns apply, with one significant exception (Table 13, line 3) to the gestures of touching analysed in this chapter.

Major notes, in support of Henley's earlier work, that 'women and girls are touched more than men or boys . . . female-female touch is slightly more frequent than male-male touch', and that 'males, older persons, and persons of higher socio-economic status are more likely to touch females, younger persons, and persons of lower socio-economic status, respectively, than vice versa' (Major, 1981, pp. 21, 23). This is borne out by Table 13.

Table 13 Touch in Relation to Gender, Age and Status

1. Being touched	female	18	vs male	10
2. Touching female →	female	11	vs male → male	4
3. Touching male →	female	7	vs female → male	6
4. Touching older →	younger	22	vs younger → older	4[*]
5. Touching higher soc-economic			lower soc-economic	
status → lower soc-economic		24	vs status → higher	4
status			soc-economic status	

[*] + 1 unknown, as ages of Mother and Madama Pace are not given.

Line 3 is interesting in that the difference in figures is not as significant as it might be. This is because the main conflict in the play is a cross-sex one between two Characters of high socio-economic status (heads of families); in other words, the Stepdaughter's high status as head of family helps to counterbalance her lower gender status. Even so, her socio-economic status is lower than that of the Father, as she is the head of the illegitimate family, while he is the head of the legitimate one (see chapter 5). Of the four gestures of touching which pass between them, only one is initiated by her. Of the six female → male gestures in this section, for which she is responsible, five are accounted for by her rough handling of the Young Boy, who, although higher than her in terms of gender status, is both younger than she is and lower down on the socio-economic scale. Another interesting point concerns the Son's two gestures of touching the Father (line 4, younger → older: line 5, lower → higher socio-economic). Both of these gestures of touch are actually reactive, in that they are responses to the Father's violent manhandling of the Son. The whole issue of reciprocity and non-reciprocity of touch will be examined later. In the terms of lines 4 and 5, then, these two gestures have a weaker value than at first sight appears. These comments on the figures in the above lines illustrate some of the complexities and difficulties involved in attempting to establish a system for the evaluation of gestures of touch in Pirandello's play. It is time now to move on to an exploratory system for the categorization of these gestures.

For the purposes of the analysis, the acts of touching as indicated in the stage directions of *Six Characters in Search of an Author* are initially divided into three categories: (1) positive acts of touching (expressing affection, comfort, warmth) (+); (2) negative acts of touching (expressing anger, aggression, violent control) (–); (3) ceremonial acts of touching (expressive of the social etiquette of the time) (=). Table 14 shows the allocation of these three categories of touching and of being touched (figures in brackets). No distinction has been made between independent gestures and frame gestures. In the discussion of this table, the utterance accompanying a frame gesture will be considered whenever appropriate.

Table 14 Touching and Being Touched

	+	–	=
Father	1 (1)	6 (2)	2 (–)
Stepd	7 (1)	6 (3)	– (1)
Son	– (–)	2 (2)	– (–)
Mother	– (2)	3 (2)	– (1)
Young Boy	– (–)	– (5)	– (–)
Little Girl	– (5)	– (–)	– (–)
Madama Pace	1 (–)	– (1)	– (–)

Of a total of twenty-eight gestures of touching, the largest category is that of negative touching (17), followed by positive touching (9) and ceremonial touching (2). This highlights the centrality of dramatic conflict in the play, as well as signalling the two Characters who are engaged most actively in conflict (the Father and Stepdaughter). This tallies, interestingly, with the findings in the turn-taking analysis of chapter 5.

This initial categorization of gestures of touching serves as a broad outline of gesture distribution from which some conclusions may be drawn. However, although some gestures are transparent in their intent (such as the Father's dominating move of pushing aside the Stepdaughter), others require further qualification. This is the case with the ceremonial gestures. It is useful to note that the Father has both gestures in this category. He alone initiates touch belonging to the code of social etiquette. However, the rules of social etiquette in themselves perpetuate the hierarchy of social relations. So, when he helps the Mother up the last few steps and leads her across the stage by the hand, there is more to this touching gesture than might appear on the surface. This gesture of apparent politeness is in fact double-edged, in that its false ceremoniality, which pretends some sort of special status for the Mother, actually demeans her by placing her in a situation of implied fragility, with the Father in a protective role.

More importantly, this gesture belies the actual violence, both physical and mental, with which the Father asserts his dominance over her. He does so not only with the violent act of lifting her veil while she struggles to stop him, but by means of two particularly southern European, non-tactile gestures. Both of them occur in the middle of one of his speeches as a reaction to the Mother's obvious disagreement with what he is saying. With the first gesture 'he opens his arms, in an attitude of desperation, on realizing the impossibility of being understood by her and turns to the Director', and with the second 'he taps his forehead'. As he does so, he refers repeatedly to her 'terrifying mental deafness', contrasting what he sees as the dullness of her reason with, significantly, her strong emotional attachment to her children.

This vehement reiteration of the traditional patriarchal dichotomy which associates men with reason and women with emotion, to the accompaniment of patronizing gestures suggesting imbecility, is a violent and demeaning attack on the Mother. Under the guise of the overt 'gentlemanliness' of the Father's ceremonial gesture, then, a covert status reminder of his actual dominance over the Mother is at work. These two ceremonial gestures, both of which are performed by the Character with the highest status in all departments, are therefore only neutral on the surface; at a covert level, they are really negative gestures of touching which assert dominance.

A couple of other gestures which are not quite transparent, and hence difficult to categorize, need further explanation. The first of these is Madama Pace's action of 'placing a hand under the Stepdaughter's chin to raise her head', the Stepdaughter having 'run towards Madama Pace, humble, as if before a mistress'. The Madama's gesture can be perceived, on the surface, as one of affection, and has accordingly been placed in the positive category. However, as in the case of the ceremonial gestures, a status reminder is present here, given the previous instruction to the Stepdaughter to move and behave towards her in a 'humble' manner, as if before a superior. In the context of this relationship of mistress-worker, then, this overt gesture of warmth takes on covert suggestions of dominance.

The second gesture which needs some clarification is the Mother's action of 'pulling' the Stepdaughter away from the Father after she has discovered them in an embrace and 'hurries over to separate them'. This is clearly a negative act, involving a certain degree of physical force, and has been categorized as such. However, although it is the Stepdaughter who is being pulled away in this manner, and who is therefore the recipient of the touch, the negativity and violence of the action inevitably affect the Father too, from whom the Stepdaughter is being forcibly removed. Despite the Father's involvement in the Mother's act, however, the Stepdaughter has been categorized as its recipient, particularly as she is the one whom the Mother addresses as she pulls her away.

Bearing these considerations in mind, then, some further conclusions may be drawn from Table 14. We have already gleaned the following from an overview of this table: the female Characters are touched more frequently than their male counterparts; the female Characters touch each other more often than the male Characters do; in cross-sex touching, slightly more touches pass from male to female than vice versa, the lack of greater discrepancy being due to the high socio-economic status of the female involved; older Characters touch younger Characters more frequently than vice versa, with the two youngest Characters performing no gestures of touch at all; Characters who are higher in socio-economic status touch those who are lower more frequently than vice versa.

Turning now to the positive category of touching (+), it is the Stepdaughter who performs most of these positive gestures (7 out of 9). (The other two gestures are, first, that of Madama Pace which has been examined above, and second, the Father's holding up of the Mother when she faints.) The main recipient of positive gestures is the Little Girl (5 out of 9). Two other female Characters receive positive touches: the Mother (2), and the Stepdaughter (1). The only male Character who is touched in this way is the Father (1). It appears, then, that female Characters both give considerably more positive touches than the male

Characters (8 vs 1) and similarly receive more (8 vs 1). Positive touching, which communicates affection and warmth, is therefore associated almost exclusively with the female Characters, and most of all with the Stepdaughter as giver, and the Little Girl as recipient. Neither the Son nor the Young Boy gives or receives any gestures of this type.

The two children are particularly interesting in this context. It will be remembered that the Young Boy dies a heroic, man's death, whereas the Little Girl dies accidentally, by drowning (see chapter 5). The allotting of gestures of touch to these two Characters is similarly gender-specific, in that the Little Girl receives the largest number of positive touches (5) of all the Characters, whereas the Young Boy receives the largest number of negative touches (5). According to Major:

> Observations of mother-infant interactions . . . indicate that gender differences occur in both initiating and receiving touch at a very early age. Within the first few months of life boy infants receive more proximal behaviors (touching, holding, rocking) than girl infants . . . By 6 months, however, this pattern reverses and girls are touched and handled more by their mothers than are boys . . . Thus, by the time children are about 1 year old, girls receive more touch and may initiate more touch with their mothers than boys do. (Major, 1981, p. 18)

As far as receiving positive touch is concerned (for neither of them initiates any sort of gesture), the Little Girl and Young Boy conform to this patriarchal pattern, which would continue into their adulthood, were they to survive. (That they do not initiate any gesture at all may stem from the fact that they are very low in status in many ways, or from the fact that, in terms of the narrative, they are already dead.)

In the negative category of touching, the Young Boy is at the receiving end of a greater number of unpleasant touches than any other Character. The Little Girl is the only one to escape being touched in this way. The Father, Stepdaughter, Son and Mother all receive similar, low numbers of negative touches. All the Characters, then, with the exception of the Little Girl, are touched negatively, which underlines the conflictual nature of their interaction, with the Father and Stepdaughter being most active in the conflict.

The final part of this analysis will concern itself with reciprocity or non-reciprocity of touch. In the words of Henley concerning touch, 'used reciprocally, it indicates solidarity; when non-reciprocal, it indicates status' (Henley, 1973, p. 430). In the context of this analysis, reciprocity is indicated by a positive reaction to touch. Non-reciprocity is indicated either by an absence of reaction or by a negative reaction. Of the Father's nine gestures of touching, none is met with a positive reaction. All are non-reciprocal, with four receiving a negative reaction (two from the Son and two from the Mother), and five receiving no reaction at all. In these terms, all the Father's gestures of touching are indicators of status, four of them particularly so in that they are contested (the Son fights back twice when the Father manhandles him, on the second occasion even throwing the Father dramatically to the ground, where he remains until his last words in the play; the Mother struggles to prevent the Father lifting the veil which is hiding her face, and when he succeeds, she rises to her feet, covering her face with her hands in despair).

Of the Stepdaughter's gestures of touching, none is reciprocal. Their non-reciprocity is indicated by an absence of reaction. Her gestures of touch can be therefore be interpreted as status indicators, but, unlike some of the Father's, none of her touches is met with a negative reaction. None of the Father's or the Stepdaughter's touches is itself reactive to the touches of others. Both of these Characters, then, perform but do not react to gestures of touch, which is indicative of their high status in relation to the other four Characters. Both of the Son's gestures of touch are, as we have seen, reactive against the Father; of the Mother's three touches, one is reactive, also against the Father; and neither the Little Girl nor the Young Boy performs or reacts to any gestures of touch at all. According to the dramatic text, then, all twenty-eight gestures of touch appear to be status indicators of one sort or another, all of them being non-reciprocal. This underlines the play's concern with conflict and hierarchy, rather than with solidarity and equality, as the basic structure dictating the relationship between the six Characters.

Frame Gestures: General Body Movement GU

These gestures differ from pure vocal modifiers in that they involve a clearly stated bodily movement (e.g. folding one's arms, smiling, getting up). In other words, although they accompany speech, they do not refer exclusively to how the words are to be spoken (as in the case of a vocal modifier such as 'with bitterness'). In practice, this is not always an easy distinction to make: all vocal modifiers obviously necessitate some kind of bodily movement, even when this is not made explicit in the stage directions. Some vocal modifiers clearly require more movement than others; for example, to say something 'with a shout', or 'in an angry outburst' involves more physical movement than to say something 'proudly' or 'immediately'.

However, as the purpose of this study is to establish if there is a qualitative as well as a quantitative difference between the types of gestures performed by the Characters, it is necessary to attempt as fine a distinction as possible. As a general rule, then, when a stage instruction includes a clearly indicated body movement, it is classified as GU. If, on the other hand, it can be interpreted as referring to the vocal aspect of an utterance, it is not included. For instance, in the case of the instruction to speak 'with an outburst of anger', although the Character in question may well not stand still as she speaks this particular line, this instruction has been considered to be a vocal modifier, as the instruction does not require her, for example, to stamp her foot at the same time.

Quantitively, then, the Father has the lowest percentage of his lines accompanied by instructions regarding bodily movement (6 per cent) and the Mother has the highest (16 per cent). In terms of the two pairs of Characters, Father-Stepdaughter and Son-Mother, each female Character has 4 per cent more of her lines accompanied by this type of instruction than her male counterpart. Once again, gesture is associated more with the female than with the male Characters.

In order to arrive at a qualitative analysis of these movements, use will be made of Habicht's three categories of gesture, which he used in his work on Middle English poetry (Habicht, 1959). The first category (A) is that of the *expressive* gestures ('*manifestierenden Gebärden*' or '*Affektausdruck*', pp. 9–10); their function is automatically to transfer affect to a manifest, physical plane, irrelevant of the will of the person concerned. Habicht cites the examples of laughing for joy, or destructive outbursts of anger. The second category (B), the *demonstrative* gestures ('*demonstrativen Gebärden*', p. 9), on the other hand, contain a wilful, even theatrical ('*theatralisches*', p. 10) element, and are meant to have an effect on others. The third category (C), the *ceremonial* gestures ('*zeremoniellen Gebärden*', p. 10), used in the previous section, refer to the realm of social etiquette. I have added a further two categories in order to represent the specifically dramatic function of some of the frame gestures of the type GU. These categories are concerned with what can be called 'stage business', and involve changing position on stage (D) and looking at/watching (E).

Table 15 Frame Gestures: Bodily Movement GUB

	A	B	C	D	E	Total
Father	4	5	1	13	5	28
Stepd	11	9	1	11	2	34
Son	1	1	—	4	4	10
Mother	7	3	—	—	—	10

Note: One group of movements, namely by a Character towards the addressee of an utterance, has not been included here, but has been counted as a deictic gesture and will be dealt with separately. These movements could be considered under D, as they clearly involve the stage business of changing position on stage. For reference, the figures are as follows: Father 7, Stepdaughter 13, Son 1, Mother 0.

From Table 15 it can be seen that the female Characters score highest in column A, the expressive gestures, in that they all have proportionally more of this type of gesture than their counterparts. The Characters who move most about the stage (column D) are those involved in the major conflict zone of the play, namely the two heads of family who are the two most powerful Characters, the Father and the Stepdaughter.

Frame Gestures: Deictic Movement GUD

Deictic movements, or kinesic markers, are, as was suggested earlier, specifically dramatic in function, in that they make obvious the particular stage context of the utterance by signalling interaction between the Characters. A considerable proportion of the stage instructions for *Six Characters in Search of an Author* calls for movements of this type, especially, as we shall see, in the case of the Father and the Step-daughter. The term 'deixis' comes from the Greek for 'pointing'. This provides the basis for the classification of deictic gestures which are specified in the dramatic text of Pirandello's play, the language of which presents many different ways of expressing the concept of 'to point'.

In the case of distal (distant) personal deixis, when a third person ('s/he') is being pointed out by the speaker, the following verbs are used: to indicate (*indicare*), to point at (*additare*), to point to (*accennare*), to point one's finger (*appuntare l'indice*), to invite someone to look at (*invitare a guardare*), and to show (*mostrare*). In the case of proximal (near) personal deixis, when the identity of the addressee ('you') is being made obvious by the speaker, whose whole body 'points' at the addressee, the following verbs are used: to turn towards (*voltarsi a*), to turn to (*rivolgersi a*), to run to (*accorrere a*), to move forward towards (*avanzare verso*), to make one's way forward to (*farsi avanti a*), and to come close to (*venire appresso*). In the rare instances of self-reflexive proximal personal deixis, when the speaker refers to the self ('I'), the verb used is 'to indicate oneself' (*indicare se*).

In examining the deictic gestures of each of the Characters, account will be taken not only of the number and type of deictic gesture instructed by the dramatic text, but also of its object. In this way, it is hoped to build up a picture of the nature of the interaction between the Characters on the basis of deictic gesture alone. Of the five types of deixis outlined earlier (personal, object, spatial, temporal and functional), only the first two, personal and object, are utilized in Pirandello's play. Of these, the personal is by far the most common.

As indicated above, there are three types of personal deixis. In order of frequency, these are (1) third person deixis GUD3 (singular 's/he', plural 'they'); (2) second person deixis GUD2 (singular and plural 'you'); and (3) first person deixis GUD1 (singular 'I', plural 'we'). Both GUD1 and GUD2 are proximal, in that they indicate the area near to the speaker, while GUD3 is distal, in that it points to an area distant from the speaker. In the case of object deixis, this can be either proximal, indicating a nearby object/s (singular 'this', plural 'these') or distal, indicating a distant object/s (singular 'that', plural 'those'). The few examples of object deixis that occur are dealt with under GUD3. Table 16 shows the instances of third person deixis enacted by the four Characters (vertical column) and the identity of the Character, or other person, who is being pointed out (horizontal column). Table 17 shows the instances of second person deixis in a similar way.

Table 16 GUD3 Distal Personal/Object Deixis

	Father	Stepd	Son	Mother	Boy	5Char	Prod/Act	MadP	Obj	Total
Father	—	5	2	10	—	2	6	—	2	27
Stepd	9	—	6	1	2	—	1	1	1	21
Son	1	2	—	2	—	—	—	—	—	5
Mother	1	2	—	—	—	—	—	—	—	3

Table 17 GUD2 Proximal Personal/Object Deixis

	Father	Stepd	Son	Mother	5Char	Prod/Act	MadP	Total
Father	—	—	—	2	—	5	—	7
Stepd	—	—	2	2	2	6	2	14
Son	—	—	—	—	—	1	—	1
Mother	—	—	—	—	—	—	—	—

There are only two instances of proximal first person deixis, both enacted by the Father.

The overall picture which emerges is that the Father and the Stepdaughter have most deictic gestures (Father 36, Stepdaughter 35, Son 6, Mother 3). This prominent deictic activity on their part once again helps to construct their dominant position at the top of the family hierarchy. Of the two, the Father has more deictic gestures directed at the Producer/acting company, and particularly at the Producer, whom he is attempting to convince of his own particular story (Father 11,

Stepdaughter 7, Son 1, Mother 0). The Mother has no specifically instructed deictic movements towards the Producer, and the Son has only one, which contributes to the low position of these two Characters in the family hierarchy. Another deictic contribution to the lower status of the Mother and the Son is the fact that they are the object of deictic gestures more often than they themselves point (the Mother points 3 times and is pointed at 17 times; the Son points 6 times and is pointed at 10 times).

The Father and the Stepdaughter, on the other hand, are more often the subject of pointing than its object (the Father points 36 times and is pointed at 11 times; the Stepdaughter points 35 times and is pointed at 9 times). Significantly, the Father is the only Character with self-reflexive deixis; he points at himself and the other Characters twice. These two gestures help to establish him as representative and head of the six Characters, not only in the eyes of the Characters, but also before the Producer, for whose particular benefit the two gestures are intended.

This raises the interesting issue of the precise locus of dramatic action in the play. As has been demonstrated, the six Characters are clearly involved in a complex of conflictual relationships with each other. A further area of dramatic interest, however, is indicated by the type of deictic gestures they employ. The Characters in fact perform only eight examples of second person proximal personal deixis (of the 'you' type) towards other Characters (Table 17, p. 189), but actually point each other out to the Producer/acting company 45 times (third person distal personal deixis of the 's/he' type, Table 16, p. 189). The prominence of these distal personal deictic gestures illustrates that the Characters talk *about* each other (in the third person) much more than *to* each other (in the second person). This signals that the central dramatic action is not actually so much between the Characters themselves, but between the Characters and the Producer/acting company before whom they are reliving their story.

What we find here, therefore, is not the most characteristic type of dramatic discourse, which would be centred on the proximal mode. It is, on the contrary, the distal mode which dominates the play. This is accounted for by the fact that the references by the Characters are to past (and even future), rather than to present, events; in other words, they are narrative rather than dramatic. This creates a tension between the simultaneous *narration* of the past (sometimes in the future tense) and the *drama* of the present re-enactment of this past, carried out for the benefit primarily of the Characters themselves, whose very existence is determined by the repeated reliving of the same events.

Woven into this deictically dramatic relationship between the Characters and the Producer/acting company, a relationship essentially founded on a power struggle which the Characters ultimately win (they manage to relive their story to the end), is the relationship between the Characters themselves. This relationship, as has been seen, is also founded on a power struggle structured by the intertwining hierarchies of family and gender. The examination of the distribution of deictic gestures amongst the Characters has, it is hoped, shown how this particular type of specifically dramatic gesture plays its part, along with other gestures, in variously positioning the Characters in the family and gender hierarchy.

In conclusion, the body politics of the play underline its concern not just with conflict, but with specific, traditional hierarchies of power. It is gender and socio-economic relations marked by conflict and inequality, rather than by solidarity and equality, which structure the relationship between the Six Characters.

Conclusion

The aim of this work has been to elucidate the ways in which gender relations are represented in the particular cultural form of the theatre to which Pirandello made a substantial contribution. The main thesis underlying this examination is that the representation of gender relations in his plays is patriarchal in orientation. In order to trace this dominant ideology in the dramatic text, and to identify precisely how its position is articulated, it has been necessary (mostly but not always) to go beyond the more obvious and accessible surface of the plays and examine their covert structurings, particularly in terms of audience identification.

As a result, aspects of the plays which are perhaps not immediately apparent have come to light. The implications of these darker areas of the plays may well surprise and even shock those for whom Pirandello represents not only a skilful playwright with a keen sense of plot development, but also one who appears actually to challenge bourgeois conventions with a humouristic flair, characterized, moreover, by an endearing sense of ironic detachment. There is no doubt that many of his plays provide this type of entertainment within a specific intellectual and philosophical framework. My point is not to dispute this, but rather to draw attention to the ideological underpinnings of this framework; in other words, to point out another, truly social, dimension to the plays, a dimension which resonates relentlessly, even though we may not be consciously aware of it. However, once we become aware, and, as it were, lose our ideological innocence, we can no longer ignore the wholesale inscription of dominant patriarchal values in Pirandello's dramatic text.

It is at this point that the issue of authorial intentionality is inevitably posited, often by those seeking to defend Pirandello from what they perceive as full-scale attack. The whole question of intentionality, however, is a red herring; the purpose of this type of study is to focus particularly on covert structures in the dramatic text in an attempt to clarify the mechanisms whereby ideology operates. The emphasis, then, is not simply on *why* the plays transmit specific ideological values, but on *how* they effect such a transmission. It would, in any case, be impossible to ascertain with any satisfactory degree of certainty, whether all the structures which go to make up the plays were intentionally, or consciously, written in. There is, moreover, frequently a lack of correspondence between authorial intentionality and the final product. (One example of such a disparity is that between the intention of Verga, Italy's prime exponent of *verismo*, to achieve authorial impersonality, and the final product, *I Malavoglia*, which betrays the practical impossibility of such an intention.)

It is now recognized that artwork, like dreamwork, is not restricted to conscious processes in its production, but also involves a high degree of unconscious input deriving from a variety of interlinking areas: the artist's particular historical, social and cultural position, family history, personality, to name but a few. And it is now generally accepted that no artist can create from a standpoint outside these areas. In other words, intentionality alone cannot account for the entirety of a creation. At most, it can only ever provide a partial explanation. Ideology itself is most powerfully both transmitted and received at the unconscious level (in other words, when it is not apparent in an overt and propagandistic manner) and it is precisely this dangerously covert and insidious level of transmission which needs to be made accessible to interpretation and exposure. There is also the argument to be made here that dominant ide-ological values which use comedy as a vehicle are particularly likely to be accepted without question, in that laughter in itself already implies a certain degree of consensus.

A more pertinent question concerns gender portrayal in Pirandello's plays as seen in relation to their historical, social and cultural context. In this regard, we can conclude that his patriarchal representations indicate a traditional position which defines him as more of a backward-looking, nineteenth-century figure than a forward-looking, twentieth-century one. In other words, in his cross-century lifespan (1867–1936) he shows a continuing affinity with traditional patriarchal values and no sympathy for feminism (despite his travels outside Sicily and in Europe). His response to feminism in his piece 'Feminism', discussed in the Appendix, reveals a profoundly negative response to this new social movement. Similarly, in the context of other cultural forms, particularly the up and coming medium of film (as I have argued in chapter 4), Pirandello is retrospective in the way he deals with issues regarding women. He does not, for instance, elect to represent women working in the expanding tertiary sector of office work, but adheres to traditional working roles. The use of contemporary statistical data in chapter 4 is an attempt to correlate his representation of women in the sphere of work with the real-life situation of working women during his lifetime.

This study, then, represents a first step in an exploration of the work-ings of patriarchal ideology in Pirandello's plays. There are, as always, many directions which could be taken by further research. For instance, in the context of the current postmodernist debate, it would be interesting to examine further the epistemological foundations of ideological aspects of Pirandello's plays (for example, the reliance on binary oppositions which, according to the postmodernist view, are in effect interrelated, rather than mutually exclusive and contradictory). As far as this work is concerned, my main intention has been to try out some methodological tools for analysing ideological aspects of the dramatic text. It is my hope that in the process I have shown that the representation of gender is indeed an area of Pirandello's theatre which deserves further attention.

Appendix

'Feminism': An Analysis

In 1909 Pirandello published an article entitled 'Feminism' in the new, tri-weekly politico-military journal *Preparation* (English translation follows analysis).[1] The typographical context of this article is interesting, in that it appears on a page also containing various articles on weaponry, military uniforms and the British naval programme. The journal dealt, for the most part, with preparations for war (from which it took its name) and specifically exhorted Italian military preparation in all spheres. In the first issue its editors, claiming to be 'interpreters of public conscience', declared, in explaining 'what we mean by 'preparation', that this should not be interpreted as a 'war cry', but that 'our country has neglected its military preparation for too long', and advocated 'preparation in arms; but also preparation of the souls of the country'.[2] It also featured articles on topics such as the theatre and art exhibitions. A particularly revealing article on the sexual etiquette of physical education for women puts forward the views of a certain E. Podesta, a 'famous advocate of physical education in France':

> He begins by suggesting that not young women, but girls of a minimum of 8 and a maximum of 14 to 15 years, should be presented in public for team gymnastics, and only the latter if they are not too grown up and too well-developed. Since – he adds – we are not yet too used to female exhibitions, so that no women should be presented in the parades and gymnastic celebrations whose presence might provoke inopportune gallantries. (*Preparation*, Year 1, no. 3)

1. Published as 'Feminismo' in *La Preparazione*, Year 1, no. 12, 27–8 February 1909, and reprinted in Pirandello (1965, pp. 1068–72). An earlier version of this analysis appears in *The Yearbook of the British Pirandello Society*, nos 8 and 9, 1988–9, pp. 91–101, under the title 'Parla pure, papà: non ti sento'. This article originated as a paper given at the Italianist Mini-Conference held at the University of Reading on 28 June 1986, and many useful points were raised in the discussion which followed. I would like to thank the following in particular for their comments on the article itself: Zygmunt Barański, Giulio Lepschy and Lino Pertile.

2. *La Preparazione*, Year 1, no. 1, 2 February 1909. All translations of passages taken from this journal, including the following piece by Podesta, are my own.

Some advertising also appeared, an interesting example being an advert for certain 'Powders of Saint Anne' to be taken by women who were either pregnant or breast-feeding. Promising to 'eliminate the sufferings of pregnancy, aid the development of the foetus and the baby, and augment the nutritive substances in the milk', it featured an illustration of a mother and child in striking Madonna and Child format.[3]

It is this particular context which provides the setting for Pirandello's article. 'Feminism', which takes the form of a short story, consists of a discussion about feminism between two male characters, the 'I' narrator and Doctor Post, two characters who also appear elsewhere in Pirandello's short stories.[4] The discussion takes place within earshot of the Doctor's daughter Pietra, who is hidden from view by her father's desk, piled high with papers which she is tidying for him. She herself takes no part in the discussion, a marginalization which is significantly underlined in various ways by the text. She is, moreover, described with traditionally pejorative physical details.

The interest and fascination of this article, particularly from the viewpoint of ideological and textual analysis, is the apparent ambivalence which it exhibits towards its main topic of feminism. The mere fact that this ambivalence even exists is somewhat unexpected, given the type of journal in which the article appeared, and Pirandello's overtly anti-feminist views expressed elsewhere in non-representational arenas (e.g. during interviews).[5] The traditional approach to this enigma would be to accept the ambivalence in the light of Pirandello's philosophy of reality itself as ambiguous, and indeed multiple, in nature. One would then conclude that any literary (as opposed to everyday verbal) expression of a point of view would, for Pirandello, necessarily entail the filtering of the viewpoint in question through this complex, fragmenting philosophical lens. However, this would be unsatisfactory in that it would ignore the fact that the discourse of philosophy, like any other discourse, does not exist in some extra-ideological universe, but is, rather, underpinned by the ideologies which in fact contribute to its construction.

Instead, we shall proceed to examine the element of ambivalence from within the confines of the text of 'Feminism', on the basis that the ambiguity is created, and can therefore be explained, by the mechanics

3. Ibid., Year 1, no. 58, 29–30 April 1909.
4. Two other pieces, similarly containing the character Paulo Post, were published in different numbers of *La Preparazione*. 'Da Lontano: Presentazione' appeared in no. 5, 11–12 February 1909, and 'Da Lontano: Ricomincio a veder l'Europa' in no. 3, 15–16 April 1909. The name Paulo Post also appears, as Pirandello's pseudonym, at the bottom of 'Una spazzola' and 'I filatori' (*La Critica*, 9 March and 18 March 1896). All these articles are reprinted in Pirandello (1965, pp. 1060–75).
5. Cf. G. Villaroel, 'Colloqui con Pirandello', *Il giornale d'Italia*, 8 May 1924, cited by Giudice (1963, p. 231).

of the text itself. The ambivalence, to be precise, can be seen to stem from the potentially contradictory attitudes to feminism which two different readings seem to indicate. However, it will be argued that one stance, namely that of anti-feminism, predominates (a conclusion which is not surprising). This reading, which we shall call (A), posits the text as an attack on feminism on both overt and covert levels. It does so particularly by virtue of its intrusion into what may be regarded as the potentially feminist, or at least not anti-feminist, reading of the text. This second reading (a) posits the text as a satire of anti-feminism. In the context of these two readings, and of their interaction, we shall then move on to investigate why the text is open to the possibility of being read as a satire of anti-feminism in the first place. We shall then attempt to clarify the purpose served by the ambivalence which the possibility of this reading encourages.

Reading (A)

This reading takes as its point of entry into the text the narrative function of the fleeting and fragmented appearance of Pietra in the context of the subsequent dialogue, in which she does not participate. The topic of the conversation about to take place is feminism, and the speaker of the words 'Do go on, father, I'm not listening' or 'I can't hear you' (*'non ti sento'*) is herself a feminist. Yet, with this utterance, the entire discourse is handed over to the Father and the male narrator by the female character (or, more precisely, is made to remain firmly within the male domain by the male author).

The discourse is relinquished specifically by means of relegating the speaker (Pietra) to the margins of both silence ('Do go on, father') and deafness, whether involuntary ('I can't hear you') or voluntary ('I'm not listening') on her part. Furthermore, given Pietra's position behind a pile of her father's books and papers, above which only a fragment of her (her head) appears momentarily, blindness can be added to her other 'disabilities' to complete the construction of her absence. In this way her presence as action (speech, hearing and sight) is made to enter the narrative (significantly as a result of her father's summons) purely in order to be dismissed, or rather, to dismiss itself, by reduction to presence as inaction: she remains physically present in the room, but is unseen, unspoken to and unheard. Her continuing physical presence therefore serves precisely to highlight the actual absence, in terms of action, of her/the feminist, voice in the text.

However, Pietra's 'presence'/feminism, is at no point felt to be impotent. On the contrary, it is regarded as a threat. It is despite the disabled nature of her position from which she neither sees nor listens, that her father initiates the summons, or self/dismissal process, after his anxious reaction of 'uneasiness' to the first mention of feminism by the 'I' narrator. The ensuing covert narrative construction of the absence of feminism, in other words, the overt narrative 'presence' of Pietra, is not sufficiently reassuring, however, and the process has to be repeated half-way through the dialogue: 'Pietra!' Doctor Paulo Post shouted again at this point. 'Oh for God's sake, father', his daughter exclaimed furiously *behind the desk* (i.e. unheard/silent, my italics), 'I've already told you, do carry on, *I'm not listening* [unspoken to/unheard]'. Only at these two points, after what amounts effectively to the actual 'disposal' of feminism by covert narrative means, does the overt narrative consideration of feminism (i.e. the dialogue between the two men) commence and recommence.

This covert narrative process of dismissing feminism (the proposed topic of conversation) before the overt narrative discussion of it has even begun clearly has important implications for what follows in the text. The result is, in effect, to invalidate the subsequent dialogue. The subject has already been closed, thereby emptying what comes next of any potential meaning. Yet the dialogue is not without significance, in that it restates the dismissal of feminism by repeating it in different terms and on another narrative level. However, since such a restatement is superfluous in narrative terms, it may be interpreted, rather, as an overstatement of the anti-feminist position. Furthermore, the dialogue consists predominantly of a detailed exposition of the anti-feminist viewpoint, to the complete exclusion of any feminist perspective, thereby exposing the reader to only one side of the argument.

The dialogue carries out what amounts to an overkill of feminism in the following ways. First, it makes use of the respected terms of philosophy and socio-economics, sanctioned *a priori* by the respectable status of their mouthpiece, the doctor/father. Feminism is thus introduced and simultaneously dismissed as yet another contemporary, abstract, philosophical construct, its 'unreal' nature automatically disqualifying it from any serious consideration. It is then further invalidated by removal to the metaphorical plane as a balloon filled with (archetypally feminine) idealist 'feeling' and not, by implication, with rational argument (which constitutes the discourse exclusively of the doctor/father/male).

This 'feeling'/'hot air' is given three possible definitions, with the ostensibly least negative one coming last: 'a puff of indignation, a brainstorm or a breath of good sense'. However, 'sense', qualified by 'good' and later also by 'natural', is instantly deprived of any inherent positive connotations (of rationality) in that it is defined as biologically female ('their natural good sense'). In other words, 'sense' is a non/sub-male, version of rational thought which is 'good', in other words, acceptable to, and indeed a necessary and integral part of, the construction of male superiority. It is then further diminished as being, in any case, out of place in a woman because it is 'the enemy of poetry', womanliness being defined ultimately as the 'dear, intimate poetry' of wifeliness. It is from this (inferior and misplaced) 'good sense' that the (inevitably) misguided feminist movement is born.

Feminism is correctly related to socio-economic considerations. It is equally correctly defined as women's desire for emancipation ('the so-called emancipation of women'), but clearly not condoned as such ('so-called'). In effect, the threatening implications of the removal of women from a situation of dependence on men, namely the diminution of male dominance by the disappearance of the dominated, leads to a male wish-fulfilment fantasy in terms of the opposite, in other words, feminism as expression of women's need to be dependent on men. Feminism is thus translated by this male fantasy into a product of women's dependence on men which takes the form of a desire 'to work to find a husband', seen as a remedy devised by 'good sense' in response to economic conditions unfavourable to taking a wife. There follows a consideration of this so-called remedy as erroneous and self-defeating, because the woman who works outside the home automatically forfeits her essential womanliness and cannot therefore make an ideal wife.[6] The equation of working woman = rational/masculine/unfeminine = unwifely = not a woman, is quickly rescued from the feminist accusation of 'prejudice' and justified as inevitable by the respectable and apparently irrefutable terms 'economic and social conditions' which give rise to it. The fatalism of these 'conditions' is compounded by the commiserative qualifiers which accompany them ('very sad' and 'sad').

The dialogue ends by re-echoing, in terms of impaired vision, the 'disability'/disabling, of Pietra (the woman without a man/husband)/ feminism. The 'I' narrator's request 'I would now like to hear the young lady, your daughter's views on this', which specifies Pietra's unmarried status ('signorina'), receives the reply: 'Women cannot see this matter [i.e. feminism] objectively. Or rather, they might, on one condition: that is, if they had a husband by their side, do I make myself clear?' Defective vision, which is the 'natural' incapacity of a woman without a man, can therefore only be remedied by marriage (in other words, by the

6. The result of married women working outside the home was, and still is, believed to be the destruction of family values. Bridental writes: 'Today, as in the nineteenth century, strains in and on the family draw public attention. . . While it has been shown repeatedly that married women take jobs either to improve their family's living standard or to keep it from falling, the interpretation persists that such work for the family is actually destroying it' (Bridenthal, 1982, pp. 230–1).

introduction/superimposition of the male view) which enables her to 'see objectively' (which eclipses the female view and thereby ensures male dominance).

Lastly, use is made in the dialogue of a patronizing tone as yet another means of re-dispensing with the topic under discussion. For instance, after the initial pretence of conceding that feminism as a topic is 'a little complicated', the doctor none the less proceeds to explain it with apparent ease and conviction. His explanation is punctuated with condescending formulations directed at feminism and feminists, in other words, at the topic itself ('this feminist balloon of theirs', 'that bit of deflated skin', 'the so-called emancipation of women', etc.) and at his interlocutor, who has raised the topic in the first place ('Let us take, dear sir', 'let us see if', 'my dear sir', etc.). The sheer blatancy of this patronizing attitude towards the 'I' narrator, in conjunction with other aspects of the relationship between the two men, contributes to the satire of anti-feminism which appears, and at first sight paradoxically so, to be a possible reading of this text.

Reading (a)

One major pointer to satire is the choice of a traditional satirical vehicle, namely the dialogue. The dialogue facilitates the interchange of opposing opinions, its non-univocal mode highlighting the possibility for dialectical development. This genre thus sets up the expectation of a potentially 'open' text while, in effect, generating the perfect space for a satirical/authorial voice. If one starts out with the premise that it is the 'I' narrator who expresses the authorial voice, this immediately places the other participant in the dialogue, Dr Post, in a position of opposition, and predisposes him for the role of satirical object. The characterization of Dr Post serves to corroborate this interpretation. Although he is momentarily set up as a potential authority by an apparently humble 'I' narrator who submits his ideas for the doctor to examine, any genuine authority the latter might have is immediately undermined, and the 'I' narrator's 'humility' called into question, by the portrayal of the doctor. He is in fact presented as a pompous, eccentric figure, rather than as someone to be taken seriously. On the level of body language, for instance, his first action in the text is the patronizing gesture of 'a slightly disdainful shrug' and a condescendingly 'pitying smile'. Then, before beginning to speak, he curtails visual communication by closing his eyes and lowering his head on to his chest, thereby pre-empting any possible interruption by his interlocutor, the 'I' narrator, to whom he clearly considers himself superior.

The doctor's self-righteousness suddenly evaporates when the topic changes from Valeriano Castiglione and D'Annunzio to feminism, at the instigation of the 'I' narrator. The latter observes somewhat ironically, 'I expected another slightly disdainful shrug, another pitying smile. Instead, Dr Paulo Post turned his head with a certain uneasiness . . . and called: "Pietra!"' The all-knowing doctor can, it seems, only begin/continue to discourse on feminism upon reassurance of his daughter's 'absence'. The result of presenting the doctor's behaviour in an eccentric light is to undercut the (anti-feminist) import of what he actually says, thereby allowing the text to be read as a satire (of anti-feminism). This clearly has implications for the character Pietra, who could then be interpreted as the long-suffering, indulgent feminist daughter who humours her father by encouraging him to continue, in full knowledge of what he will say, and who is, moreover, in a position where she can in fact hear very well. However, it is in the description of Pietra that the satirical reading of the text begins to fall apart. Such a reading, with Dr Post/anti-feminism as the object of satire, would logically entail a positive, or at least a neutral, representation of his feminist daughter, and this is certainly not how she is portrayed, as far as description of her is concerned.

We shall now leave reading (a), and concentrate both on the description of Pietra and on the nature of the 'I' narrator, as we begin to investigate how the two readings relate to each other. An analysis of the description of Pietra, given through the 'I' narrator, entails an examination of how the 'I' narrator functions in relation to the other characters. We need, in other words, to delimit the exact zone of narrative influence within which this character operates. The 'I' narrator, as was suggested above, begins by 'humbly' introducing Dr Post as an authority to whom matters of intellectual import may be submitted for comment. It very soon transpires that this humility is affected, and that the 'I' narrator's attitude towards the doctor is in fact none other than the mock respect of the devil's advocate who does not himself participate fully in the discussion, but operates from a position of detached irony. He does not express any direct views, but elicits those of the doctor while himself remaining non-committal. He can thus by no means be seen to be in sympathy with the doctor, and is indeed instrumental in setting him up as an object of satire.

The 'I' narrator is not in sympathy with Pietra either, retaining a distanced stance of overall bemusement as far as she is concerned. He displays stupefaction at hearing her voice, timidity and confusion when asking whether she is a feminist, dismay when she appears and relief when she disappears. The 'I' narrator is thus presented as a non-omniscient, unsuspecting, essentially naive Everyman type of figure who appears to maintain a position of ironic detachment from both father/anti-feminism and daughter/feminism.

The narrative ends in the same way, with the somewhat ambivalent departure of the 'I' narrator. He goads the doctor by declaring that he would like to hear Pietra's views and then makes a hasty exit after the doctor's response. The reason for the 'I' narrator's swift retreat is not completely univocal. The dominant meaning is certainly that he is escaping from the threat of marriage/a husband-seeking daughter/feminism itself. This would be a suitable end to reading (A) of the text as condemnation of feminism, and reduces the entire discussion finally to the traditional comic topos of the bachelor-victim pursued by the the unattractive, husband-seeking woman. Another possible interpretation is that he is fleeing from the stupidity of the doctor's last analysis, in other words, a suitable end to reading (a) of the text as satire of anti-feminism.

The problem of the apparently ambivalent, non-committal position of the 'I' narrator which is instrumental in generating the ambiguous nature of the text as a whole can be resolved by charting the precise limits of the narrative domain within which each character operates. So, although the 'I' narrator appears to be in control of the entire narrative, and it is through him that we are presented with the other two characters, he is in reality only in command of his own perception of them, and of his own speech, actions and reactions. It is in the description of Pietra that this distinction of narrative responsibility proves especially revealing, in that negative (and so by implication anti-feminist) terms are used to portray her not only by the 'I' narrator as character, by means of value-judgements, but significantly also by the third person narrator, Pirandello himself. When Pietra's head appears, the 'I' narrator describes it as 'a red, dishevelled head with glasses which enlarged her eyes enormously and confusingly'. It is thus a narrative fact, rather than the 'I' narrator's impression, that she wears strong glasses and that she therefore has faulty vision, while only the adverbial qualifiers emphasizing the actual degree may be attributed to the 'I' narrator ('that enlarged her eyes *enormously* and *confusingly*' (my italics)). The narrative fact of Pietra's strong glasses clearly supports Dr Post's opinion that feminists cannot 'see objectively' (literally, 'see from a distance' ['*veder da lontano*']) and that feminism is, by implication, short-sighted. It also ties in with the scientific belief current at the time that education was physically damaging to women.[7]

The 'I' narrator also distances himself, and the reader, from Pietra's voice, thereby establishing an immediate hostility towards it, by the manner in which he introduces it: 'a guttural, masculine voice replied, to my great astonishment'. In this way the voice is not presented by the

---

7. In particular, education was supposed to have a detrimental effect on the woman's reproductive apparatus (Sayers, 1982, pp. 7–27).

narrator to the reader, but is 'heard' unexpectedly by both narrator and reader simultaneously. Moreover, it appears as a voice that *is* guttural and masculine, in other words, without the attenuating effect of, for example, a verb such as 'seemed' (*'pareva'*), or an adverb such as 'like' (*'come'*). Having established that this voice is guttural and masculine, it reappears as 'the' rather than 'a' in 'the guttural, masculine voice', and is thus tacitly and indisputably confirmed as such. Both here and in the unflattering description of Pietra's head, then, the stereotype of the masculine, unattractive and unfeminine feminist is reinforced.

In other words, although Pietra's words could be seen to fit either reading (A) or (a), as has been shown, and the 'I' narrator's bemused and unsuspecting reactions to her make him appear ironically detached, it is clear that, as far as description of Pietra is concerned, representation of her is far from positive, or even neutral, as the satirical reading of the text would require. Reading (a) of the text as satire of anti-feminism is thus intruded upon and, effectively, dismantled, when the two readings are juxtaposed in this way, thereby revealing the anti-feminist reading (A) to be dominant.

Given the predominance of reading (A) of the text as covert as well as overt attack on feminism, the function of reading (a) may perhaps be construed to be that of cosmetically mollifying the severity of the anti-feminist position which underlies the mechanics of the text. Another way of approaching the relationship between the two readings might be to draw an analogy with Freud's theory of negation.[8] Freud says:

> [T]he content of a repressed image or idea can make its way into consciousness, on condition that it is negated . . . With the help of negation only one consequence of the process of repression is undone – the fact, namely, of the ideational content of what is repressed not reaching consciousness. The outcome of this is a kind of intellectual acceptance of the repressed, while at the same time what is essential to the repression persists. (Freud, 1925, 19, pp. 235–6)

He gives as an example 'You ask who this person in the dream can be. It's *not* my mother', and adds, 'We emend this to: 'So it *is* his mother' (ibid., pp. 235–6). For our purposes, we might substitute as follows: 'You ask what 'Feminism' is about. It's *not* anti-feminist' (i.e. reading (a)). We then emend this to 'So it *is* anti-feminist' (i.e. reading (A)). In other words, reading (a), by satirizing anti-feminism, operates as the negating element (*not* anti-feminist). This provides a vehicle for the surfacing into consciousness of the ideational content (namely, the transmission of anti-feminist values, reading (A)).

8. See Freud, 'Negation' (1925, in Freud, 1953–74).

In conclusion, then, 'Feminism' represents an attack on feminism, an attack which is particularly aimed at attempts by feminists to gain wider access to the world of work. Having established this, we are still left with a question mark regarding an explanation for the ambivalence which is such a feature of this text. One possible answer would be to locate the roots of this ambivalence in the actual struggle of the text to produce a coherent anti-feminist discourse. In other words, it is by virtue of its ideological partiality that any anti-feminist discourse necessarily contains the seeds of its own deconstruction.

'Feminism' by Pirandello

The reaction of Doctor Paulo Post this morning to all the topics which I submitted for him to examine, and exercise his powers of reduction upon, topics chosen for what seemed to me the excellence of the individuals they concerned, as well as the importance of their subject matter, was to give a slightly disdainful shrug and a pitying smile, as if to say:
– Come along! Surely you do not believe this?
The doubt, or rather the fear, which I expressed, like a sting in the tail, at the end of my last article, was unfortunately being borne out; namely that once placed before the reversed telescope of this doctor of mine, the many heroes of our time, together with the many political, social and literary questions which so engross us nowadays, and to which we attach so much significance, would vanish out of sight.
– How do you mean? – I tried to protest. – Is it really possible that men of such high repute can actually be as nothing, dear doctor? Just think! Try to see them . . .
Doctor Paulo Post closed his eyes at this plea of mine. He bowed his head and began to recite in a voice that seemed to come from far away:
– Don Valeriano Castiglione was a most famous man; the greatest literary figures vied with each other to exalt him; the greatest personages of his time fought for his attention. And Pope Urban VIII honoured him with magnificent praise; and Cardinal Borghese and the Viceroy of Naples, Don Pietro of Toledo, solicited his description, in the former case, of the deeds of Pope Paul V, and in the latter, of the wars of the Catholic king in Italy; and both were unsuccessful. On the suggestion of Cardinal Richelieu, he was nominated by Louis XIII, King of France, to be his historiographer. And he was also nominated historiographer by the Duke of Savoy, Charles Emmanuel. In his praise, leaving aside other glorious testimonies, Duchess Cristina, daughter of the most Christian king, Henry IV, affirmed in a diploma, together with many other titles, 'the certain fame which he is gaining in Italy as the foremost writer of our time'.

When he had recited this passage, Doctor Paulo Post opened his eyes, raised his head and said to me:

– This is how they appear in history, dear sir, these literary figures of yours, who today are of such high repute: Gabriele d'Annunzio, for example; correct me if I'm wrong, but if we were to glorify him thus, *for the certain fame which he is gaining in Italy as the foremost writer of our time*, surely three centuries from now, might it not be impossible not to laugh at him, just as we laugh today at the most famous Don Valeriano Castiglione, pride and joy of the library of Manzoni's incomparable Don Ferrante? Remain here and look at him there, this D'Annunzio of yours.

– In the seventeenth century?

– Three centuries back in time. I can see him there, and yet it is as if these three centuries had not yet passed for him. To conclude, he is present and in the seventeenth century. Take heed, my dear sir, for here lies the true essence of my philosophy. Do you see him? In front of you and alongside Don Valeriano Castiglione. Now do you not feel it would at least be prudent not to hold him in the sort of esteem that Castiglione was held by Don Ferrante in his day?

– Maybe, – I said. – Let's forget about D'Annunzio. I really would like to consider from afar, my dear doctor, some of the more hotly debated social questions of our time. Feminism, for example.

I expected another slightly disdainful shrug, another pitying smile. Instead, Doctor Paulo Post turned his head around with a certain uneasiness from the old leather armchair in which he sat buried in front of me by the study window, and called out:

– Pietra!

A guttural, masculine voice replied, to my great astonishment, from the depths of the study, where, amid bookcases crammed with books, there towered a huge desk, also completely overloaded with books and piles of papers.

– Do go on, father – said that voice.

I was not in the least aware of the presence of another living being in the study.

– My daughter, the second, – the doctor explained to me. – For the past few days she has been attending to the re-ordering of my filing system. I would not like to speak in front of her on the subject you are proposing.

– Feminist? – I enquired with a certain air of timidity and confusion.

– Yes sir! – came the firm reply, from, as it leapt up from all that profusion of books and papers, a red, dishevelled head with glasses which enlarged her eyes enormously and confusingly.

I was somewhat dismayed.

The head immediately disappeared, fortunately, behind the books; and from there, as if from somewhere underground, the guttural, masculine voice repeated:

– Do go on, father: I'm not listening.

– Well now, – Doctor Paulo Post then said, – it's a little complicated, this particular matter. Feminism, like so many other things these days, is an ideal construction. Let us, dear sir, take a sac and fill it with air. We now have a nice balloon. Let's let it out on a piece of string and leave it, in its inflated state, up in the air for a day. The following day we shall find it a little less inflated, and so on after the second, third and fourth day. The string slackens more and more, and the balloon, becoming progressively smaller and more shrivelled, drops lower until it falls, a deflated sac once again. But it is not just feminism, dear sir, which turns from a sac into a balloon and then back into a piece of skin again. This is the fate of all ideal constructions. They hold together and stay up for as long as they are filled with air, that is, with our feelings. Gradually, in time, these feelings, with which we have filled them, become faint and fade away. History is full of these deflated balloons, which you might even re-inflate skilfully by blowing your feelings into them, in other words, more of that air with which women have filled this feminist balloon of theirs.

– Pietra! – Doctor Paulo Post shouted again at this point.

– Oh for God's sake, father – his daughter exclaimed furiously behind the desk. – I've already told you, do go on, I'm not listening!

– All right, all right! Well now – the doctor resumed – let us see if this air is a puff of indignation, a brainstorm or a breath of good sense. It is common knowledge that life nowadays is very hard. Everything is expensive! All the professions and jobs pay badly and inadequately. Now women, my dear sir, have understood correctly, poor things, why it is becoming more and more difficult to find a husband. They have been made a little exasperated and a little crazy at having to suffocate their instinctive needs, and seeing their natural inclinations frustrated (for just as man desires woman, woman desires man, even though she is often unable, or unwilling, to say so openly). But all this ideal revolt of theirs against so-called social prejudices, and all this fervent preaching of theirs in favour of the so-called emancipation of women, what else is it, basically, if not a disdainful masquerade of physiological needs stirring underneath? Women want to work in order to find a husband, my dear sir. This is a remedy suggested to them by their natural good sense. But good sense, alas, good sense is the enemy of poetry! And women understand this too: that is, they understand that a woman who works like a man, amongst men, outside the home, is no longer considered by the majority to be the most ideal of wives, and they rebel against this way of thinking which goes counter to their remedy, and they call it prejudice. Here lies their mistake, albeit, in the last analysis, quite understandable. To suppose that a woman who associates continually with men must in the end become too masculine; to foresee that the home, once deprived of the assiduous, intelligent and loving care of a woman, must lose that dear, intimate poetry which is the major attraction of marriage for a man; to suppose that a woman who also contributes to the maintenance of the home with her own earnings, must no longer have for the man that devotion and respect in which she delights so much: these are not prejudices; they are sad necessities, on account of which the ideal composition of feminism disintegrates and dissolves into wider questions concerning the very sad economic and social conditions of our day. It dissolves without trace, my dear sir, do believe me. Only that bit of deflated skin . . .

– I would like – I said quietly in the doctor's ear, before rising to take my leave – I would now like to hear the views of the young lady, your daughter, on this . . .

– Dear sir – replied Doctor Paulo Post, opening his arms. – Women cannot see this matter objectively. Or rather, they might, on one condition: that is, if they had a husband by their side, do I make myself clear?

I am still running away.

My translation

Bibliography

Pirandello's Plays

The dates of the following completed plays are taken from the bibliographical section of the *Mondadori Teatro e Cinema* Edition of the plays, on which my translations are based. The dates refer to the first published edition of each play. References to Pirandello's other writings can be found in the notes. * signifies no English translation available.

The Epilogue (La morsa), 1898
Sicilian Limes (Lumíe di Sicilia), 1911
A Doctor's Duty (Il dovere del medico), 1912
Cecé (Cecé), 1913
As Others See It* (La ragione degli altri), 1916
At the Exit (All'uscita), 1916
Think It Over, Giacomino* (Pensaci, Giacomino), 1917
Liolá (Liolá), 1917
That's How It Is (If You Think So) (Cosí è (se vi pare)), 1918
The Licence (La patente), 1918
The Pleasure of Honesty (Il piacere dell'onestá), 1918
Cap and Bells* (Il berretto a sonagli), 1918
The Rules of the Game* (Il giuoco delle parti), 1919
Man, Beast and Virtue* (L'uomo, la bestia e la virtú), 1919
But It's Not Serious* (Ma non è una cosa seria), 1919
All For the Best (Tutto per bene), 1920
The Grafting (L'innesto), 1921
As Before, Better Than Before* (Come prima, meglio di prima), 1921
Six Characters in Search of an Author (Sei personaggi in cerca d'autore), 1921
Henry IV (Enrico IV), 1921
Mrs. Morli, One and Two* (La signora Morli, una e due), 1922
Clothing the Naked (Vestire gli ignudi), 1923
The Life I Gave You (La vita che ti diedi), 1924
The Festival of Our Lord of the Ship (Sagra del signor della nave), 1924
Each in Their Own Way (Ciascuno a suo modo), 1924

The Other Son (L'altro figlio), 1925
The Jar (La giara), 1925
The Imbecile (L'imbecille), 1926
The Man With the Flower in His Mouth (L'uomo dal fiore in bocca),
    1926
Diana and Tuda (Diana e la Tuda), 1927
The Wives' Friend (L'amica delle mogli), 1927
The New Colony (La nuova colonia), 1928
Bellavita (Bellavita), 1928
I Dream (But Perhaps Not) (Sogno (ma forse no)), 1929
*Belonging to One Person or to No-One** (O di uno o di nessuno), 1929
Lazarus (Lazzaro), 1929
Tonight We Improvise (Questa sera si recita a soggetto), 1930
As You Desire Me (Come tu mi vuoi), 1930
Finding Oneself (Trovarsi), 1932
When One Is Somebody (Quando si è qualcuno), 1933
*The Fable of the Changeling** (La favola del figlio cambiato), 1933
One Doesn't Know How (Non si sa come), 1935

English Translations

To date, nine of Pirandello's plays are unavailable in English (see * in
above list), although unpublished translations for some of them do exist
(see Bassnett-McGuire, 1989). Editions of published translations appear
below:

Henry IV
The Man With the Flower in His Mouth
Right You Are (If You Think You Are)
Lazarus
    Collected Plays, ed. R. Rietty (London, Calder, 1987, vol. 1)

Six Characters in Search of an Author
All For the Best
Clothe the Naked
Limes From Sicily
    Collected Plays, ed. R. Rietty (London, Calder, 1988, vol. 2)

The Rules of the Game
Grafted
The Other Son
    Collected Plays, ed. R. Rietty (New York, Riverrun, 1992, vol. 3)

Liolà
It Is So (If You Think So)
Henry IV
Six Characters in Search of an Author
Each in His Own Way
　　Naked Masks, ed. E. R. Bentley (New York, Dutton, 1952)

The Rules of the Game
The Life I Gave You
Lazarus
　　The Rules of the Game, ed. E. M. Brown (Harmondsworth, Penguin 1952)

Right You Are! (If You Think So)
All For the Best
Henry IV
　　Right You Are! (If You Think So), ed. E. M. Brown (Harmondsworth, Penguin, 1962)

Six Characters in Search of an Author
Henry IV
The Rules of the Game
　　Three Plays, ed. R. Rietty (London, Methuen, 1985)

Each in His Own Way
The Pleasure of Honesty
Naked
　　Each in His Own Way and two other plays, tr. A. Livingston (London, Dent; New York, Dutton, 1923)

The Mountain Giants (left incomplete by Pirandello)
　　The Yearbook of the British Pirandello Society, tr. F. Firth, no. 10, 1990

The Mountain Giants (incomplete)
The New Colony
When Someone is Somebody
　　The Mountain Giants and other plays, tr. Marta Abba (New York, Crown, 1958)

Tonight We Improvise
　　tr. C. Fredericks (London, Samuel French, 1960)

A Dream, But Perhaps Not

tr. S. Putnam, *This Quarter*, vol. 2, 4, June 1930

As You Desire Me
 tr. S. Putnam (New York, Dutton, 1931)

Diana and Tuda
 tr. Marta Abba (London, Samuel French, 1950)

The Wives' Friend
 tr. Marta Abba (London, Samuel French, 1959)

To Find Oneself
 tr. Marta Abba (London, Samuel French, 1959)

No One Knows How
 tr. Marta Abba (London, Samuel French, 1961)

The Vice (La morsa)
The Doctor's Duty
Chee-Chee (Cecé)
At the Exit
The Jar
The Licence
Our Lord of the Ship
The Other Son
The Imbecile
Bellavita

 Pirandello's One-Act Plays, tr. W. Murray (New York, Doubleday, 1964)

Secondary Texts

Ardener, E. (1975) 'Belief and the Problem of Women', and 'The 'Problem' Revisited' in Ardener (1975), pp.1– 17, 19–27
Ardener, S. G. (ed.) (1975) *Perceiving Women*, London, Dent
Ardener, S. G. (ed.) (1978) *Defining Females: The Nature of Women in Society*, London, Croom Helm
Armstrong, J. (1976) *The Novel of Adultery*, London, Macmillan
Austin, J. L. (1962) *How To Do Things With Words*, Oxford, Clarendon Press
Barański, Z. G. and Vinall, S. W. (eds.) (1991) *Women and Italy: Essays*

on Gender, Culture & History, London, Macmillan

Barker, F. et al. (1980) *1936: The Sociology of Literature*, University of Essex

Bassnett-McGuire, B. (1983) *Luigi Pirandello*, London, Macmillan
_____ (1989) *File on Pirandello*, London, Methuen

Beardsley, R. K., Hall, J. W., Ward, R. E. (1959) *Village Japan*, Chicago, University of Chicago Press

Belsey, C. (1980) *Critical Practice*, London, Methuen
_____ (1985) 'Constructing the Subject: Deconstructing the Text', in Newton and Rosenfelt (1985) pp. 45–64

Benson, R. G. (1980) *Medieval Body Language: A Study of the Use of Gesture in Chaucer's Poetry*, Copenhagen, Rosenkilde and Bagger

Birdwhistell, R. L. (1971) *Kinesics and Context: Essays on Body-Motion Communication*, Harmondsworth, Penguin

Borzello, F. (1982) *The Artist's Model*, London, Junction Books

Brecht, B. (1986) 'On Gestic Music', in *Brecht on Theatre*, tr. J. Willett, London, Methuen, pp. 104–6, written 1932. first publ. as 'Über gestische Musik', *Schriften zum Theater* (1957)

Bridenthal, R. (1982) 'The Family: A View from a Room of Her Own', in Thorne and Yalom (1982), pp. 225–39

Brilliant, R. (1963) *Gesture and Rank in Roman Art: The Use of Gestures to Denote Status in Roman Sculpture and Coinage*, Memoirs of the Connecticut Academy of Arts and Sciences, Connecticut, Academy of Arts and Sciences, vol. 14, February

Brown, P. (ed.) (1973) *Radical Psychology*, New York, Harper & Row

Brušák, K. (1976) 'Signs in the Chinese Theater', in Matejka and Titunik (1976), pp. 59–73, first publ. 1939

Caldwell, L. (1986) 'Reproducers of the Nation: Women and the Family in Fascist Policy', in Forgacs (1986), pp. 110–41

Cameron, D. (1985) *Feminism and Linguistic Theory*, New York, St Martin's Press

Case, S. E. (1988) *Feminism and Theatre*, London, Macmillan
_____ (1990) (ed.) *Performing Feminisms: Feminist Critical Theory and Theatre*, Baltimore, Johns Hopkins University Press

Chodorov, N. (1978) *The Reproduction of Mothering: Psychoanalysis and the Sociology of Gender*, Los Angeles, University of California Press

Clark, M. (1984) *Modern Italy 1871–1982*, London, Longman

Clemen, W. (1987) *Shakespeare's Soliloquies*, London, Methuen

Clerice, S. and Di Pierro, A. (1991) '1951–1991: Quarant'anni di numeri che fanno la storia', *Il Venerdí*, 18 ottobre, pp. 73–94

Cook, C. (1990) 'Unbodied Figures of Desire', in Case (1990), pp. 177–95

Creed, B. (1986) 'Horror and the Monstrous-Feminine: An Imaginary Abjection', *Screen*, Jan.–Feb., pp. 44–70

Cuddon, J. A. (1982) *A Dictionary of Literary Terms*, Harmondsworth, Penguin

Dashwood, J. R. and Everson, J. E. (1991) *Writers and Performers in Italian Drama From the Time of Dante to Pirandello*, Lampeter, Mellen

Diamond, E. (1990) 'Refusing the Romanticism of Identity: Narrative Intervention in Churchill, Benmussa, Duras', in Case (1990), pp. 92–105

Dolan, J. (1990) '"Lesbian" Subjectivity in Realism: Dragging at the Margins of Structure and Ideology', in Case (1990), pp. 40–53

Ducrot, O. and Todorov, T. (1981) *Encyclopedic Dictionary of the Sciences of Language*, tr. C. Porter, Oxford, Blackwell; first publ. as *Dictionnaire encyclopédique des sciences du langage*, Paris, Seuil, 1972

Elam, K. (1980) *The Semiotics of Theatre and Drama*, London, Methuen
_____ (1984) *Shakespeare's Universe of Discourse: Language Games in the Comedies*, Cambridge, Cambridge University Press

Fanning, U. (1991) 'Angel vs monster: Serao's use of the female double', in Barański and Vinall (1991), pp. 263–92

Ferris, L. (1990) *Acting Women: Images of Women in Theatre*, London, Macmillan

Forgacs, D. (ed.) (1986) *Rethinking Italian Fascism*, London, Lawrence and Wishart

Forte, J. (1990) 'Women's Performance Art: Feminism and Postmodernism', in Case (1990), pp. 251–69

Foucault, M. (1987) *Discipline and Punish: The Birth of the Prison*, Harmondsworth, Penguin Books, first publ. as *Surveiller et punir*, Paris, Éditions Gallimard, 1975

Freud, S. (1925) 'Negation', in *The Standard Edition of the Complete Psychological Works of Sigmund Freud*, London, Hogarth Press, 1953–74, vol. 19, pp. 234–9, first publ. as 'Die Verneinung', in *Gesammelte Werke*, London, Imago, 14, pp. 11–5

Garvin, P. (ed.) (1964) *A Prague School Reader on Esthetics, Literary Structure and Style*, Georgetown, Georgetown University Press

Ginsburg, M. P. (1982) 'Free Indirect Discourse: A Reconsideration', Language and Style, 15, 2, Spring, pp. 133–49

Giudice, G. (1963) *Pirandello*, Torino, UTET

Glass, D. V. (1967) 'The Italian Struggle For Population', in *Population Policies and Movements in Europe*, London, Cass, pp. 219–68; first publ. 1940

Golini, A. (1988) 'Profilo demografico della famiglia italiana', in

Melograni, 1988, pp. 327–81

Greimas, A. and Courtes, J. (1983) *Semiotics and Language: An Analytical Dictionary*, Bloomington, Indiana University Press, 1983, first publ. as *Sémiotique: dictionnaire raisonné de la théorie du langage*, Paris, Hachette, 1979

Gumperz, J. J. (ed.) (1982) *Language and Social Identity*, Cambridge, Cambridge University Press

Günsberg, M. (1983) 'The Mirror Episode in Canto XVI of the *Gerusalemme liberata*', *The Italianist*, 3, pp. 30–46

_____ (1991) 'Donna Liberata? The Portrayal of Women in the Italian Renaissance Epic', in Barański and Vinall (1991), pp.173–208

_____ (1992) 'Hysteria as Theatre: Pirandello's Hysterical Women', *The Yearbook of British Pirandello Studies*, no. 12, pp. 32–52

Habicht, W. (1959) *Die Gebärde in englischen Dichtungen des Mittelalters*, München

Hall, E. T. (1959) *The Silent Language*, New York, Doubleday

_____ (1966) *The Hidden Dimension*, New York, Doubleday

Hall, J. (1974) *Dictionary of Subjects and Symbols in Art*, London, John Murray

Halperin, D. M. (1986) 'Plato and Erotic Reciprocity', *Classical Antiquity*, 5, pp. 60–80

_____ (1990) *One Hundred Years of Homosexuality and Other Essays on Greek Love*, London, Routledge

Hamilton, R. (1980) *The Liberation of Women: A Study of Patriarchy and Capitalism*, London, Allen & Unwin

Hastrup, K. (1978) 'The Semantics of Biology: Virginity', in Ardener (1978), pp. 49–65

Hay, J. (1987) *Popular Film Culture in Fascist Italy: The Passing of the Rex*, Bloomington and Indianapolis, Indiana University Press

Helms, L. (1990) 'Playing the Woman's Part: Feminist Criticism and Shakespearean Performance', in Case (1990), pp. 196–206

Henley, N. (1973) 'The Politics of Touch', in Brown (1973), pp. 421–33

_____ (1977) *Body Politics*, Englewood Cliffs, NJ, Prentice-Hall

Hinde, R. A. (ed.) (1972) *Non-Verbal Communication*, Cambridge, Cambridge University Press

Honzl, J. (1976) 'Dynamics of the Sign in the Theater', in Matejka and Titunik, (1976), pp. 74–93

Horkheimer, M. (1972) 'Authority and the Family', in *Critical Theory*, tr. M. J. O'Connell, New York, Herder and Herder, pp. 47–128; first publ. as 'Autorität und Familie', 1936

Irigaray, L. (1977a) 'Le Marché des femmes', in Irigaray (1977), pp. 165–85

_____ (1977b) 'Des marchandises entre elles', in Irigaray (ibid., pp. 187–93)

_____ (1977c) 'Ce sexe qui n'en est pas un', in Irigaray (ibid., pp. 21–32)

_____ (1977) *Ce sexe qui n'en est pas un*, Paris, Minuit

Istituto Centrale di Statistica (abbr. Istat):

_____ (1911) *Censimento della popolazione del Regno D'Italia*, vol. 7

_____ (1919–21) *Annuario statistico italiano*, seconda serie, vol. 8

_____ (1921) *Censimento della popolazione*, relazione generale

_____ (1922–5) *Annuario statistico italiano*, seconda serie, vol. 9

_____ (1927) *Annuario statistico italiano*, 5, terza serie, vol. 1

_____ (1931) *Censimento generale della popolazione*, 21 aprile, vol. 9

Jacobus, M. (1982) 'Is There a Woman in This Text?', *New Literary Theory*, 14, pp. 117–41

Kuhn, A. (1982) *Women's Pictures: Feminism and Cinema*, London, Routledge & Kegan Paul

Lacan, J. (1966) 'Le Stade du miroir comme formateur de la fonction du Je', in *Écrits*, Paris, Seuil, vol. 1, pp. 89–97, first publ. 1949

Laplanche, J. and Pontalis, J. B. (1980) *The Language of Psycho-Analysis*, tr. D. Nicholson-Smith, London, Hogarth Press; first publ. as *Vocabulaire de la Psychanalyse*, Paris, Presses Universitaires de France, 1967

Laslett, P. (1977) 'Characteristics of the Western Family Considered Over Time', *Journal of Family History*, 2, 2, pp. 89–115

Lepschy, A. L. (1988–9) 'The Treatment of Antefact in Pirandello's Theatre', in *The Yearbook of British Pirandello Studies*, pp. 68–89

_____ (1991) 'The Treatment of Antefact in Pirandello's Theatre in the Theatre', in Dashwood and Everson (1991)

Lévi-Strauss, C. (1969) *The Elementary Structures of Kinship*, tr. J. H. Bell et al., Boston, Beacon Press; first publ. as *Les Structures élémentaires de la parenté*, 1949

Lloyd, G. (1984) *The Man of Reason: 'Male' and 'Female' in Western Philosophy*, London, Methuen

Lloyd, G. E. R. (1971) *Polarity and Analogy: Two Types of Argumentation in Early Greek Thought*, Cambridge, Cambridge University Press

Maclean, I. (1985) *The Renaissance Notion of Woman: A Study in the Fortunes of Scholasticism and Medical Science in European Intellectual Life*, Cambridge, Cambridge University Press

Major, B. (1981) 'Gender Patterns in Touching Behaviour', in Mayo and Henley (1981) pp. 15–37

Maltz, D. N. and Borker, R. A. (1982) 'A Cultural Approach to Male-Female Miscommunication', in Gumperz (1982), pp. 195–216

Marinetti, F. T. (1968) *Teoria e invenzione futurista*, ed. L. De Maria, Milano, Mondadori

Matejka, L. and Pomorska, K. (eds) (1971) *Readings in Russian Poetics:*

Formalist and Structuralist Views, Cambridge, Massachusetts, MIT

Matejka, L. and Tutinik, I. R. (eds.) (1976) *Semiotics of Art: Prague School Contributions*, Massachussetts, MIT

Mayo, C. and Henley, N. (eds.) (1981) *Gender and Nonverbal Behaviour*, New York, Springer-Verlag

Melograni, P. (ed.) (1988) *La famiglia italiana dall'ottocento a oggi*, Roma, Laterza

Michaelson, E. J. and Goldschmidt, W. (1971) 'Female Roles and Male Dominance among Peasants', *Southwestern Journal of Anthropology*, 27, pp. 330–52

Miller, J. (1979) 'Plays and Players', in Hinde (1979), pp. 359–72

Montroni, G. (1988) 'La famiglia borghese', in Melograni (1988), pp. 107–40

Mulvey, L. (1989) 'Visual Pleasure and Narrative Cinema', in *Visual and Other Pleasures*, London, Macmillan, pp. 14–26, first publ. *Screen*, 1975, 16, 3, pp. 6–18

Nelson, C. and Grossberg, L. (eds) (1988) *Marxism and the Interpretation of Culture*, Urbana and Chicago, University of Illinois Press

Newton, J. and Rosenfelt, D. (eds) (1985) *Feminist Criticism and Social Change*, London, Methuen

Ortner, S. (1974) 'Is Female to Male as Nature is to Culture?' in Rosaldo and Lamphere (1974), pp. 67–87

The Oxford English Dictionary (abbr. OED)

Pavis, P. (1981) 'Problems of a Semiology of Theatrical Gesture', *Poetics Today*, vol. 2, 3, pp. 65–93

_____ (1982) 'Gesture and Body Language', in *Languages of the Stage: Essays in the Semiology of the Theatre*, New York, Performing Arts Journal Publications, part 2, pp. 37–66

_____ (1987) *Dictionnaire du théâtre*, Paris, Messidor

Pirandello, L. (1965) *Saggi, Poesie e Scritti Varii*, ed. M. Lo Vecchio-Musti, Milano, Mondadori

Rackin, P. (1990) 'Anti-Historians: Women's Roles in Shakespeare's Histories', in Case (1990), pp. 207–22

Ragusa, O. (1980) *Luigi Pirandello: An Approach to his Theatre*, Edinburgh, Edinburgh University Press

Ravera, C. (1978) *Breve storia del movimento femminile in Italia*, Roma, Riuniti

Roessler, E. W. (1966) *The Soliloquy in German Drama*, New York, Ams Press, 1966; first publ. 1915

Rosaldo, M. and Lamphere, L. (eds) (1974) *Women, Culture and Society*, Stanford, Cal., Stanford University Press

Rose, J. (1986) *Sexuality in the Field of Vision*, London, Verso

Bibliography

Sacks, H., Schegloff, E. A. and Jefferson, G. (1974) 'A Simplest Systematics for the Organisation of Turn-Taking for Conversation', *Language*, 50, 4, pp. 696–735

Sapir, E. (1958) 'The Unconscious Patterning of Behavior in Society', in *Selected Writings of Edward Sapir*, ed. D. G. Mandelbaum, Berkeley, University of California, pp. 544–59; first publ. in *The Unconscious: A Symposium*, New York, Knopf, pp. 114–42, 1927

Sayers, J. (1982) *Biological Politics: Feminist and Anti-Feminist Perspectives*, London, Tavistock

Searle, J. R. (1969) *Speech Acts: An Essay in the Philosophy of Language*, Cambridge, Cambridge University Press

Searle, J. R. and Vanderveken, D. (1985) *Foundations of Illocutionary Logic*, Cambridge, Cambridge University Press

Silverman, K. (1983) *The Subject of Semiotics*, Oxford, Oxford University Press

Šklovsky, V. (1976) *Teoria della prosa*, tr. C. G. de Michelis and R. Oliva, Torino, Einaudi

Spivak, G. C. (1988) 'Can the Subaltern Speak?', in Nelson and Grossberg (1988), pp. 271–313

Stone, J. (1980) 'Mirror Image/Collage: Reality, Representation and Revolution in Pirandello', in Barker et al. (1980), pp. 37–71

Theweleit, K. (1990) *Male Fantasies*, tr. S. Conway, Minnesota, Polity; first publ. as *Männerphantasien*, 1977

Thorne, B. and Henley, N. (eds) (1975) *Language and Sex, Difference and Dominance*, Rowley, Mass., Newbury House

Thorne, B. and Yalom, M. (eds) (1982) *Rethinking the Family: Some Feminist Questions*, New York, Longman

Todorov, T. (ed.) (1968) *I formalisti russi*, transl. C. Riccio et al., Torino, Einaudi

Veltruský, J. (1964) 'Man and Object in the Theater', abridged in Garvin (1964), pp. 83–91; first publ. 1940

_____ (1976) 'Dramatic Text as a Component of Theater', in Matejka and Titunik (1976), pp. 94–117; first publ. 1941

Warner, M. (1976) *Alone of All Her Sex: The Myth and Cult of the Virgin Mary*, London, Picador

Williman, D. (1986) *Legal Terminology: An Historical Guide to Technical Language of Law*, Canada, Broadview Press

Zimmerman, D. H. and West, C. (1975) 'Sex Roles, Interruptions and Silences in Conversation', in Thorne and Henley (1975), pp. 105–26

Name and Text Index

Subject Index